The Buckeyes

A Story of Ohio State Football

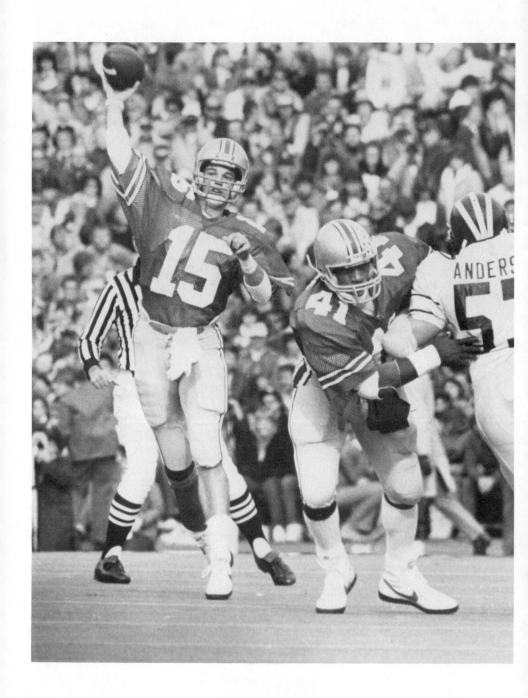

MIKE TOMCZAK   **1984**   **OHIO STATE**

The Buckeyes:

Ohio State Football

by

Wilbur Snypp

and

Bob Hunter

THE STRODE PUBLISHERS
Texas, 1988

Originally Published 1974
Revised And Updated 1982

Published in the United States of America by
Strode Publishers Division, Circle Book Service
P.O. Box 626, Tomball, TX 77375

"Then strip, lads, and be to it, tho sharp be the weather.

"And, if by mischance, you should happen to fall,

"There are worse things in life than a tumble on heather,

"For life, itself, is but a game of foot ball."

—Sir Walter Scott

Photographs Courtesy Of
The Columbus Dispatch, The House Of
Portraits, The Ohio State University
Department Of Photography, Bill
Foley, Malcolm Emmons, Lester Nehamkin,
And The Ohio State University Department
Of Athletics

Contents

Introduction

The graveyard of the coaches, as Ohio State was known before Woody Hayes' 28-year reign, hung out a "Back in Business" sign a few months before this book was to be updated.

OSU President Edward Jennings' firing of Earle Bruce, who had the best record in the Big Ten for his nine years there, created the biggest stir in Buckeye football circles since Hayes' punch of Clemson linebacker Charlie Bauman opened the job for Bruce after the 1978 Gator Bowl.

In researching this update, my second since the late Wilbur Snypp released the book in 1973, I gained a new perspective of the Bruce era. A game-by-game study of several seasons together provides a different view than the one received by a weekly, one-game-at-a-time analysis stretched over several years. In retrospect, the six-year string of 9-3 records and the disappointing 6-4-1 campaign that ended it, seems to have been marked more by bad luck than bad coaching.

If Bruce didn't possess the emotion of Hayes or the playbook of Francis Schmidt, he also didn't have their timing or their good fortune: he seemed eternally dogged by last-minute easy misses by his place-kickers or the mental mistakes, like a fourth down pass to stop the clock by his quarterback. One promising season was wrecked by a star tailback's broken ankle, another setback by a quarterback's broken leg and his last damaged by the loss of the school's career pass reception leader to an agent, illegal under NCAA rules.

But if Bruce wasn't treated fairly in his firing, he can take some solace in the fact that he isn't alone. This book is littered with cases of Ohio State football coaches done wrong, of men sent to the coaching graveyard when their won-loss records indicated good health.

John Cooper, the former Arizona State coach chosen as Bruce's successor and the subject of this book's last chapter, looks healthy and robust, and more than able to fend off the school's statewide army of football morticians.

But looks can be deceiving, especially in the vicinity of the horseshoe. Bruce, two points from an almost-certain national championship in his first season, once appeared so too.

Bob Hunter
Columbus, Ohio
February, 1988

The Beginning

During Ohio State's early years little was said about sports and even less about football, then a two-word game. The university opened its doors in 1873, and what sports fans there were spoke mainly of tennis and track and field. But seventeen years later, in 1890, Ohio State football began officially, and it was not long before the gridiron sport took over in Buckeye land. Then, as now, it provided most of the livelihood of the athletic program, small as it was.

When Professor William Lyon Phelps, the eminent Yale authority on English literature, was asked which he preferred, a perfect recitation in Chaucer or a victory over Harvard, he replied that he always appreciated a perfect recitation but it never made him throw his hat away. This typifies the interest and excitement identified with Ohio State football over the years.

Commencement time, 1890, found a petition signed by nearly 200 students requesting the board of trustees to enclose an athletic field which would contain, among other things, "foot ball grounds, or that a sum of $200 be set aside annually to be expended under the direction of the athletic association on baseball, foot ball, tennis and general athletics."

As Dr. James E. Pollard wrote in his book, *Ohio State*

The first Ohio State football team, 1890, played with an oval ball resembling the present-day basketball. Holding it is captain Jesse Jones.

Athletics, the petition was referred to the president and the executive committee. Five months later a faculty committee recommended that "special pains should be taken to furnish facilities for field sports." A grandstand seating 300 was recommended also, with "special practice grounds for foot ball so that baseball could be played at the same time without interference."

It was estimated that 5½ acres would be required at a cost of $1,950, but after hearing the report the trustees voted $200 for the athletic association to be expended under its direction for the furtherance of its objects.

By 1890 athletics had gained enough prominence to warrant considerable mention in the annual report of President W. H. Scott, who said there was a "new and unprecedented interest in athletics with teams in baseball, foot ball and tennis."

President Scott let it be known that he was concerned about absence from class by the athletes. He cited that the baseball team had made a tour to play three games, causing "an absence of two and a half days from college exercises." There also was one match game of foot ball, he said, with a team of another college, unidentified. It is presumed that this was the spring game of 1890 with nearby Ohio Wesleyan University, carried in the records as a 20 to 14 victory for the neophyte Buckeyes.

President Scott had more to say on the subject, particularly about football:

"Most of the time, there is but little practice; then comes a tremendous overstrain. Lawn tennis is not subject to criticism, as practice is more regular and match games are less violent. To foot ball, on the other hand, the criticism is especially applicable, as in this game accidents are frequent. Another evil that attends the present system of athletics is its interference with university work. This is particularly true of intercollegiate games. An effort is made to restrict them to Saturdays and other holidays, but it is apparently impossible to play them without more or less neglect of regular studies, not only at the time when they are played but during the period of training for them."

"The faculty has adopted no plan for regulating these

18

games so as to abate the evils that already exist or to prevent those that seem likely to arise. We have great confidence in the loyalty and earnestness of our students. Some of our most loyal and earnest are members of the various teams and others are zealous friends and supporters of the association. Yet the history of athletics in eastern colleges and the manifest tendency of those of Ohio indicate that some limits should be prescribed."

In 1891 the football squad petitioned to be excused from military drill "in order that they might devote that hour to foot ball practice." This had the endorsement of athletic association managers and of the commandant, with the suggestion that football practice, if the petition was granted, "be made subject to the same rules as govern military drill." On this condition the request was granted by a 3 to 2 vote. At the same meeting the athletic association managers petitioned the trustees to fence the athletic grounds and erect a grandstand at an estimated cost of $1,150. This was refused "because of lack of funds."

Slowly, but effectively, football and other sports gained favor. In the spring of 1892 the trustees granted the athletic association permission to erect a fence and grandstand at a place to be designated by the chairman of the executive committee and the secretary of the board. In line with the previous action in excusing the football squad from military drill the trustees granted a request to have certain members of the baseball squad excused. The nine starters were in this group.

In 1893 the general faculty took an action on athletic eligibility which resulted in student disapproval. The discontent lay in an action to the effect that no student or preparatory pupil of the Ohio State University be allowed to take part in intercollegiate games "unless his record in the past has been above average. The president of the university is to decide what constitutes such record." Apparently the students thought the rule was too exacting, for they petitioned the faculty to reconsider the matter, which was done the following month.

The earlier rule was amended to read that "no student or preparatory pupil of the Ohio State University be allowed to take part in intercollegiate games, who has, within two preceding terms, incurred a failure in any subject or has incurred conditions in more than five hours' work. This

19

regulation shall go into effect at the opening of the university year 1893-94." The amended rule was less stringent and was not to take effect until the start of the next school year.

The university's fourth president, James H. Canfield, moved ahead to take the lead in what nowadays would be termed a housecleaning of intercollegiate athletics. The regulations were the consummation of student and faculty efforts "to place Ohio State athletics on a basis of absolute purity." Of the seven regulations the two most important were:

1. No person shall represent Ohio State in any athletic games or other public events who is not a student doing full work in the regular course.

2. No student shall take part in any intercollegiate contest unless he has been in regular work for at least six months of the academic year in which said contest takes place.

While the first varsity football was not played on the campus until the autumn of 1890, dormitory grounds were the scene of impromptu activity as early as 1881. The *Columbus Dispatch* of October 8, 1887, reported that "a new foot-ball was obtained today at the dormitory and promises to furnish considerable amusement for the boys."

It was not long before talk began of meeting teams from other Ohio colleges. Thus the *Lantern*, Ohio State student daily, reported on April 21, 1887, that Marietta College students had sent word that they were "willing to play us a game of foot-ball."

Footballs were so rare they belonged to individuals of considerable means. Often the balls were home-made, and on other occasions a collection had to be taken from several boys to get a "store-bought" ball.

In 1893 the *Dispatch* recalled the beginnings of college football in Ohio, although the details were at variance. In its November 27, 1893, issue, the newspaper said..."figuratively speaking, the students of colleges of Ohio had never seen a foot ball until the fall of 1890 when several of them organized an intercollegiate association and Columbus was represented by the OSU eleven. The game did not receive a very enthusiastic reception, as it was, locally, a new one and consequently a very small number were acquainted with it." But interest, the story added, increased rapidly.

George N. Cole, of the Ohio State class of 1891, was credited with being one of those influential in introducing football to the campus. Cole had gone to school in Columbus with Alexander S. Lilley, who then attended Lawrenceville Prep. and Princeton. Lilley and K. L. Ames, an early Princeton all-American, were in Columbus later.

Cole said he helped Ohio State get started in two ways: by writing Spaulding's for a rule book and talking Lilley into coaching the team without salary. According to Cole's account, Lilley, who lived several miles from the campus, rode an Indian pony to practice while Ames, also working without pay, taught the squad how to kick the ball.

So, 21 years after the first college game was played between Rutgers and Princeton, the stage was set for a spring game May 3, 1890, involving Ohio State and Ohio Wesleyan at Delaware, 25 miles north of Columbus.

"Anything went except brass knuckles," Cole reported in an interview in 1938. There was no passing or razzle-dazzle, he said, but emphasis on power plays and wedge work. Cole said it was all right to step on a man's face as long as care was exercised in the performance.

These tactics were later confirmed by Campbell Graf, captain of the 1914 team, who played as a sophomore in the 1912 game against Penn State. Graf said the Penn State linemen were expert spitters of tobacco juice. "They were both powerful and accurate," Graf reported. "They blinded us most of the afternoon by using our eyes as targets."

Neither the *Columbus Dispatch* nor the *Ohio State Journal* made any immediate mention of the May 3 game, which also was ignored by the *Delaware Democratic Press,* a weekly. The student *Lantern,* however, carried an account of the game, which was called for 9:30 a.m.

With touchdowns counting four points and goals-after counting two, Ohio State led at the half 14 to 6. With 10 minutes to play in the second half, the *Lantern* said Ohio Wesleyan tied the score but that Ohio State formed a flying wedge and scored on the second attempt from four feet out. The kick was good, making the final score 20-14.

The *Delaware Gazette* reported: "The game was a spirited one, and from the interest aroused, it is safe to say that foot

Alexander S. Lilley was Ohio State University's first football coach in 1890. His team played a spring and fall schedule, winning one game and losing three.

ball has taken a firm hold upon both the students and citizens."

The *Gazette* also needled losers by stating: "Had our boys worked a little harder and displayed a little more head work in the first half of the game, there is reason to believe that the result would have been different."

A Challenge From Otterbein

In the beginning of college football in Ohio, an undergraduate team manager handled all details and arrangements for a game. The young man did everything from getting the team to bed to actual scheduling of the games. He had charge of finances, headed the ticket selling, and made all trip arrangements. He actually bought the equipment and was responsible for it, along with having other sundry jobs, now so highly departmentalized in athletic environment.

Thus it was on November 26, 1890, that the following letter arrived on the Ohio State campus from Westerville, Ohio, 12 miles away. It was signed by B. V. Leas, student manager of the Otterbein University football team.

> *"Manager, Football Team*
> *Ohio State University*
> *Columbus, Ohio*
>
> *Dear Sir:*
>
> *"Can we arrange a game of ball to be played on our grounds, Saturday, December 6? We will give you $10 and hotel expenses while here. You can get here at 1:00 p.m. and leave at 7:00. We are very anxious for our team to meet yours as we never have contested for any honors before.*
>
> *"If Saturday is taken, can you come Thursday or*

Friday of the same week? Hoping you will give this your
careful consideration, we remain,

> *Respectively yours,*
> *(Signed) B. V. Leas, Manager Otterbein*
> *University Football Team"*

Apparently the Ohio State manager, later determined to be Charles B. Mowry, failed to reply in time for the game to be scheduled. A letter dated December 5, 1890, was written to Mowry by Otterbein manager Leas.

The letter said:

> *"We sent you a challenge on November 26 and expected an early reply. Just having one-half day to advertise the game, it will be necessary to cancel the date.*
> *"I had excused two of our men from town, thinking you would not answer at such a late date. We will accept a later date if you notify us at once. Hoping this will not put you to any inconvenience, reply soon.*
> *(Signed) Yours, B. V. Leas*

There is no record if Mowry or anyone else responded to Leas' second letter. The two schools did not meet on the gridiron until the opening game of the season for both teams in 1893.

Perhaps Otterbein gained some measure of satisfaction for being ignored, winning the game, 22 to 16.

When football was resumed in the fall of 1890, it was not so successful as the spring game.

Wooster was the opening opponent, the first team to play in Columbus. The *Columbus Dispatch,* in an announcement several days before the game, attempted to shed some optimism on the game by saying, "Our boys will use every endeavor to win and a splendid contest may be expected."

The sad result was 64 to 0 in favor of Wooster, and it was noted that "A number of ladies were present and attempted to cheer the OSU boys to victory, but to no avail, as there was not the remotest possibility of their winning."

The other two games of the 1890 schedule also were

losses—to Denison, 14 to 0, and Kenyon, 18 to 10.

When the first two games of the 1891 schedule resulted in losses to Adelbert (later Western Reserve) and Kenyon, the situation was pretty gloomy, particularly when the respective scores were 50 to 6 and 26 to 0. The Adelbert game was played at Recreation Park, then in the southern part of the city, while the Kenyon game was played at Gambier.

The student daily, the *Lantern,* said that the Adelbert game "has sadly confirmed the fact there must be an awakening in our interest in athletics if we wish to be recognized with any degree of respect among the colleges of Ohio." The *Dispatch* called the game "a match of boys on one side and men on the other."

In regard to the Kenyon loss, the *Lantern* reported that the game "was not as unequal as the score would indicate." It called the Kenyon field "very poor" and charged the umpire, furnished by Kenyon, with being "clearly and stubbornly unfair and prejudiced."

The five-game losing streak came to an end, appropriately enough, on Thanksgiving morning when Denison was defeated 8 to 4 at Recreation Park. On the following day the *Lantern* said that the team had worked out beforehand in "the drill house" and that this extra preparation had been instrumental in winning the game.

The following week the team went to Akron to play Buchtel (now Akron University) and won 6 to 0. Despite the *Lantern's* report that "both teams played like high school boys," the young Buckeyes were happy with a 2-2 season.

It appeared that the up-and-down team had turned the corner.

The season of 1892 proved to be a winner, 5-3, but Oberlin inflicted two of the defeats in convincing style, 40-0 and 50-0. The other loss was to Western Reserve, 40-18.

Thanksgiving Day proved to be a good omen for the Buckeyes, as arch rival Kenyon was defeated for the first time, 26 to 10. Since Kenyon fielded good teams consistently in the early days, this was a big home town victory. The *Columbus Dispatch* praised the team as one that could hold its own with any in Ohio and also patted coach Jack Ryder on the back. The "coacher," the paper said, was a "mighty man and a mighty

25

With officials wearing black suits and sporting derbies, Ohio State played Denison University at Recreation Park on November 26, 1891. Ohio State won, 8 to 4, much to the satisfaction of the Thanksgiving morning crowd.

27

player."

Dr. Pollard reported in his athletic history book that quarterback Homer Howard told him that Kenyon had its choice that day of taking a cash guarantee of $85 or 60 percent of the gate. Kenyon decided to take the cash, and the receipts were $1,134. It was a bad day for Kenyon all around.

This game boosted public interest considerably, and the *Dispatch* gave more space to the team, including listing of menus at the training table. The newspaper also pointed out that a new formation, known as the "Ryder wedge," was instrumental in winning the game. Inasmuch as a dismal financial picture had been painted in some quarters for the 1892 season, the $1,049 net from the Kenyon game gave everyone a big lift, including the worried administrators.

The team scored in all nine games in 1893, but this time lost twice to Kenyon, 42-6 and 10-8, the latter on Thanksgiving Day, ending the Turkey Day good-luck pattern. After losing

An Ohio State football practice session in 1892 resembled mob action. In the center of this skirmish in the dark jersey is coach Jack Ryder, Williams College alumnus, who later became a prominent Cincinnati sports writer.

Jack Ryder established a coaching record at Ohio State by serving three different "hitches." His 1890 team, the Buckeyes' first, failed to win in three starts. He then coached from 1892 through 1895, when his combined record was 19-17-1. After a two-year lay-off from coaching, Ryder returned for the 1898 season, winning three, losing four, and tying one. Tired of playing "catch up" in an effort to establish a winning record, Ryder quit with an overall six-year record of 22-24-2.

four of the first five games, the team righted itself and put on a three-game winning streak at the expense of Akron, Cincinnati, and Marietta, but the season-end loss to Kenyon chilled the fans more than usual during the winter months that followed. When Kenyon came from behind to win, the *Dispatch* reported that the crowd of 4,000 tore down portions of the fence and the game had to be stopped "until police cleared the grounds."

In 1894 Ohio State football games were made a part of State Fair Week, and contests were scheduled with Antioch, Wittenberg, and Buchtel. The *Dispatch* pointed out that these games should be classed as "exhibitions" and scores not counted in the regular season. However Ohio State records show 12 to 6 and 32-0 victories over Buchtel and Antioch respectively and a 6-0 loss to Wittenberg.

Popular Jack Ryder came back as coach in mid-season after M. C. Lilley, a Yale alumnus, had directed the team in early games. The team won four of its last five games and finished with a 6-5 record. As usual Kenyon was played on Thanksgiving, and it was a 20 to 4 victory, noteworthy, the *Dispatch* pointed out, for being "free from slugging and dirty work." No players were injured, but the 17th Regiment, stationed at Columbus Barracks, was present to keep "the field clear and maintain order on the outside."

The 1895 season was highlighted by a four-game schedule in eight days, although one—with Starling Medical—was not played. There were two precedents: back-to-back games on Friday and Saturday, and a tie game. The Buckeyes defeated Kentucky 8 to 6 at Lexington and then played and lost to Centre at Danville, 10 to 0, the next day.

The first tie game involving football occurred when an 8-8 deadlock was played with Ohio Wesleyan in mid-season. Oddly there were one or more tie games during each of the next seven seasons. Again Kenyon was defeated on Thanksgiving Day, 12 to 10, and the *Dispatch* said that the "crowd went wild and carried the winners off the field."

That long hair was common among players in 1895, as it is today, is evidenced in the *Dispatch's* observation that "The players will now seek the barber shops to be shorn of their lengthy locks."

As a tribute to William McKinley, the Ohio State-Otterbein game of 1896 was shifted to Canton, Ohio, the president's home. There is no indication he attended the game, won by Ohio State 12 to 0. The game started late in the afternoon and was called on account of darkness by mutual agreement. The season's record was 5-5-1, with the Buckeyes taking a 34-18 pasting from Kenyon in the finale. The 52 points represented the highest-scoring game up to that time and only the second time the Buckeyes had lost with an 18 point total. The team had two coaches, Sid Farrar, a former Princeton player, who was an Ohio State medical student, and Charles Hickey, captain of the 1895 Williams College team.

The roof fell in during the 1897 season, resulting in the most disastrous campaign on record. The new coach was David F. Edwards, a Princeton grad of '96, who had starred as a halfback for his alma mater. The team won one game, lost seven, and tied one. The only victory ended in a row, a 6-0 affair with Ohio Medical, with Ohio State claiming a forfeit.

The team failed to score in its seven losses, getting on the scoreboard only in a 12-12 tie with Otterbein. Meanwhile the opposition ran up 170 points. The highlight of the season was playing Michigan for the first time, a game at Ann Arbor, won by the Wolverines 34 to 0. Michigan had just played Ohio Wesleyan, and the Ann Arbor fans were still objecting to the fact that Fielding H. Yost had played, as well as coached, the Wesleyan eleven. As a result Ohio Wesleyan was dropped from the Michigan schedule, and managers of athletic teams were warned by the administration not to make any engagements with any team representing the Delaware school.

Ohio State wound up the season playing Yost's team on Thanksgiving, losing only 6 to 0. This must have been a good showing in an otherwise deplorable year, as the *Lantern* pointed out that "Despite trick plays by their crafty coach, Yost, only one touchdown was scored."

Having experienced a season they wanted to forget and also one they reviewed with bitterness, campus editors demanded some changes before another year rolled around. In language which was to have a familiar ring 40 to 50 years later, the *Lantern* not only advocated alumni coaching, but, as Dr. Pollard points out in his book, it said: "The experience the Ohio State University has had during the past two years with high-salaried eastern coaches who were supposed to know the game, but who did not, has taught a lesson not to be forgotten soon. If the Ohio State University could secure the services of several of its alumni to coach the team next year, as is done at the University of Michigan and eastern schools, it would undoubtedly put a winning team on the gridiron and would meet with hearty approval of the alumni faculty and student body."

.31

Yost Applies For Coaching Job

It is almost unbelievable, but the same Fielding Yost applied for the head coaching job at Ohio State in February of 1897. He might have gotten it, too, but for his own exuberance. According to Fred E. Butcher, of the class of 1901, Yost, who had coached and also played at West Virginia University, wanted to demonstrate his physical prowess while on the campus. This he did, first on a student and then on a faculty member. The performance was so vigorous the professor called Butcher to "get rid of that wild man." It is an open secret that Yost's later successes at Michigan were painful to Ohio Staters.

Capable Jack Ryder came back as head coach for his sixth and final season in 1898, winning three, all by shutouts, losing four, and tying one. The team blanked Heidelberg, Denison, and Ohio Wesleyan, and tied Ohio Medical. Losses were to Ohio Medical in a return game, Case, Kenyon, and Western Reserve. Ryder's teams had always averted losing streaks, but in between the Denison and Ohio Wesleyan victories were the four losses. He was particularly discouraged by successive defeats at the hands of Kenyon, 29-0, and Western Reserve, 49-0.

The season of 1899 was as pleasantly shocking as the previous year had been disappointing.

John B. C. Eckstorm, a student of physical fitness and hard as a rock, took over as head coach. All he did in his first year was post an undefeated season of 9-0-1. It was the first in Ohio State history and was not to be repeated until 1916, when the Buckeyes won their first Big Ten championship.

The most successful football coach in the early days was Dr. John B. Eckstorm. His teams of 1899-1900-1901 won 22 games, lost only 4, and tied 3. The 1899 team was undefeated but tied Case 5 to 5. It was Ohio State's first undefeated season, and the next one did not occur until 1916.

A strong Case team held the Buckeyes to a 5-5 tie, but all other opponents not only were defeated but shut out. Only three games were close, 6-0 with both Oberlin and Western Reserve, and 5-0 with Kenyon. Meanwhile the Buckeyes piled up 185 points in an amazing showing of both offensive and defensive strength.

WA-HOO! WA-HOO! NEITHER SIDE SCORED
NINE HUNDRED OHIO ROOTERS
CHEER ON THEIR HUSKIE TEAM
Three Thousand People Witness the Great Game of Football

Those were Page One headlines of the *Ann Arbor Daily Argus* on Saturday evening, November 24, 1900, after a scoreless tie between Michigan and Ohio State that afternoon. It was another great day for Coach Eckstorm and his improving Buckeyes, who had to be quite an underdog, as they were to be for many years to come whenever Michigan was played. The story indicates that 25 minute halves were played, with officials being Fred Haynon of Lake Forest as referee and Bob Wrenn of Harvard as umpire. Ohio State was permitted to have one of the linesmen and the timer.

The "play-by-play" reads, as the score would indicate, that the game featured punting and defense. Michigan reached Ohio State's 30-yard line in the first half, but a field goal try failed. The Buckeyes came back to Michigan's 25, but a penalty stopped the drive. In the second half Michigan reached the Ohio State 37 but was stopped, after which Michigan blocked a Buckeye punt but the visitors were fortunate and recovered on their own 15. Michigan had another chance when Ohio State fumbled, the Wolverines recovering on the Ohio 22, but again the Buckeyes held at the 18. The game ended with Ohio State back on its own 10-yard line. It is indicated that several punts by halfback Westwater of Ohio State and fullback Sweeley of Michigan carried 40 to 50 yards.

Editorial comment at the end of the story reads:—"Ohio State takes it as virtually a victory, their band playing and the crowd gathering."

Judging from the pre-game excitement, the only difference between 1900 and recent years is the size of the crowd, yet the

Daily Argus says, "It was the biggest crowd that ever invaded Ann Arbor. The guests had the keys to the city and were welcomed here by the U of M band and 300 Michigan students. As the two sections of the train pulled into the Ann Arbor depot, the rival yells went up and the lung duel had commenced. Ohio State brought a band of 20 pieces and it marched down Main St., thence to the campus, where visiting students were given a glimpse of what Michigan thinks is the greatest state institution in the country."

The *Argus* goes on to relate early-day gambling on the outcome "...at the hotels, the Ohio boys wore an air of confidence, but when the question of backing up their opinion with money was brought up, they demanded odds."

Evidently coaches "scouted" games in those days, too. In the stands was Amos Alonzo Stagg, of Chicago, and one of his assistants. Chicago was scheduled to play Michigan at a later date.

Such was the high point of the 1900 schedule, which saw the Buckeyes win eight, lose one, and gain their "moral" victory over Michigan. The loss was to neighboring Ohio Medical, 11 to 6, one of three teams to score on Eckstorm's lads. The other teams to score were Case, beaten 24 to 10 and Kenyon, defeated in the season's finale, 23 to 5. In 20 games over a two-year span only 31 points were scored against the Buckeyes.

A Successful Turn

Ohio State University made the turn of the century with only four losing seasons out of eleven.

It was a good omen, despite the fact that Coach Eckstorm had his poorest year in 1901 of 5-3-1. All three losses came together against Michigan, Oberlin, and Indiana, the Hoosiers being played for the first time. An 11-6 victory over Kenyon in the usual Thanksgiving Day finale helped to ease the pain.

Perry Hale took over the head coaching duties in 1902-03 and received a rough initiation from Michigan to the tune of 86-0. However there were several bright spots, including ties with favored Illinois and Indiana and a 51-5 trouncing of arch rival, Kenyon. The 1903 schedule included 11 games, and the Buckeyes won 8 of them, losing, as predicted, to Michigan, Indiana, and Case, the Cleveland school that always gave Ohio State a hard time.

E. R. Sweetland became the head coach in 1904 for two seasons. His team broke even in 10 games during his first year, winning the first 4 games by shutouts for a fast start. Then Michigan inflicted the usual defeat, 31-6; Illinois made it worse, 46-0; Oberlin won an oddity, 4-2; and then the Carlisle Indians were played for the first time. The redskins scalped the Buckeyes, 23-0, and Indiana took an 8-0 decision back to Bloomington.

A 12-game schedule was played for the first and last time in 1905. It was a good season at 8-2-2, the two losses being to Michigan and Indiana. The ties were with Otterbein and Case.

36

Perry Hale was Ohio State's head coach in 1902-03, during which his teams won 14, lost 5, and tied 2. One of the 2 losses in 1902 was an 86-0 whomping by Michigan. The Wolverines did it again in 1903, but the outcome was a more respectable 36 to 0. Easing the pain over the two-year span were victories over West Virginia and tie games with Illinois and Indiana.

37

Fans came to early Ohio State games in Columbus in buggies, surreys, and tally-hos. Here they watch a game with Michigan in 1901, won by the Wolverines 21 to 0. Spectators later protested that they could not see the game because people stood on top of their horse-drawn vehicles. This resulted in their eventual removal from the field.

Wooster was back on the schedule for the first time since 1890, and the Buckeyes gained some measure of revenge for the early 64-0 spanking by winning, 15-0.

E. R. Sweetland, from the University of Chicago, was Ohio State's head coach in 1904-5. The 1904 team broke even in 10 games, but the 12-game season in 1905 resulted in 8 wins, 2 losses, and 2 ties.

40

Proudly displaying his "M" for Michigan, no less, Al Herrnstein was Ohio State's head coach from 1906-09. He had winning teams each year and had a three-year record of 28-10-1. He was not able to stop his Alma Mater, however, as Michigan won all four games by scores of 6-0, 22-0, 10-6, and 33-6. Two intersectional victories were scored over Vanderbilt, 17 to 6 and 5 to 0.

Al Herrnstein, a native of Chillicothe, Ohio, took over the coaching reins in 1906, and the former Michigan athlete and alumnus had four successful seasons. He had good information on his alma mater, but Michigan edged the Buckeyes, 6-0, for the only loss in 1906. Ohio Medical scored eight points, and the fourteen points comprised the season's total by the opposition.

Hall of Fame Coach Howard Jones tutored the Buckeyes in 1910. He came to Ohio State by way of Syracuse and Yale. He later coached at Iowa, Duke, and Southern California. His 1910 team won six, lost one, and tied three, one being a 3-3 deadlock with Michigan.

The 1907 season was 7-2-1, Michigan and Case inflicting the defeats while Wooster was tied, 6-6. Northeastern Ohio schools, Case, Reserve, and Wooster, joined Michigan in stopping the Buckeyes in 1908, but the Wolverines did not run away with this one, the score being 10-6. Herrnstein bowed out after 1909 when a 7-3 record was posted. Oberlin and Case joined Michigan in thumping the Buckeyes, but Wooster was trampled 74-0 and Vanderbilt was defeated for the second time, 5-0.

Howard Jones, who showed great promise as a coach at

Without previous coaching experience Harry Vaughn, a Yale law student, had charge of the 1911 Ohio State football team. He did an outstanding job, winning five games, losing three, and tying two.

Syracuse and Yale, assumed command in 1910 and continued his good work which was to become even more prominent at Iowa and Southern California. His one-year stint showed six wins, one loss, and three ties, a record for deadlocked games which stood until 1924. One of the ties was a 3-3 battle with Michigan, which pleased the Buckeye fans no end. The others were with Denison and Oberlin. The loss was 14-10 to Case, the old Ohio nemesis.

Harry Vaughn took over for the 1911 season which resulted in 5-3-2. Only four teams scored on the Buckeyes, but three of them won: Michigan, Case, and a new opponent, Syracuse. Cincinnati scored but was defeated 11-6. Old rival, Kenyon, which had been met on 20 previous occasions, was dropped from the schedule after the Buckeyes won 24 to 0. It was evident that the teams from Gambier could no longer compete with the up-and-coming Buckeyes.

Vaughn, who had no previous coaching experience, was lauded before he returned to Yale to resume his law studies. His supporters pointed out that he had inherited only three regulars from the previous season, yet had done a fine job. It was a good year, financially, too, as the athletic association paid off $3,500 in notes.

The conclusion of the 1911 season marked the end of an era. The year of 1912 was to see the Buckeyes move in with the "big boys."

A New Era — Important Personalities Move In

The year of 1912 could be called the turning point on Ohio State's football highway. The Buckeyes were taken into the Western Conference.

The year of 1912 also brought in John R. Richards from Wisconsin to be athletic director and football coach. Although Richards had been successful at Wisconsin and elsewhere, his tenure at Ohio State was a one-year stand. His team started well, with one-sided victories over Otterbein and Denison. After losing to Michigan 14 to 0, refreshing triumphs were recorded over Case, the old nemesis, 31 to 6, and a good Oberlin team, 23-17.

Then a game was played in Columbus with Penn State which undoubtedly changed the future of Richards as well as Ohio State football.

The visitors came to town undefeated, numbering among their victims strong Cornell and Washington & Jefferson teams. With the score 37 to 0 in Penn State's favor and nine minutes to play in the fourth quarter, Richards ordered his team off the field. He said the visitors were guilty of unsportsmanlike conduct and that officials were lax in calling or enforcing penalties. Ohio State records show the score as standing 37-0, but others say the official result was a forfeit, 1 to 0.

The student *Lantern* said the officials should have banished the offenders in the third quarter, then the contest likely would have been completed in orderly fashion. Richards claimed it was a case of "sportsmanship vs muckerism" and issued statements defending his action.

It was an embarrassing day in other ways. President Edwin E. Sparks of Penn State, an alumnus of Ohio State, was in the stands after spending part of the day with his Chi Phi fraternity brothers. He was forced to watch the Penn State colors burned on the goalposts, for which a freshman took the blame. A committee of alumni and students apologized to Dr. Sparks before he left the city, and a student apology was sent to Penn State.

The season ended with a 36-6 victory over Ohio Wesleyan and a 35-20 loss to Michigan Aggies (now Michigan State). Although the Buckeyes had won the "Ohio championship" for the first time, the Penn State fuss lingered on, and Richards resigned both suddenly and voluntarily, effective January 1, 1913.

So, the youngest member of the Western Conference had a schedule for its first season in the league, but no coach. Neither was there a director of athletics.

The athletic directorship was decided first.

Lynn Wilbur St. John, who had earned a letter as a halfback in 1900, was already on the staff as football line coach and head basketball and baseball coach. He also served as business manager. In his book, *Ohio State Athletics,* Dr. Pollard points out that St. John was not consulted about his promotion but merely told about it after it occurred. For more than 10 years St. John had wanted a medical career, but this move ended all thoughts of becoming a doctor.

Another sudden turn of events authorized the employment of Carl Rothgeb of Colorado College as football coach, but Rothgeb declined, leaving the door open to John W. Wilce, a star Wisconsin football and basketball player, as well as a member of the Badger crew. Wilce, who had been teaching and coaching at LaCrosse, Wisconsin, High School, accepted the Buckeye challenge from his new post as freshman coach at Wisconsin.

Under the new regime, Wilce had general responsibility; St. John was to coach the line and Frank Castleman, who was brought from the University of Colorado as track coach, was to assist with the backs. When spring practice opened, George Little, a former Ohio Wesleyan star, assisted on a part-time

46

John R. (Jack) Richards was both director of athletics and head football coach in 1912, but he resigned suddenly after one season. Many thought his decision was based on an incident in the Penn State game of that year when he took the Buckeyes off the field for what he claimed was unsportsmanlike conduct.

Lynn W. St. John served as Ohio State's director of athletics from 1913 to 1947, during which he elevated the Buckeye athletic program and became a powerful personality in the Big Ten and NCAA.

basis.

Three opponents were scheduled in the first conference season: Indiana, Wisconsin, and Northwestern. It was an oddity that Michigan, considered a rival by this time, was not a member on the league in 1913. The Wolverines had withdrawn from the conference in 1908 over disputes involving training table issues. Many faculty members and students expressed a desire for Michigan to return to the conference, which it did after the 1917 season.

Schedules had been running as high as eleven and twelve games per season, but now that the Buckeyes were in the conference, schedules dropped to seven games. Wilce's first year was 4-2-1 with losses in the conference to Indiana, 7-6, and Wisconsin, 12-0. However Northwestern was beaten solidly, 58 to 0. Three of the four Ohio games were won with Ohio Wesleyan, Western Reserve, and Case, while Oberlin was tied, 0-0.

Another important factor in the transition to the conference was the improvement of academic standards. The registrar's office reported that only a handful of men from teams of previous years would have been eligible on the 1913 squad.

Dr. John W. Wilce, an alumnus of Wisconsin, was Ohio State's coach from 1913 through 1928, a 16 year regime which saw the Buckeyes win three conference championships and finish second in three other seasons.

The record continued to improve in 1914 when Indiana was defeated for the first time, 13 to 3. Northwestern again was beaten 27 to 0, but losses were to Wisconsin, 7-6, and Illinois, 37-0. The three state rivals, Ohio Wesleyan, Case, and Oberlin were defeated.

It was amazing, but true, that young Wilce, not yet 27, could improve upon his record for the third straight time.

The 1915 team won the first two games from Ohio Wesleyan and Case, 19-6 and 14-0, then tied a strong Illinois team, 3-3. After losing to Wisconsin for the third straight time, Indiana was shaded 10 to 9. It was the second straight win over the Hoosiers, who had spoiled the Buckeyes' inaugural in the conference, 7-6. Oberlin was blanked the following week, 25-0, and again Northwestern was easy, falling 34 to 0. It was the third straight whitewash for the Wildcats, who gave up 119 points in the process.

Not only was the offense improving, but the defense was tightening. The 1915 team gave up only 39 points to 55 the previous year. Ohio Wesleyan's lone touchdown was the only one scored by the three state rivals and Illinois had failed to cross the goal line.

Meanwhile a strong freshman team was waiting in the wings, headed by a slight, shy youngster from Columbus East High School who was destined to carry the Buckeyes right to the top, and thousands of fans with him. It is true that the "glory days" were just ahead.

"Chic" Harley — Legend
Of Success

It is doubtful if any college football player ever made a greater impact on his eventual alma mater than did Charles W. (Chic) Harley.

Harley came to Ohio State from Columbus East High School, where he had established an enviable record as an all-around athlete, a career he was destined to follow as a Buckeye.

Born in Chicago, Harley moved to Columbus when he was 12 years old along with three brothers and three sisters. After eight years the Harleys decided to return to Chicago, a decision which disturbed John D. Harlor, principal of East High School and John Vorys, captain of the 1913 team, on which Harley had played as a junior. They along with other friends persuaded Chic's mother to let him finish high school at East.

Many colleges sought the fleet-footed Harley, but members of the Phi Gamma Delta fraternity, with which he eventually became affiliated, influenced him to stay in Columbus, a choice which later was to be applauded by thousands of Buckeye followers.

After completion of his freshman year in 1915, Harley lost no time in making his presence felt in the varsity lineup a year later.

In his first conference game as a sophomore against Illinois, Ohio State had the ball on the Illinois 13-yard line with one minute and 10 seconds remaining. Harley faded back to pass, but, finding all receivers covered, faked a pass, cut around

51

Charles W. (Chic) Harley, 1916-17-19, was Ohio State's first all-American. More than just a triple threat, Harley was a dropkicker and place-kicker as well. On defense he was a vicious tackler, often giving away 30 or 40 pounds in stopping opposing runners. In 21 intercollegiate games, Harley scored 201 points made up of 23 touchdowns, 39 extra points and 8 field goals. Harley passed away April 21, 1974.

left end, evaded three tacklers, and scored standing up, tying the score at 6-6.

Then came one of the real dramatic moments in Ohio State history. Inasmuch as the field had been mud-laden with Illinois clay from an all-day rain, Illinois had missed the extra point. This was Harley's chance to put Ohio State ahead, and he did after changing his shoes for a dry pair. The 7 to 6 margin stood up, and Illinois had lost its first conference game at home in four years—all because of an upstart sophomore.

This was just the beginning.

Always-tough Wisconsin followed. Harley, playing safety, received a punt on his own 22-yard line. With one-man interference Harley brushed past the first would-be tackler, out-ran the next, and then dodged, feinted, and out-raced the remaining Badgers for a 76-yard touchdown run. Harley also scored the other Buckeye touchdown and kicked both extra points as Ohio State won another big game by one point, 14 to 13.

Elated over their success as neophytes in the Big Ten, the Buckeyes ran rough-shod over Indiana the following week, 46 to 7. Harley gained 107 yards in eight minutes of the first quarter and was removed from the game.

The homecoming game with Northwestern placed the championship "on the line" for the Buckeyes.

Again it was Harley who set the pace. He ran 63 and 15 yards for touchdowns, passed 40 yards to put the ball on the 2-yard line for an eventual score, kicked a field goal from the 40-yard line, and added 2 extra points. The score had been a 3-3 tie early in the fourth quarter until Harley broke the game wide open, 23-3.

Thus ended Ohio State's first title season in which Harley scored eight touchdowns, kicked seven extra points, and one field goal for fifty-eight points.

By the time the 1917 football season rolled around it was evident the Buckeyes had picked up hundreds of new followers and revived many old ones. People who previously had little or no interest in Ohio State football wanted to learn what it was all about.

When the first four opponents—Case, Ohio Wesleyan, Northwestern and Denison—failed to score while the Buckeyes

Dr. John W. Wilce, Ohio State football coach from 1913 to 1928, called this the "perfect offensive play." Made against Northwestern on Ohio Field in 1916, Chic Harley (at left with ball) went the distance for a touchdown, Ohio State winning 23 to 3 in a game that gave the Buckeyes their first Big Ten title.

ran up 209 points, interest continued to grow,

The next game, with Indiana, was played at Indianapolis instead of Bloomington or Columbus as both schools had men in the World War I camp at nearby Ft. Benjamin Harrison.

It did not make much difference to Harley where the game was being played. Withheld until late in the second quarter, "Chic" subsequently ran for the four touchdowns scored by his team on rambles of 40, 11, 33, and 8 yards. He also kicked two extra points, scoring all of the Buckeye points in a 26 to 3 victory.

An account of the game reads: "'Chic' was the only consistent ground gainer. His open field runs of 25 to 50 yards, his change of pace, dodging, squirming and diving, were nothing short of phenomenal."

Wisconsin's big, experienced team was a heavy favorite the following week, but, like Indiana, the Badgers were held to a field goal in a 16 to 3 triumph for Harley & Co. For the first time in more than a year the Buckeyes had to come from behind to win as the Badgers went ahead 3 to 0 on a 43-yard drop kick. With his running stopped by some sensational defensive play, Harley resorted to passing. With the ball on Wisconsin's 44-yard line, third down and 20, Harley dropped back as if to punt but instead wheeled and passed the distance to Charles (Shifty) Bolen in the end zone.

This put the Buckeyes on the way again, and Harley passed to Howard Courtney for a touchdown, then kicked an extra point and a 40-yard field goal to have a hand in all 16 points.

A 13 to 0 victory followed over Illinois in which Harley almost duplicated the routine employed against Wisconsin. He again passed to Courtney for a touchdown, then kicked an extra point and two field goals from the 14 and 29 yard lines.

For the benefit of service men two post-season games were played that year, a scoreless tie with Auburn at Montgomery, Alabama, and a 28 to 0 victory over Camp Sherman at home. The game at Montgomery was scheduled largely because numerous Ohioans were training there with the 37th Division (Ohio National Guard). Team members expressed over-confidence against Auburn and were annoyed considerably by having their winning streak stopped at 17.

Although his passing had replaced much of his running,

Charley Seddon, weighing only 147 pounds, was a regular guard on the Ohio State football teams of 1915, 1916, and 1917. Known as the "watch charm" guard, Seddon was the lightest player ever to play for the Buckeyes. The 1916 and 1917 teams were champions of the Big Ten.

First Title Team—The Ohio State team of 1916 was the first to win a Big Ten championship. Conference victories were scored over Illinois, Wisconsin, Indiana, and Northwestern. A record Ohio State scoring mark was established of 128 points against Oberlin College. Charles W. (Chic) Harley, fourth player from left in second row, was named to Walter Camp's first all-American team, first Ohio State player so honored.

Harley still scored 72 points during the season, 14 more than his 58 as a sophomore. Included were 8 touchdowns, the same as in 1916, 15 points after touchdown, and 3 field goals.

With its goal line uncrossed, the team scored 292 points compared to 6 by the opposition: the field goals by Indiana and Wisconsin.

Shortly after the season Harley, along with most of his teammates, entered the service.

Harley's senior year of 1919 picked up where 1917 left off, despite a six game schedule in 1918 when most of the football talent was in service. The war shortened all schedules in the Big Ten, and Ohio State lingered through a 3-3 season, saddened by two war casualties, halfback Fred Norton and tackle Harold (Hap) Courtney.

With Harley as captain, playing one of the halfbacks, and another all-American to-be at the other spot in Gaylord (Pete) Stinchcomb, the Buckeyes rambled over Ohio Wesleyan 38 to 0, Cincinnati 46 to 0, and Kentucky 49 to 0. None of the three teams threatened to score, and Harley collected 52 points.

Then came one of those first-ever triumphs, a 13 to 3 victory over Michigan at Ann Arbor. With the exception of a scoreless tie in 1900 and a 3-3 deadlock in 1910, Michigan had inflicted 11 straight defeats on the Buckeyes, a source of annoyance that since has carried on for more than 50 years. As usual Harley sparked the Buckeye attack with a 42-yard touchdown, and tackle Iolas Huffman set up the other touchdown by blocking a punt.

After Purdue was blanked 20 to 0, in which Harley ran 30 yards for a score and passed to end Bill Slyker for another, Wisconsin was edged 3 to 0 on Harley's 22-yard drop kick.

Up to this point Ohio State's goal line was uncrossed. Only Michigan's field goal appeared in the opponents' scoring column.

Then came the heart-breaker, a game the old-timers wish they could forget, particularly for Harley's sake.

Illinois came to Columbus with a good team, but Ohio State held a 7-6 edge by reason of Harley's pass to Clarence McDonald which put the ball on the one-yard line. "Chic" ran it over and kicked the extra point. That is the way the score stood until only eight seconds remained.

Then it happened! Illinois coach Bob Zuppke, playing a "hunch," sent reserve Bob Fletcher into the game to try a place kick. Fletcher split the uprights from 30 yards out and with it went several items: an undefeated season, a championship which would have meant three in a row, and a three-year unbeaten career for Harley. Thus "Chic" suffered the same experience he had in high school, an undefeated career wiped out in the final game.

So the championship went to Illinois by the margin of eight seconds.

Harley scored 71 points during the season, one less than in his junior year. His three-year contributions showed 23 touchdowns, 39 extra points, and 8 field goals for a total of 201. This was a varsity scoring record until Howard (Hopalong) Cassady scored 222 points. However Cassady played four years, 1952-1955.

"Harley could do everything. He was the complete player."

Thus did Gaylord (Pete) Stinchcomb recently describe his former running mate, "Chic" Harley, Ohio State's first all-American.

"'Chic' was like a cat. you know how hard it is to catch a cat. It usually takes more than one person. It always took more than one player to catch Harley.

"He could dodge, feint, and run fast. In addition he used a straight-arm to ward off tacklers like nobody else could."

When Stinchcomb was a freshman in 1916, he watched Harley become an all-American, then played the opposite halfback in 1917 and 1919. After Harley finished in 1919, Pete went on to become an all-American himself in 1920.

"Harley's versatility showed in our game with Wisconsin at Madison in 1919," Stinchcomb added. "He missed three chances to place-kick a field goal, so we decided he should try a drop-kick. This he did, and we won the game, 3 to 0."

Stinchcomb's first Big Ten game was against Northwestern, and the defense was geared to stop Harley. "I scored three times, but 'Chic's' blocking was superb. Without it I would have been lost."

Pete's second Big Ten start was against Indiana in a game that was played at Indianapolis as a favor to men in service.

Gaylord R. (Pete) Stinchcomb was an all-American halfback in 1920 and recently elected to the Football Hall of Fame. He played opposite "Chic" Harley in the latter's all-American years of 1917 and 1919. Stinchcomb passed away in August of 1973 at the age of 78.

"For some strange reason we forgot to take our white jerseys, so both teams wore red. I was utterly confused. Harley told me to run interference for him, but I just saw too many red shirts. He told me to forget it and follow him. So we switched tactics and won easily 26 to 3.

"It was real fun beating Michigan for the first time,

The late Charles W. (Chic) Harley, left, and the late Gaylord (Pete) Stinchcomb, both 155 pound players, were Ohio State's first all-American halfbacks. Harley was named in 1916-17-19 and Stinchcomb in 1920. Here, they met on the campus in 1923 as youthful alumni.

particularly at Ann Arbor right after Michigan returned to the conference.

"Harley got away for 95 yards, and after that we stayed ahead to the end, 13-3.

"I had a peculiar experience in that game. Playing quarterback I passed against the wind, and when Sunday morning newspapers criticized Coach Wilce for my tactics he was upset. We had a squad meeting Sunday, and I thought he would be elated that we had won. Instead I was deflated and never played quarterback again.

"Harley had a way of staying out of trouble on the football field; in fact he was always helping some other player out," Stinchcomb said.

Harley never weighed more than 157 pounds, and Pete was usually five pounds lighter. "There is no substitute for speed. Both of us could run," said Pete.

Both were four-sport men. Both were outfielders on the baseball team; both played guard in basketball. Stinchcomb was a broad jumper in track and held the university record at 23 feet, 2 inches. Harley ran the dashes and held the school record for 50 yards.

Pete had to go without Harley in 1920 but led the team to the title. He helped pull two big ones out, 13 to 7, against Wisconsin and 7-0 with Illinois. In addition Purdue, Chicago, and Michigan were beaten.

"We knew the stadium campaign was coming up, so we dedicated the season in that direction.

"When we beat Winconsin in the last 50 seconds, I recall $100,000 was raised for the building fund," Stinchcomb said.

Rose Bowl Game —
January 1, 1921

Preparation for Ohio State's first Rose Bowl game in December of 1920 was vastly different from plans involving the several trips made since that time. Anticipating that an invitation might be received to play in Pasadena, the athletic board on November 24 authorized acceptance. Definite word did not come until after the conference meetings in December, however.

"We were on edge for a couple of weeks, wondering what the outcome would be," says "Pete" Stinchcomb, all-American halfback of the 1920 team.

The team practiced in the snow before leaving by train and also encountered snow in Iowa City, Denver, and even Sacramento, according to Pete. The last stop, for one night, was at Palo Alto.

"We did not start our Pasadena practices until four o'clock because of the heat, but it was still hot. We went from snow to seeing people faint from the humidity on the morning of the game. The temperature was 85, and moving the starting time up to 1:00 p.m. did not help, either," says Stinchcomb.

In explaining, in part, the 28 to 0 loss to the California Bears, Pete says, "Our reflexes were bad. We could not coordinate. We would call 'time out' and it would do no good. The heat really had us down. We did have a revival of sorts toward the end of the game when we moved from our own five yard line to the California five."

California, coached by Andy Smith, went into the game

EY - WARD ·
ER   ASST. COACH
5 - MILLER - KAPLOW - PATCHELL - WEISS - LUSK
- COTT - WIPER - WILDER - ISABEL - JOHNSON , E·Y · - DR.WILCE
-WEICHE - NEMECEK - TAYLOR ,J.L· MYERS - WILLAMAN ·
· WESTERN · CONFERENCE · 1920 ·

© F·H· HASKETT
COLUMBUS, O.
COACH

*This 1920 team won Ohio State's third Big Ten title within a
five year period but lost to California in the Rose Bowl 28 to 0.
It was the first appearance of a Big Ten team at Pasadena since
the first Bowl game in 1902, involving Michigan and Stanford,
won by the Wolverines 49 to 0. Rose Bowl relationships with
the Big Ten were not renewed until 1946.*

67

with an 8-0 record, while the Buckeyes were undefeated in 7.

The passing combination of Harry (Hoge) Workman to Stinchcomb made the Buckeyes a slight favorite, but California fans were high on Harold (Brick) Muller, truly an all-around performer.

Writing in the *Pasadena Star-News*, Charley Paddock, the Olympic sprinter said, "Muller did everything a great end should do. He covered punts so swiftly he often beat the ball to the receiver. He caught every pass that was thrown to him. His passing, too, was phenomenal."

Writing in his book, *The Tournament of Roses*, Joe Hendrickson says that Paddock told of a play in which Muller

Pesky Sprott of the California Bears tackles all-American Pete Stinchcomb of Ohio State in this 1921 Rose Bowl action.

caught a trick flip behind the line from Pesky Sprott and then completed a long pass to Brodie Stephens in the end zone.

This resulted in a discussion of long duration involving the distance of the pass. Maxwell Stiles, a Los Angeles sportswriter, after considerable research stated that the figure was 53 yards. A *Spalding* record book originally said that it was 70.

Sprott later told George Davis of the *Los Angeles Herald Express* that it was his recollection that the play started on Ohio State's 38-yard line. "I handled the ball," Sprott said, "some 10 yards back of the line of scrimmage before flipping it to Muller, who dropped back another 15 yards before throwing it to Stephens on the goal line."

California won, 28 to 0, but the Buckeyes then won four straight in the Pasadena classic.

The play is said to have opened when fullback Archie Nesbet faked an injury. Then he suddenly jumped up, not as a fullback but as the center, and snapped the ball to Sprott. Actually the ball was handled by four players, with the scoring play being from Muller to Stephens.

California lost no time getting an early lead, recovering an Ohio State fumble and scoring in slightly over six minutes.

Howard (Red) Blair took the ball to the Bears' eight-yard line, but another fumble spoiled scoring chances. Early-game injuries to Workman and Stinchcomb lessened Buckeye opportunities, too. This passing combination had a fine record during the 1920 season, but against the Bears, Ohio State completed only eleven of twenty-five aerials.

The attendance was announced as 41,500, which prompted W. L. Leishman, tournament president, to say, "We can't go on much longer like this. Soon there won't be enough lumber in the city to seat them. We have to get started on our new stadium."

The Stadium Era

It was obvious that work should move fast toward a new stadium following three Big Ten championships and a second place finish in a five-year period. First plans were announced in the winter of 1919 and 1920. The original goal was $600,000, and plans called for a seating capacity of 50,000, with the first games to be played there in 1921.

A stadium edition of the *Alumni Monthly* in February of 1921 said that the stadium was to be horseshoe-shaped, with soccer fields, running track, and tennis courts. Inasmuch as the university was founded in 1870, it was decided that a 50-year mark, 1920, would be a good time to open the stadium campaign, and the week of October 18-23 was set. Not only Columbus but the entire state, as well as alumni centers all over the country, joined in the "kickoff."

All male students participating in athletics or engaged in physical education were asked to march downtown in athletic costume. Some 4,000 joined the parade, while artillery regiments and campus infantry marched in full equipment.

Historian Pollard notes that the downtown papers carried reams of publicity and that billboards were used and a huge horseshoe with electric lights denoting the progress of the campaign was suspended in front of the Deshler hotel, since razed.

By January 20, 1921, pledges stood at $1,001,071, with citizens of Columbus accounting for approximately one-half of the total. The contract was let on a bid of $1,341,017, some

Ohio Stadium has been one of America's leading attendance magnets. Here, the giant horseshoe, dedicated in 1922, holds one of its capacity crowds. Twenty-one gatherings in excess of 85,000 have watched the Buckeyes in the last four seasons. Standing room has been permitted only since 1969. Ohio State has led the nation in college football attendance in 21 of the last 23 years.

$300,000 more than could be accounted for. It was stipulated that the university itself was to incur no financial obligation in connection with the stadium and that the cost of the structure was not to exceed $930,000. In the final analysis it was to cost twice that much.

Meanwhile the 1921 season was another successful one, although clouded by two thoroughly unexpected defeats. A small but talented Oberlin college team defeated the Buckeyes 7 to 6, and Illinois inflicted a 7 to 0 loss in the final game of the season and also the last game to be played on old Ohio field.

Coach Wilce was both angry and depressed after the loss to Oberlin and ordered the squad to a practice session after the game. It is believed that this was the first and only time a workout was called for after a varsity game.

Illinois had not won a conference game and the Buckeyes were undefeated when the old rivals clashed, but wily Bob Zuppke was up to date on Ohio's tricks and the home team failed to threaten. The Illinois touchdown resulted in considerable discussion, many fans believing that the receiver of the scoring pass had allowed the ball to first touch the ground.

Prof. Thomas E. French, chairman of the engineering drawing department, is credited with being the father of Ohio Stadium plans. He served as faculty representative from Ohio State's entry in the conference in 1912 until his death in 1944, longer than any other man in Big Ten history.

The loss was hard to take as it allowed Iowa to win the title and relegated the Buckeyes to a second-place tie with Chicago.

Prior to the loss the Buckeyes had defeated Michigan 14-0, Minnesota 27-0, Chicago 7-0, and Purdue 28-0. The touchdowns scored by Oberlin and Illinois not only inflicted two defeats but were the only points scored by seven opponents.

One of the big features of the Ohio State University football program is the 150 piece Marching Band which plays before each home game and between halves. One road trip is made each year and sometimes two, depending upon finances available. Until recently the band had only 120 pieces, but now the student total is actually 187, with 150 of these appearing on the field and 37 remaining on the sidelines to handle props and act as alternates. Competition is keen, with all spots being open. Normally at least 250 appear for fall tryouts.

An all-male organization throughout its recorded history, the present band grew from a drum corps and a military band to

The crowd stands in Ohio Stadium as the Marching Band plays the National Anthem. The band has become an integral part of the football season.

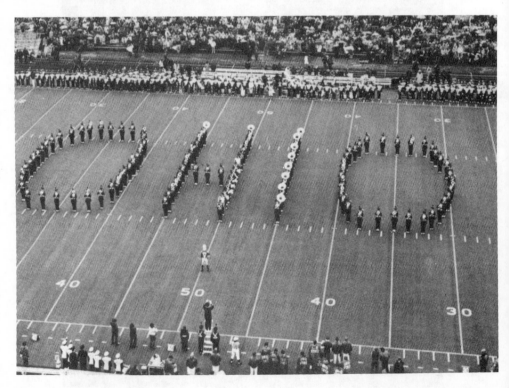

its present size. Since Ohio State began playing football, only seven men have directed the Marching Band. Paul Droste, the current director, is the first former member of the band to be selected as its director. In 1973, coeds could try out.

Ohio State has had an all-brass and percussion marching band since 1934. It is the largest band of this type in the United States—perhaps in the world. All music performed by the band is specially arranged to suit the instrumention and style of the band. All music played on the field is memorized.

The Marching Band has pioneered many techniques that have been copied by other bands. Such innovations as floating formations, animated movement of formations, scriptwriting, measured step marching, and the fast cadence and the high step were first tried and proven at Ohio State.

Unlike most marching bands the Ohio State band plays at least one concert per season and has released many commercial recordings.

The band stepped off toward its present place as an all-American football accessory when it first used formations in 1921. The first maneuvers were rather simple compared to present standards. The band just walked into an "OHIO" to the beat of drums. But soon the craze for band formations was sweeping the country.

Drum majors soon discovered that the position they occupied was more dramatic than anyone had noticed. The first Ohio State major to exploit the potentialities of the job was Edwin (Tubby) Essington. His high-stepping, spirited strut in his $500 (1920 prices) gold-belted regalia is still a vivid memory among old-timers in Columbus.

In 1947 Professor Manley Whitcomb put the basses and drums in the middle, making it the only reversible marching band in the country. Music sounds the same on both sides of the stadium and the band can reverse direction without interfering with the quality of the music. He also introduced the pictorial technique with appropriate song script and the impressive ribbon outline.

The band has marched in presidential inaugural parades in Washington, D.C., and in seven Rose Bowl parades. In the Pasadena marches, which are five miles long, the band members carry an extra pair of socks. This precaution permits more

75

C. Edwin (Tubby) Essington was Ohio State's first drum major, serving in the 1920, 1921, and 1922 football seasons. In his first appearance on the football field at the head of the Marching Band, he wore regulation dress with a pillow stuffed under his coat. His high stepping was an immediate hit, which led to friends producing a gala Scarlet and Gray uniform for him. He wore this for the first time at Illinois in 1920 and continued to wear it every game for the next two years.

comfortable footing for the hours ahead in the Rose Bowl.

In the early days of Ohio Stadium, buckets were passed through the crowd at half time to solicit funds to send the band on an out-of-town game trip. Later students were assessed 50 cents on their season tickets. This plan soon was abandoned, and now the athletic department underwrites traveling expenses from football receipts.

Holstein Cow Wins Election

Election of a Homecoming Queen always has been a serious business. But one of the greatest college stunts of all time was perpetrated on the Ohio State campus in the fall of 1926 when a pure-bred Holstein cow, Maudine Ormsby by name, was elected Homecoming Queen.

In this case fraternities and sororites had their own candidates and students who did not belong to either felt they had been shunned. It was this independent group that decided to do something about it.

They came up with "Miss Ormsby," who really was Ohio Maudine Ormsby, a prize-winning cow. She had the instant support of the College of Agriculture, where students were fully aware of the identity of Maudine.

The university enrollment was only 9,000 then, but more than 13,000 ballots were cast, counterfeit fee cards resulting in a stuffed ballot box. Maudine won going away, which is what university officials wished—far away.

Chaperones of Maudine (after all, she was only three years old) would not permit her to appear in all of the homecoming festivities. This really was too bad, the "Ag" students protested, because Maudine really was No. 1 at the milk bucket. At the age of one year, nine months, and fifteen days she had produced 22,049 pounds of milk, containing 782 pounds of butterfat, an all-time record for any cow her age. Later, in a seven day test, she produced 743 pounds of milk and 28 pounds of fat, another world record.

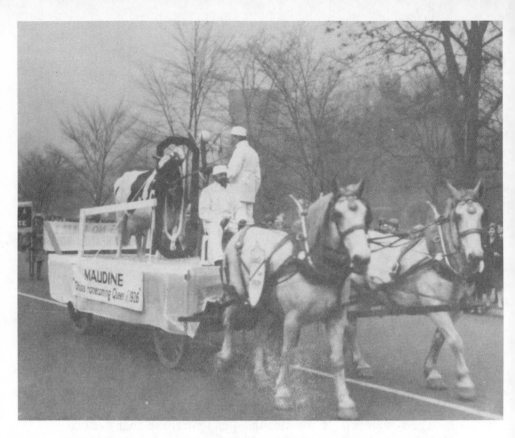

Maudine Ormsby, a pure-bred Holstein cow, rode majestically in the 1926 Ohio State homecoming parade, having been elected queen when students stuffed the ballot box. The hoax, regarded one of the best college pranks of all time, eliminated the legitimate contenders for the honor.

There was nothing phoney about Maudine, but a more crooked election never has been held. Perhaps this had something to do with Ohio State losing to Michigan the next day—an "udder" disappointment.

First Years In Stadium

The first game played in the stadium, October 7, 1922, with Ohio Wesleyan University, was a rain-drenched affair won by the Buckeyes 5 to 0. After Oberlin was defeated 14 to 0, the official dedication game followed with Michigan on October 21, a courtesy move as the Buckeyes had helped dedicate the enlarged Ferry Field the year before.

Three Columbus newspapers, the *Dispatch, Citizen,* and *Ohio State Journal,* published stadium editions of considerable size, with each advertisement linked with the stadium or university. The two campus publications, the *Lantern,* and *Alumni Monthly,* also printed all of the historical and current facts they could research in behalf of the occasion.

Policies established at the dedication game have prevailed over the years, such as pennants of all Big Ten schools flying from "C," or top deck. Another is having the Buckeye gridders emerge from a southeast tunnel in full view of their supporters on the west side of the horseshoe. The question was raised concerning what air currents would do with the ball. More than 50 years later this is still a subject discussed by coaches in post-game interviews.

Several Ohio State player-pictures were used in advertisements, a practice no longer permitted by the NCAA. Such a policy today could result in the player's ineligibility.

Thirty former football captains had the privilege of sitting on the sidelines during the dedication game, but they were disappointed in what they saw as Michigan won, 19 to 0. The story listing the names of the captains pointed out that "All of those old leaders would have given up a year of their life to beat Michigan." The story went on to say that when the 1900 team held the Wolverines to a scoreless tie "the university declared a semi-holiday."

Two predictions cited in 1922 have proven true. M. A. Carter, architectural draftsman of the stadium, said that the seating capacity of 62,110 would not be sufficient to accommodate the crowds. He predicted that a miniature stadium, seating 15,000, would be erected adjoining the stadium within 10 years. He missed his guess about a second stadium, but he was right about greater crowds soon wanting to get into the horseshoe. The other prediction said that there would be an increased interest in co-ed sports as a result of the stadium. This definitely became true.

The Michigan game was a case of too much Harry Kipke, whose "coffin corner" punting kept the Buckeyes on their heels all afternoon. The Wolverines scored in every quarter with field goals in the first and final quarters and touchdowns in the second and third. Ohio State had eleven first downs to six for Michigan and once moved to the Wolverines' four-yard line but failed to score. So, for the first time in four years, the Buckeyes had lost to their rivals.

After such success wrapped around World War I seasons, it was ironical that fortunes should swing downward, particularly with the stadium, still to be paid for, as a drawing feature.

During the next 4 years the teams won 12 games, lost 14, and tied 5. By contrast the record from 1916-1921 was 33-4-1. Despite a 7-1 season in 1926, the only loss being to Michigan 17-16, the natives became restless and the alumni critical.

Marty Karow, 1926 fullback and captain, and currently Buckeye baseball coach, says that the score with Michigan might have been tied but for a disagreement over how one of the extra points was to be attempted—the one that failed.

Unfortunately for Dr. Wilce (he had gotten his medical degree while coaching), he was unjustly criticized for the downward trend of the team. Part of the difficulty stemmed from sharp differences between the head coach and members of his staff, particularly Grant P. Ward who was assistant line coach and intramural director.

The upshot resulted in Ward's resignation and a resolution of confidence in behalf of Dr. Wilce, which read, as follows: "The athletic board expresses its full confidence in Dr. Wilce, both as to his professional qualifications as a coach, his ethical standards, and his leadership. He has the entire support of this board and merits the loyalty of all those who have the best interests of Ohio State football at heart."

Despite a break-even season in 1927 and an exceptionally good year in 1928, Wilce turned in his resignation on June 2, 1928, which was to become effective June 1, 1929. He said that he wanted to enter the active practice of medicine and teaching. At the end of the 1928 season, which had included a 19-7 victory over Michigan and a 5-2-1 record, the athletic board granted him a leave of absence for the rest of the academic year, including the summer quarter.

The athletic board then turned its attention to obtaining a new head coach. Historian Pollard reported that director St. John was anxious to obtain Knute Rockne from Notre Dame and that at one time it was felt he was available.

Early in 1929, when it was evident that Rockne could not be obtained, St. John told the athletic board that in his opinion the choice should be Sam Willaman, former Ohio State fullback and later coach at Iowa State. George Hauser, Minnesota line coach, was hired also, along with Don Miller, one of Notre Dame's "Four Horsemen."

It was rather difficult to quarrel with Sam Willaman's five-year coaching record of 26-10-6. Nonetheless two items seemed to have brought on complaints against him—the manner in which he handled the squad and his style of play, which could not be termed glamorous.

He started well, winning from Iowa and Michigan in the first two conference games in 1929, then Indiana was tied 0-0. The Buckeyes then lost to Pittsburgh, Northwestern, and Illinois. In four games Ohio State had scored but eight points.

The 1930 season was better, five victories being credited against two losses and another scoreless tie, this time with Wisconsin. The losses were to Northwestern and Michigan. The score was evened with Pittsburgh, and Illinois was defeated for the first time in four years, 12-9. The first of a home-and-home series with Navy was played, the Buckeyes winning, 27 to 0.

Sam Willaman, former Ohio State player, was coach of the Buckeyes from 1929 through 1933. He followed Dr. J. W. Wilce and was succeeded by Francis Schmidt.

After finishing in a tie for fifth in the conference standing in 1929 and a tie for fourth in 1930, the Buckeyes held fourth place undisputedly in 1931. Three losses, to Vanderbilt, Northwestern, and Minnesota, were offset with six victories, including conference wins over Michigan, Indiana, Wisconsin, and Illinois.

It can be said that Willaman's teams were consistent, as another fourth place finish occurred in 1932. They also managed to be involved in many tie games, six to be exact, in five years. Three of them happened in 1932, Indiana and Wisconsin, 7-7, and Pittsburgh, 0-0. The only loss was to Michigan, 14-0, but that, as usual, was the big one.

By this time the coaching staff had been reorganized. George Hauser returned to Minnesota, leaving the line job open, and Don Miller, backfield coach, returned to Cleveland to devote more time to his law practice. Ernie Godfrey, former football coach at nearby Wittenberg College, had charge of the freshmen and was to assist with the line. Floyd Stahl, Illinois alumnus and a highly successful high school coach in Ohio, had the reserve squad and assisted with the backs. Wesley Fesler, an all-American under Willaman in 1929 and 1930, who later was to become head coach, assisted Godfrey. Dick Larkins, later to become director of athletics, was to have charge of the freshmen, under Godfrey's direction.

Willaman's fifth and final season was his best, with seven victories and only one loss—to Michigan again. The team finished third in the final standings.

Meanwhile there was pressure from within as well as from the outside. There is evidence that director St. John wanted a change, along with several members of the athletic board, because, on January 24, 1934, Willaman was asked to announce his plans by February 4. In other words he was being pressured to resign, which he did in a letter of January 31.

Temperament was said to be the chief cause of unrest, but there were other obvious factors, too. Ohio State had not won a Big Ten championship since 1920, and Michigan had won nine of the last twelve games. It was to prove amazing how much the Michigan game affected the lives of Ohio State coaches. In later years at least two others felt the bite of the Wolverine.

Willaman went to Western Reserve University as athletic director and head coach. He asked that Ohio State be placed on the Reserve schedule the following year, which was arranged. The Buckeyes won, 76 to 0, and it was the last time Ohio State played another team from within state boundaries.

Francis Schmidt Arrives

It is doubtful if any college football coach had more loyal, enthusiastic players—and friends for life, than Francis Aloysius Schmidt. Athletic Director St. John could not have made a more popular choice if he had spent a lifetime of picking and choosing, when he recommended the tall Texan to take over Buckeye football fortunes in the spring of 1934.

Not a "name" coach to Ohio State fans, Schmidt came from Texas Christian University, where, oddly enough, he spent the same years, 1929 through 1933, that his predecessor Sam Willaman had served at Ohio State.

Small wonder that St. John looked in Schmidt's direction. His five-year record at TCU defied the odds-makers. It showed forty-six victories, only six losses, and five ties. In each of the five years his teams won nine or more games and twice were undefeated. On two occasions he had undefeated strings of nineteen and then sixteen games. He coached at TCU for nearly two years before losing to Texas 7 to 0. That ended the non-losing streak of 19. TCU schedules ranged from ten to twelve games each year.

Schmidt had an undefeated record against some of the leading rivals, Texas A&M, North Texas State, Rice, Southern Methodist, and Hardin-Simmons. He lost to Arkansas once. Only Texas and Baylor could beat him twice. The sixth loss was to Tulsa, where he had coached, 1919-1921.

In 34 of Schmidt's 57 games at TCU the opponents failed to score. This prompted Ohio State halfback Dick Heekin to say

Francis Schmidt, the popular razzle-dazzle coach, headed Buckeye grid fortunes from 1934 through 1940. The gold football pants on his watch chain indicate victories over Michigan in 1934, 1935, 1936, and 1937.

in later years. "Schmidt knew something about defense, too."

When Schmidt arrived on the Buckeye scene, he seemed to

turn things completely around. Always wearing a bow tie, he resembled a successful businessman rather than a college football coach.

When someone asked him, "What about Michigan?" he replied, "Well they put their pants on one leg at a time, the same as the rest of us."

From this remark came formation of the Michigan Pants Club, which was made up of alumni and downtown businessmen. After each victory over Michigan, a dinner was held, attended by coaches and players as well as club members. Miniature gold pants were presented honored guests.

Schmidt was eccentric and, with it, amusing. He was constantly drawing plays and formations, whether in notebooks or on tablecloths. He also was absentminded on these occasions and once, while sitting in his hoisted car as it was being serviced, almost stepped out. Gas station attendants prevented him from falling to the concrete floor. He also was secretive with his new plays, often hiding them from his assistants while he went to lunch. Other times he would lock them securely in his desk. He also insisted that quarterbacks paste or draw plays inside their helmets to help them remember the offense.

Although he rated high in the profanity league, to which many of the faculty objected strenuously, Schmidt also had a soft approach. Many times during practice he would say, "Now, lookie." It became one of his favorite expressions.

Schmidt picked up at Ohio State where he had left off at TCU, a winner. His first Buckeye game was a 33-0 victory over Indiana, and after a 1 point loss to Illinois, 14-13, his team won all others, including Michigan, which was defeated, 34 to 0. It was a 7-1 season, the same that Willaman had had the year before, but there was much glamour and fanfare this time.

Schmidt's background would not have indicated that he some day would be a football coach. He held a law degree from the University of Nebraska, and his military career would have suggested that he had graduated from West Point. He was bayonet instructor with the 87th division and commander of Headquarters Company, 347th Infantry, AEF. Later he was captain of the 50th Infantry of the regular army. He was a Presbyterian and a Mason, being a member of Knight Templar, Scottish Rite, and Shrine.

Despite a heart-breaking loss to Notre Dame, which had no bearing on the Big Ten race, the Buckeyes won a share of the title in 1935, first since 1920, so Schmidt's record after 2 years was 14-2. He was a hero, not only on the campus but with the downtown followers and alumni as well.

Three losses were suffered in 1936 by a total of 12 points, 14-13 with Northwestern, 7-2 Notre Dame, and 6-0 Pittsburgh. Michigan was defeated for the third time 21 to 0, and it came on the heels of 2 other shutouts, 44-0 over Chicago and 13 to 0 with Illinois.

Indiana, which had failed to beat Schmidt's teams thus far, turned the tables in 1937 for a 10-0 victory, and Southern California edged the Buckeyes 13-12 for 2 defeats against 6 victories.

The 1938 season was Schmidt's poorest to date, a 4-3-1 year, with Michigan winning for the first time in 5 years. Southern California and Purdue joined the victorious Wolverines. Northwestern was tied 0-0.

Despite a season's ending loss to Michigan, 21-14, the Buckeyes won the Big Ten title outright in 1939 with victories over Northwestern, Minnesota, Indiana, Chicago, and Illinois. Cornell, being played for the first time, inflicted the other loss, 23 to 14.

Schmidt's final year was 1940 when he broke even in 8 games, his poorest season. The 40 to 0 loss to Michigan was the big blow, but losses also were inflicted by Northwestern, Minnesota, and Cornell again.

Schmidt's 7-year record added up to 39 victories, 16 losses and 1 tie, along with 2 titles, 1 outright and 1 shared.

The Notre Dame Game Of 1935

It has been nearly 39 years, but people are still talking about it. Meaning the Ohio State-Notre Dame game of 1935 in jam-packed Ohio Stadium. The attendance was announced as 81,018.

It was the first meeting of the two football giants, both undefeated at the time. The Irish had rolled over Kansas, Carnegie Tech, (then a football power), Wisconsin, Pittsburgh, and Navy. The Buckeyes had stopped Kentucky, Drake (85-7), Northwestern, and Indiana.

The Buckeyes were favored. Perhaps enthusiasm stemmed from the manner in which the team had finished the 1934 season as Francis Schmidt's first campaign showed only a one-point loss to Illinois, 14-13, and six straight victories to close the season. Included was a rollicking 34-0 triumph over Michigan and a season-ending 40 to 7 spanking of a good Iowa team.

A feeling prevailed through Buckeye-land: "We just cannot lose this one."

Many football games have been played in Ohio stadium since November 2, 1935, but none will leave a greater impression.

Fr. John Cavanaugh, president of Notre Dame University at the time, has said: "The game defied description." He has plenty of believers.

Sportswriters said it was fantastic (a word not used as much then, as now). Others said it was unbelievable.

The Buckeyes scored early in the first quarter after Frank Antenucci intercepted a pass on the Ohio State 24-yard line. He then lateralled to Frank Boucher, who, behind fine blocking, raced 76 yards down the west sidelines for a touchdown. With Stan Pincura holding the ball, Dick Beltz place-kicked the extra point.

The Irish came back to the Ohio 25 but failed to gain in 3 tries and a short punt was returned to the Buckeye 29 to get out of the hole. When the period ended, the Buckeyes were on the Irish 16, "Jumping Joe" Williams having been knocked out-of-bounds after a 1-yard gain.

As the second quarter opened, Boucher on a power drive went to the Notre Dame ten-yard line. Charley Hamrick then opened a hole for Boucher, who went to the four and a first down. After Pincura gained one on a sneak, Williams went over the Irish left tackle for a touchdown. This time Sam Busick missed the extra point.

The Buckeyes continued to play good defensive football, and the closest the Irish could get during the remainder of the half was the 29. Ohio State moved to Notre Dame's 31, but three successive passes failed, forcing John Kabealo to punt to Andy Pilney on the Irish eight-yard line. During this episode Coach Schmidt called for one of his famous triple laterals, and it gained five yards. It went from quarterback "Tippy" Dye to halfback John Bettridge to fullback Kabealo, and back to Dye again.

With the half ending 13 to 0, and the Irish really never threatening, it looked almost a cinch for the Buckeyes.

The Irish made their best penetration of the game toward the end of the third period when they marched to the Ohio 10, but there they lost the ball on downs.

Then came the big play of the day and one that swung the momentum toward Notre Dame. Kabealo got off another of his good punts, but this time Pilney took it on Ohio's 35 and zig-zagged 53 yards to the Ohio 12 before Boucher brought him down as the quarter ended, with Ohio still in front, 13 to 0.

Pilney later was carried off the field with a twisted knee and replaced by William Shakespeare, who was to have a big hand in the Irish comeback.

As the fourth period opened, two plays were stopped, but

Ohio State's pint-sized quarterback, William (Tippy) Dye, No. 50, carries the ball against Notre Dame in 1935. Notre Dame jerseys were numbered only on the back. Dye now is athletic director at Northwestern University.

on third down Pilney passed to Francis Gaul for a first down on the Ohio two, and from there Steve Miller, a substitute back, hit center for a touchdown. When the extra point was missed, Buckeye fans breathed easier.

This only served to make the Irish line battle furiously, and 2 plays lost 15 yards. When Notre Dame next got the ball in midfield, it put on a dedicated march that ended with a pass from Pilney to Mike Layden, good to the 1-yard line. Here, Miller hit the center of the line but fumbled, and Ohio State recovered back of the goal line for a touchback. It was a temporary reprieve.

The Buckeye offense failed again, which gave the Irish a new spark, and a pass from Pilney to Wally Fromhart put the ball on Ohio's 33. Two more passes took the ball to the 15, from where Pilney pitched to Layden for a touchdown. When Fromhart's placement try was low, the Buckeyes were still hanging on, 13 to 12.

Less than 2 minutes remained to be played, and Notre Dame attempted an onside kick. It failed to work, and Ohio State came up with the ball on its own 47-yard line.

At this point there was an opportunity to freeze the ball and run out the clock. However Pincura called for a direct pass from center to halfback Beltz, who fumbled after an eight-yard gain, being hit hard by a savage tackle. The ball was close to the sidelines, and Henry Pojman, a substitute Notre Dame center, touched it with his fingertips just before it went out-of-bounds. Present-day rules give out-of-bounds fumbles to the last team in possession. However, in 1935, fumbles out-of-bounds went to the team which last touched the ball.

The Irish knew this was their last opportunity, and they made the best of it. Pilney dropped back as if to pass, but finding no receiver open made a magnificent run to the Ohio 19. It was on this play that Pilney, who played his greatest game, suffered a wrenched knee. Shakespeare rushed in as his replacement and threw a long pass which Beltz partially intercepted, but could not hold on to.

This gave the Irish another opportunity, and this time Shakespeare passed high to end Wayne Millner who leaped between two defenders. When he came down he was in the end zone. It mattered little that the extra point was missed again.

There was just enough time left to take the kickoff and run one play, good for 3 yards. The Irish won, 18-13, all points coming in the final quarter.

It was a strange game, one that helped make Notre Dame football history and one that stunned Buckeye fans to the point many have not recovered yet. Certain it is the first half

From graduate manager to "father of athletics" to president of the university. This was the rapid step-up of George W. Rightmire who served as graduate manager in 1893, Ohio State's first. He became so active in sports administration that he was affectionately known as "father" and then became president of the university in 1926, serving until 1938.

belonged to Ohio State and the second to Notre Dame. Figures show that Ohio's pass defense, which paved the way for two scores through first-half interceptions, collapsed completely after intermission.

Notre Dame completed only 2 of 7 passes in the first half for a gain of only 12 yards and had 3 intercepted, including 1 which resulted in Ohio's first touchdown. In the second half the Irish aerials succeeded 8 times in 12 attempts and produced 128 yards, scored two touchdowns and set up the third. All told, Notre Dame advanced the ball 477 yards to Ohio State's 134, a convincing margin.

The game drained both teams, physically and mentally.

Notre Dame lost the following week to Northwestern 14 to 7, and Ohio State was hard-pressed to beat an inept Chicago team 20-13. The Irish also were tied by Army, 6-6, but did defeat USC in the final game, 20-13.

Ohio State fared somewhat better, defeating Illinois 6 to 0 and Michigan 38 to 0. The Buckeyes tied Minnesota for the championship, first since 1920. It was the second season for both Elmer Layden, Irish coach, and Schmidt. Notre Dame was still recovering from the shock of Knute Rockne's tragic death. Now a great victory had reduced the gloom.

The return game at South Bend the following year was a flat anti-climax. Notre Dame again won by 5 points, 7-2, in a game played in rain and mud.

The two schools have not met on the gridiron since. Unfortunately the games revealed religious overtones and differences among the faculty. President George W. Rightmire is said to have remarked that no football game was worth dividing the university. He did not elaborate, but athletic administrators got the message.

Schmidt was invited to speak at a Notre Dame football banquet at which he said, "I keep running and re-running the films of the second half of the 1935 game. Some day Millner is going to drop that ball."

He never did.

The Sarkkinen Brothers

One of the amusing stories to stem from military service during World War II involved the Sarkkinen brothers, Esco, an Ohio State all-American end in 1939 and his younger brother, Eino, a third string halfback on the 1940 and 1941 squads.

Esco was stationed at New London, Connecticut, with the US Coast Guard Academy while Eino was in the Air Force at Midland, Texas, along with Don Scott, a former Buckeye halfback teammate of Esco's.

One day a call came from the PR office, stating that Scott and Eino had been selected for the Army all-star team that was slated to work out at Yale University under the direction of Major Robert Neyland, former Tennessee coach. Another all-star squad was to train at Denver under Wallace Wade of Duke University.

Major Neyland said to Scott and Eino; "Go ahead. There will be no problems."

On the side, however, Eino said to Scott; "They think I am Esco. I think I ought to tell them."

At the urging of Scott, Eino decided he could have some fun.

The first conflict arose when Scott was sent to Denver, breaking up whatever collusion they might have had in mind.

This setback was overcome at Yale, however when Eino found Esco's college roommate, Frank Clair, on the squad.

"We had a ball for two weeks," Eino relates, "as we did nothing except go through calisthenics. And with Esco at

Esco Sarkkinen

Eino Sarkkinen

nearby New London we could get together often."

It was not long before Major Neyland decided to step up the program with pass patterns. But, with Clair on the opposite team giving signals and clues, Eino was able to cope with his faster company.

Soon the pinnacle of success was to be achieved, temporarily.

George Cafego, all-American quarterback from Tennessee, one of Neyland's own proteges, was directing the squad on which Eino was playing. With Cafego pumping the ball prior to a pass, Eino found himself on the receiving end of a button hook, but only after a defensive back had over-committed himself. The result was that Eino ran 80 yards for a touchdown following a nifty catch and dazzling sprint.

"THAT," yelled Major Neyland "is the way an all-American end performs." Assistant coaches applauded and shouted encouragement.

Needless to say, Eino, Clair and Esco, who was a visitor that day, were soon rolling on the ground with laughter.

Adding to the luster of the day was the presence of a Pathe News photographer who filmed part of the scrimmage, including Eino's triumphant appearance in the end zone.

Then the truth had to come out.

Neyland decided to switch Eino to defensive end, a position he knew nothing about. Unfortunately Clair was on the same team, putting an end to their trickery.

"I went to the major," Eino relates "and told him I had never played end in my life.

"He took our little joke in stride, merely sending me back to Midland to fly bombers again."

This move prompted Joe Williams, sports editor of the New York *Herald-American,* to write, "Major Neyland must have quite a team at New Haven. He has just cut an all-American from the squad."

An amusing aftermath developed, however when Esco, scouting for the Coast Guard eleven, met Herman Hickman after an Army game.

"You don't look like the Sarkkinen I saw at New Haven," said the jovial Herman.

"You are right," replied Esco. "That was my brother."

"I have not been sure during these two months," said Hickman, "because the name is unusual. But I will tell you one thing. He never did line up like an end."

Yes, it was a sad day when Major Neyland decided to have Eino, otherwise known as "Shorty," try to play defensive end.

Paul Brown Succeeds Schmidt

Even if it was good, (and the *Alumni Monthly* of December, 1940, says it could not be), Ohio State partisans would never like a 40-0 shellacking at the hands of Michigan, but even the most rabid Michigan-haters were willing to admit that Tom Harmon and his associates on November 23, 1940, were one of the greatest aggregations that ever played in Ohio Stadium.

The answer seemed to be that Michigan players were keyed up as never before. They were playing their last game for Fielding H. Yost, who was retiring in the spring of 1941 as athletic director. They also were inspired by the great Tom Harmon who seemed to be at his best for his last game. This was a tough combination to face.

There was no dampening of enthusiasm at the football banquet, however. President Howard Bevis said, "We are not going to quit playing football here. There will be another season next year, and our team will be out there battling with chins up. As long as we observe the tenets of good sportsmanship, we can tell the rest of the world go hang."

Vice-president Lew Morrill said, "Winning the game is not the most important consideration in football. While we would rather win than lose, the experience of being a good loser is worth a hundred victories won unworthily."

L. W. St. John, director of athletics, said, "We will go right on playing football here. The fact that 73,000 fans came out to see us last Saturday after the team lost three previous games

Paul E. Brown, former coach of the Cleveland Browns and now coach of the Cincinnati Bengals, was Ohio State's head coach for the three seasons of 1941, 1942, and 1943. Brown was an instant success, winning the Big Ten and national titles in 1942 after a 6-1-1 record in 1941. After a 3-6 season in 1943, Brown enlisted in the Navy and did not return to Ohio State.

proves that fans are more interested in seeing a good game than the winning of it."

Captain Jim Langhurst of the 1940 team pulled the surprise of the banquet evening when he presented Coach Schmidt with a gold trophy from the seniors "In Appreciation of Your Efforts."

Schmidt, always highly emotional, broke down in tears and was only able to say, "This gets my goat. It means a lot to me."

Despite all of the fanfare that 1940 was not such a bad season after all, Schmidt and all five assistants were asked to resign December 16. This followed an "investigation of the football situation" by a special committee of the athletic board.

The No. 1 choice, by the proverbial country mile, to succeed Schmidt was Paul E. Brown, known as the "miracle man" of Massillon High School. Brown's teams won 81 games, lost 8, and tied 1 during his 9-year regime there. While numerous names of the coaching fraternity wanted the Ohio State job, it soon became "Brown against the field." The press was in his corner, as well as 500 members of the Ohio High School Coaches' Association, who were asked by the officers of the association to write a good word about Brown—which they did.

Brown seemed to make a hit with certain members of the athletic board when he said there would be no winter practice, as Schmidt had held.

"I do not believe in it," Brown said. "The boys are fed up with football when they get too much of it."

Impressed with the new coach, one board member said, "Mr. Brown may be the find of the country, or he may explode into a thousand pieces."

Answering a question on the difference between high school and college football, Brown said, "Football is football, wherever it is played. They still block and tackle and run with the ball, whatever the league. College players are high school players just one or two years older. I am not the least bit fearful of the difference."

Speaking of Brown's Massillon teams, St. John said, "Their success came from soundness in the fundamentals of blocking and tackling and better execution of the ABC's of football than their competitors. Out of it came a splendid spirit of loyalty to the coach and to each other, calculated to make them go on the field and give everything they had at all times. In short, the secret of Brown's success has been his genius of organization, his capacity for hard work and thoroughness, and a fine understanding and liking for boys."

It was apparent from the start that Brown was not going to require that players be 6 feet tall and weigh 200 pounds. He had entered Ohio State as a freshman in 1926 weighing 136 pounds after some experience as a high school quarterback. Realizing that he was too small for the Buckeyes, Brown went to Miami University at Oxford, Ohio. He had planned to be a lawyer but decided to switch to coaching and then earned a master's degree at Ohio State during summer periods. Meanwhile he played quarterback at Miami in the 1927 and 1928 seasons.

So at 32 Brown became the youngest coach in the Big Ten and one of the youngest in the nation.

President Bevis was quite impressed. He said, "I have talked with Mr. Brown and I am delighted. His qualities as an athletic coach have been explored thoroughly by the athletic board. My conversations with him have convinced me that his

Ohio State's first national championship team was the 1942 eleven coached by Paul E. Brown, later head coach of the Cleveland Browns and now with the Cincinnati Bengals. The

WESTERN CONFERENCE AND
BROWN-McGRANAHAN-BIXLER-SOUDERS-COLEMAN-REES-TAYLOR-WILLIS-S
DYE-MACKEY-WIDDOES-DEAN-ANTENNUCI-SLUSSER-CLEARY-SELBY-VICKROY-
DURTSCHI-FRYE-HORVATH-JAMES-HOUSTON-SCHNEIDER-PALMER-HACKETT-

other qualities will make him a welcome and respected member of the university staff; one who will exert a wholesome influence upon the entire student body as well as upon the members of his own squad."

Brown was given a one-year contract, plus a gentleman's agreement of three.

He stayed three noteworthy years, 1941, 1942, 1943.

Football at Ohio State in 1942 was the realization of long-standing dreams of students, alumni, and fans. Each Saturday proved to be a big thrill as Paul Brown's precision-like Buckeyes won the Big Ten championship and was acclaimed the nation's No. 1 team by the Associated Press, representing 156 writers. Talent was both plentiful and individually outstanding, headed by timely strategy of quarterback George Lynn, regarded by many as one of Ohio State's all-time fine quarterbacks.

team lost to Wisconsin but won nine of ten games. The team produced three all-Americans in end Bob Shaw, tackle Charles Csuri, and guard Lindell Houston.

NATIONAL CHAMPIONS - 1942
TE-EICHWALD-SHAW-McCAFFERTY-DUGGER-STEINBERG-LAVELLI-FEKETE
USCH-APPLEBY-PRIDAY-MATUS-McCORMICK-DRAKE-DIESEN
ING-McDONALD-LAPUJ-STAKER-CSURI-SARRINGHAUS-NAPLES-BIGGS

Brown, selected that year as one of the 10 most outstanding young men in the country, had his team in excellent condition from the start. The team rolled up 337 points, blanked Purdue and Fort Knox, and finished with a 9-1 record.

A football team seldom figures in one "overtime" game, much less two. This rarity came to the Buckeyes within a five-year period, both resulting in victories in 1943 and 1947.

With the score tied 26-26 and the game to all intents and purposes ending in a tie, the head linesman threw a flag at the close of the Illinois-Ohio State game in 1943. Dr. Walter E. Duffee, Buckeye team physician, now deceased, saw the flag go down from the west side of the field, while the late Paul Walker, a *Dispatch* reporter, heard a horn on the east side. The flag, for an Illinois offside on the final play, was thrown as the crowd was starting to file out of the stadium and players of both teams were going to their dressing rooms.

Assistant coach Paul Bixler, later head coach, says that the officials had forgotten just where the ball had been but placed it in the vicinity of the 18-yard line.

Coach Paul Brown ordered John Stungis, who never had attempted a field goal before, to try for three points. He succeeded, and the Buckeyes won, 29-26, with some of the players standing around in street clothes.

Coach Ray Eliot of Illinois was in a daze, as were hundreds of spectators, who had left with the score tied. Most of them did not know until Sunday morning that Ohio State had won. Among them were President Howard L. Bevis, Lieutenant Governor Paul Herbert, and Lieutenant Colonel James H. Leusley, head of the university ASTP program.

While newspaper photographers had approximately 12 minutes to get set for the place-kick "added attraction," only one caught it, and he got it on a film he had exposed previously. His newspaper, the *Columbus Dispatch,* used it in four columns anyway, with the caption, "Excited? Who's Excited?"

The other half of the story occurred November 8, 1947, also in Ohio stadium.

Northwestern was leading 6 to 0 with 13 seconds to play. The Wildcats intercepted a pass by Pandel Savic, but Northwestern was penalized back to the seven for having 12

John Stungis, who never attempted a place-kick before, booted one successfully in an "overtime" game to beat Illinois 29 to 26 in 1943.

men on the field.

One second remained on the clock. Rodney Swinehart made three yards, but Northwestern was offside and penalized to the three. Savic then passed to Don Clark in the end zone for a touchdown.

Emil Moldea's try from placement was blocked, but again the Wildcats were penalized for offside, giving the kicker another try. This time, with no seconds left on the clock, Moldea made good, and the Buckeyes walked off with the charitable 7 to 6 decision.

Widdoes Takes Command

With Paul Brown in the Navy, Carroll Widdoes, his assistant at both Massillon High School and Ohio State, took command in 1944. His 2-year stint was one of the brightest since the early days of Dr. J. W. Wilce. The 1944 team won the Big Ten title in an undefeated season; it was acclaimed "national civilian champion," and Widdoes himself was named "College Coach of the Year." The 1945 team lost only to Purdue and Michigan, the latter 7 to 3 when an offside penalty put the Wolverines in scoring position.

Born in Philippines of missionary parents, Widdoes was a reserved, religious man. When he was six years of age, his parents received leave to return to Dayton, Ohio, for one year where he entered school, but he then returned to Manilla and remained there until he was thirteen. He then came back to Ohio and entered the United Brethren Home at Lebanaon, Ohio. With no football team there Widdoes participated in baseball, basketball, and track. He later became an all-around athlete at Otterbein College in Westerville, Ohio.

Widdoes' parents were captured by the Japanese during the war but eventually were released unharmed in 1946. Thus he was able to have a reunion with them while he was a member of the coaching staff.

While many thought Widdoes' selection as successor to Brown was a surprise, he soon made his presence felt as a fundamentalist and good organizer. He liked to teach blocking techniques, and in this department the Buckeyes stood out.

Soft-spoken Carroll Widdoes was Ohio State's head coach in 1944 and 1945 when his two-year record was 16-2. He was named College Coach of the Year in 1944 when the undefeated Buckeyes won the Big Ten title. The team also was acclaimed "national civilian champions."

There was some fine talent on the 1944 team, headed by Les Horvath, a 23-year-old "coach on the field." He worked with 4 outstanding freshmen, all under 18 years of age. The group consisted of Bob Brugge, Ollie Cline, Dick Flanagan, and Tom Keane. In addition Widdoes inherited tackles Bill Willis and Russ Thomas, end Jack Dugger, and guards Bill Hackett and Warren Amling. All made all-American except Thomas.

The team opened the 1944 season by swamping Missouri 54 to 0 and followed with a 34-0 triumph over Iowa—88 points in 2 games and the opposition had not scored. People were beginning to whisper. When a good Wisconsin team was defeated at Madison 20 to 7, they were talking out loud.

It was no problem to get the fans excited about the fourth

Ohio State's war-time team of 1944 produced a Big Ten champion and the unofficial title of "national civilian champions." While nearly all other major college teams had Army, Navy, Marine, or Air Corps assistance, the Buckeyes were

game of the season, for Paul Brown was bringing the Great Lakes Naval team to Columbus. It was a case of teacher vs student, and Ohio State won the decision, 26 to 6. More than 73,000 people were in the stands as a tribute to Brown's homecoming. The game was tied 6 to 6 going into the last period, but Horvath led the Buckeyes in a strong rally. Horvath played under 3 coaches at Ohio State, but it was the first time he had a hand in defeating 1 of them.

Minnesota, Indiana, Pittsburgh, Illinois, and Michigan fell in order. Illinois was played at Cleveland before 83,627, the largest crowd to witness an athletic event during the war. Defense against the speedy "Buddy" Young paid off in this one. He was held to 61 yards in 9 carries, his lightest output of the season. The Michigan game was an Ohio State epic, a 52-yard march late in the final quarter, culminating in a touchdown, naturally, by Horvath, for an 18-14 victory.

For the first time since 1920 there was talk of a Rose Bowl

made up of freshmen and military—deferred students. The team produced four all-Americans and a Heisman award winner in Leslie Horvath, who was one of the all-Americans. The others were end Jack Dugger, tackle Bill Willis, and guard Bill Hackett.

bid. That was the last time any Big Ten team had been invited and it was Ohio State, which had lost to California, 28 to 0. A special meeting of faculty representatives was held in Chicago on Sunday following the Michigan game, but the answer was "No." It was reported that the vote was 7 to 3 against sending a representative to Pasadena. Tennessee went instead, playing Southern California. Director St. John was pretty bitter but said he would abide by the wishes of the majority.

Widdoes' second season was approached with optimism, but even the most ardent fans could not expect a duplicate of 1944. Horvath had graduated along with Willis and Dugger. Brugge was in the Navy while Hackett had been injured in an auto accident during the winter. He suffered a head injury and was advised not to play football again. There were two valuable additions, however. Dick Fisher, who played halfback for Brown in 1941, returned along with Paul Sarringhaus who had played the same position in 1942.

William (Bill) Willis, all-American tackle in 1944 and an all-pro lineman with the Cleveland Browns, had the unusual distinction of playing on two national champions while a member of the Buckeyes. The 1942 team was so acclaimed, as was the war-time eleven of 1944. Willis, an outstanding student and campus leader, has been a member of the Ohio Youth Commission since retiring from professional football. He was elected to the National Professional Football Foundation Hall of Fame in 1972.

The first 3 games were on the right side of the ledger against Missouri, Iowa, and Wisconsin. The good offense and defense which had marked the beginning of 1944 again were in evidence, 101 points being scored against 6. The winning streak stopped at 12 in a row when Purdue rocked the Buckeyes 35 to 13. Bob DeMoss, recent Purdue head coach, threw 2 touchdown passes, and Ed Cody rambled for 3 more.

The Buckeyes went right back to their winning streak, however, waltzing over Minnesota, Northwestern, Pittsburgh, and Illinois. Only the 16-14 game with the Wildcats was close.

Both Michigan and Ohio State were in the title chase as they had been the year before. The Buckeyes led in this tight struggle at Ann Arbor until late in the fourth quarter, 3 to 0, by means of a 17-yard field goal by Max Schnittker. A 5-yard off side penalty against Ohio State, when the ball was on the 6, moved the Wolverines up to the 1, and on the second effort Henry Fonde scored on a reverse. The extra point was good, so, as Ohio State had won by 4 points in 1944, Michigan took this one by the same margin, 7 to 3.

Leslie Horvath:
An All-Time Favorite

The 1944 football team of Ohio State University not only proved to be the No. 1 civilian 11 in the nation but produced the No. 1 player in Leslie Horvath. A senior in the College of Dentistry, 167-pound Horvath was the inspiration which helped carry his younger teammates through the Buckeyes' first undefeated and untied season since 1916.

Deprived of varsity participation in 1943 because of the army specialized training program on the campus, Horvath reported for practice September 1, after his dental unit had been discharged from military obligations in August. Flattering offers to play professional football came to the Buckeye ace, but he voluntarily elected to remain with the Scarlet and Gray. Despite a heavy schedule of studies, Horvath never missed a practice and often was the first man on the field.

The 24-year-old star not only directed the team's play but participated in more actual combat than any other member of the squad. Though playing only 8 minutes against Pittsburgh that season, Horvath played 402 minutes of football, a full quarter more than any of his teammates. The lightest regular on the team and one of the slightest-built players in the Big Ten, Horvath carried the ball 163 times and gained 924 yards, an average of nearly 6 yards per try. He led the team in scoring with 72 points, 30 more than Bob Brugge, the runner-up. In forward passing Horvath completed 14 aerials in 32 attempts, thereby adding 344 more yards to Ohio State's offense. Despite lack of ruggedness Horvath was one of the team's big defensive

Leslie Horvath

cogs and often prevented touchdowns when he was the lone defender between the ball carrier and the goal line.

It is doubtful if any player in Big Ten history, before or since, has received as many individual honors as Horvath. Recipient of the John Heisman award, first Ohio State player to be so honored, Horvath likewise was voted the most valuable man to his team, a step which led to his selection as the outstanding player in the conference for 1944. Newspapers in all sections of the country voted him the "Player of the Year."

Equally efficient in both the single wing and T-formation attacks, Horvath played under three head coaches during his varsity career, the late Francis Schmidt, the late Carroll Widdoes, and Paul E. Brown—the only Ohio State football player to have had that experience.

Horvath had the personality and quality of leadership to inspire his mates to almost unbelievable achievements. The best example was his direction of the winning touchdown against Michigan in 1944, the victory meaning the Big Ten title for the Buckeyes. With Ohio State trailing 12-14 and 8 minutes remaining, Horvath led a sustained march of more than 50 yards.

Calling his younger mates together in the huddle preparatory to launching the successful march, Horvath said, "We are not going to pass. We are not going to fumble. We are not going to give up the ball. We are going right in with a series of first downs. Now, everyone block as he never has blocked before."

The result was just as Horvath ordered—no passes, no fumbles—superb blocking through 4 first downs on short gains—1 first down being made on a "4th and 5" situation.

Leslie Horvath, modest and unassuming, will live in the minds and hearts of every Ohio State University supporter: always a gentleman, student, and athlete.

Season Of 1946:
One Of Peaks And Pitfalls

The season of 1946, when Paul O. Bixler served his one year as head coach after being an assistant under both Paul Brown and Carroll Widdoes, was one of peaks and pitfalls.

The peaks came in a fine 21 to 0 intersectional victory over Southern California at Los Angeles and a thrilling 39 to 27 triumph over previously-undefeated Northwestern at Evanston.

Inasmuch as this was the first year of the pact with the Pacific Coast Conference to permit the Big Ten winner to appear in the Rose Bowl, hopes were high for a championship team.

Wisconsin, however, pricked the bubble 20 to 7 at Madison; Illinois came from behind to win 16 to 7 at Champaign; and then Michigan really unloaded to hand the Buckeyes a 58 to 6 lacing in Columbus. Since it was the last game of the season and on the home field, at that, bitter memories lingered through the winter months.

The season had not been all bad, though, as the Buckeyes had tied Purdue and Missouri, and defeated Minnesota and Northwestern.

While the Northwestern games appeared to be nothing more than another Big Ten tilt, since both teams eventually finished in second division, it established a precedent in Buckeye football history as follows: BOTH TEAMS SCORED IN EVERY QUARTER.

This had never been done before and has not been matched since, despite some high-scoring games such as 46-34,

Paul O. Bixler was 39 years old when he assumed charge of the Ohio State football squad in 1946. He came to the university in 1941 as a member of Paul Brown's staff, coaching the ends and wingbacks. He served only one year as head coach.

44-20, 83-21, 34-32, and 35-34.

From the time Ohio State scored on the seventh play of the Northwestern game, when Bob Brugge went 13 yards, it was a parade of touchdowns and missed extra points which prevented a safe margin for either team.

Fullback Pete Perini, who was the only starter who scored for the Buckeyes, tallied in the second quarter, but this was

Fullback Joe Whisler was the star of the Ohio State's epic game with Northwestern at Evanston in 1946 when both teams scored in every quarter. It was an unprecedented feat and has not been repeated in the past 27 years.

matched by two Northwestern touchdowns, one in each period. Each team missed a conversion attempt, making it 13-13 at the half.

Northwestern went ahead 20 to 13 after 2 minutes and 35 seconds of the third period, but Jerry Krall, who like Brugge did not start, rambled 21 yards for 6 points. John Stungis missed the conversion attempt, keeping the Wildcats ahead 20-19. Moments later Krall scored again on a 20-yard pass, but for the third time Stungis missed the extra point.

With a precarious 25 to 20 lead going into the fourth period Joe Whisler, another non-starter, pushed the Buckeyes ahead, scoring from the 1-yard line. This time Stungis kicked the point for a 32-20 lead.

The Wildcats came right back with an 81-yard touchdown run by Fred Aschenbrenner, and the kick was good, so once more the Ohio State advantage was the unsafe margin of 5 points, 32-27. Only 2 minutes and 39 seconds had been played in the fourth period, so it was still anybody's game.

At that point the Buckeyes received a break when Tony Adamle intercepted a pass and returned to the Northwestern 30. Whisler caught a pass good for 19 yards, then, with the exception of 2 plays carried the ball the rest of the way, the last bolt for a touchdown. Stungis added the 39th point.

In the last 3 minutes and 25 seconds the Wildcats reached the Ohio State 30, and the Buckeyes went back to the Northwestern 8 when time ran out on the wild-scoring orgy.

Score by quarters of historical game;

Ohio State	7	6	12	14—39
Northwestern	7	6	7	7—27

Bixler recalls the flight to Los Angeles in three DC-3's as being more frightening than any of the football games in 1946.

"We had a big plane lined up, but at the last minute the government cancelled our plans. In the smaller planes we had to stop at St. Louis, Oklahoma City, and Albuquerque. The squad voted to practice there, so we stayed overnight at an Army base. Nearly everyone got sick from the stopping and starting. Oddly enough the sickest player was Hal Dean, a guard who had been a parachute jumper during the war. However he recovered rapidly and played a fine game against USC."

The Buckeyes won the game, 21 to 0.

Returning to Columbus the squad had planned to stay in Texas Sunday night, but fog forced another landing at Albuquerque. This caused an all-day flight Monday, with school classes being missed as well as the coaches missing a staff meeting.

To shorten the week further the team had to leave by train Thursday night for Madison, Wisconsin, where the Badgers thumped the Buckeyes on Saturday, 20 to 7.

Small wonder! It was a rough week.

118

The Fesler Regime

Following Bixler's resignation it was evident that the first choice of athletic director St. John was Wesley E. Fesler, then coaching at Pittsburgh.

Fesler, one of Ohio State's all-time great athletes, was a nine-letter winner, three each in football, baseball, and basketball. In addition he was a three-time all-American football selection, joining the great "Chic" Harley as Ohio State's only representatives in this category.

Versatile on the gridiron as an end or fullback, Fesler was even more so on the baseball diamond, where he played first base, second base, and center field. On May 18, 1931, Fesler had one of the greatest days at bat in the history of Ohio State baseball. He hit two doubles and three home runs, two of the homers coming with the bases full. With a total of sixteen bases he accounted for nine of ten runs as Ohio State defeated Illinois, 10 to 5.

In addition to being all-American in football, Fesler was all Big Ten in basketball. He also was named the most valuable player in the Big Ten in 1930.

Because Fesler began his college career in engineering, a course he followed for more than one year before transferring to commerce, his graduation was delayed until 1932. In the fall of 1931, and for one season following his graduation, Fesler was a member of the Ohio State football coaching staff. In 1933 he went to Harvard University as head basketball coach and assistant in football.

Wesley E. Fesler, one of Ohio State's all-time great athletes, was head football coach from 1947 through 1950.

In 1942 Fesler joined the staff of Connecticut Wesleyan University as head football and basketball coach and freshman baseball coach.

During 1944 Fesler received a leave of absence to join the Office of Strategic Services but in February of 1945 became head basketball and assistant football and baseball coach at Princeton University. In the spring of 1946 Fesler was named head football coach at the University of Pittsburgh, his last stop before coming to Ohio State.

Vic Janowicz: All-American

When Vic Janowicz, from Elyria, Ohio, enrolled as a freshman at Ohio State University in the fall of 1948, he had just finished being the most widely-recruited high school athlete in the history of the state. In 1947 Janowicz had led his high school football team to the championship of the Lake Erie League, a rugged circuit of good teams. He scored 101 points and ran away with all-Ohio honors. It was reported that 61 colleges and universities expressed interest in getting Janowicz' talents.

Vic said that he always wanted to go to the state university and play in the big stadium. He regarded it as a patriotic gesture, he said, indicating that Ohio boys should play in their home state. He added that he was impressed with Wes Fesler, who was beginning his second year as head coach. Since Janowicz also played baseball and basketball, he relished the opportunity to play these sports on the university level.

As a sophomore Janowicz played largely on defense, including safety. He also kicked off, punted, and booted extra points. Later he added field goals to his category of scoring.

Playing sparingly on offense in his first year, Vic scored only 14 points on 2 touchdowns and a pair of extra points. He rushed 30 times for 121 yards, caught 1 pass for a 24-yard touchdown, and punted 4 times for an average of 34.8. Injured in the third game of the season against USC, Janowicz missed the next four games but finished strong against Illinois, Michigan, and California in the Rose Bowl.

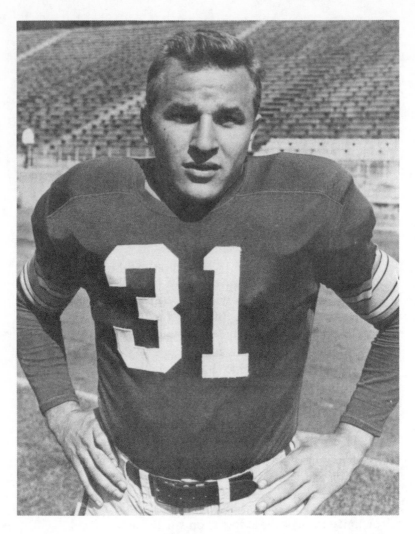

Vic Janowicz

Janowicz had his best year as a junior in 1950 when he received the Heisman award in a landslide vote, the first junior to win the honor. He also was a unanimous choice for first team all-American.

Vic played in all 9 games and scored 65 points, including 5 touchdowns, 26 extra points, and 3 field goals. In addition he passed for 12 touchdowns, including 6 against Pittsburgh and 4 against Iowa. He also punted 54 times for an average of 36.5 yards. In an incredible all-around performance, Janowicz carried the ball 114 times for 437 yards. It is true that he did everything except sell programs at half time.

In the game with Iowa, which Ohio State won 83 to 21, Janowicz established a record for points-after-touchdown with 10 in 11 attempts.

His place-kick against Michigan in the "Blizzard Bowl," described elsewhere, is an historical event among Buckeye fans.

In 1951, Woody Hayes' first year as successor to Fesler, Vic scored only one touchdown himself but passed for two others, kicked nine extra points, and booted three field goals. His punting average went up to 39.4, one of the best in the country. Carrying the ball 106 times, he averaged 3.5 yards per try.

During Vic's 3-year varsity career of 26 games he scored 8 touchdowns, gained 982 yards from scrimmage, and passed 102 times, completing 39 for 635 yards and 14 touchdowns. One of the most active kickers of that period, Vic punted 120 times for 4,532 yards, more than 2½ miles, for an average of just under 38. He also kicked 6 field goals, 2 of which won games from Pittsburgh and Northwestern in 1951.

Small wonder that he was a wanted young man in 1948.

Rose Bowl — January 1, 1950

Preparations for the first Rose Bowl trip in December of 1949 (first since the trip by invitation in 1920) caused quite a stir among members of the athletic board who had the responsibility of making all plans, paying the bills and selecting the personnel whose bills would be paid by the athletic department.

When the budget for the Rose Bowl was discussed, it was to include all expenses for 55 persons designated as the official party, plus all other related projects in connection with the Tournament of Roses. Estimated costs of these expenses were placed at $41,000, to be paid by the Tournament of Roses Committee.

Richard C. Larkins, then athletic director, submitted a list of 11 additional persons to be taken on the trip to properly take care of details of operation. These included ticket sales people, publicity man, auditor, an additional coach, 2 managers, an injured squad member, and an office manager.

Dr. Howard L. Bevis, then university president, now deceased, brought up the matter of the board of trustees' jurisdiction in the selection of the official personnel to represent the university at the Rose Bowl. These, he said, included the trustees, administrative personnel, and the athletic board representatives, all of whom would be subject to the state auditor's approval.

The auditor's office, he said, would conduct a post audit on Rose Bowl accounts, therefore all transportation expenses

Richard C. Larkins, former Buckeye football and basketball star, served as Ohio State's director of athletics from 1947 to 1971. Larkins, second director in the school's history, succeeded L. W. St. John, who pioneered activities from 1913. Larkins now is retired. Larkins built the varsity program up to 18 sports, one of the largest in the nation, and was widely-known as a leader in the intercollegiate field. He was active in NCAA, Olympic, and physical fitness programs as well as the National Association of Collegiate Directors of America. Under his supervision Ohio State University was the first to conduct a summer youth program, whereby hundreds of underprivileged children have benefited through use of the university facilities. The winner of the James J. Corbett Memorial Award, Larkins also was elected to the Helms Hall of Fame for athletic directors. Only two men in addition to Larkins have received the Corbett award to date: H. O. (Fritz) Crisler of Michigan and the late William R. Reed, commissioner of the Big Ten.

125

First Ohio State squad to play in the Rose Bowl under the modern agreement with the west coast was the 1949 team which defeated California, 17 to 14, on a fourth quarter field goal by Jimmy Hague. The team won seven, lost to Minnesota

would have to be officially approved before they could be expended. After considerable discussion it was decided that the matter of athletic board personnel selection representing the university at the Rose Bowl be left to the board of trustees.

Being consistent with rising prices, inflation, and increased costs the $41,000 budget of 1949 jumped to $119,535 in 1972, with the official traveling squad of players moving up from 44 to 60.

Ohio State's first appearance in the Rose Bowl in 30 years was achieved after a tie game with Michigan, 7 to 7. Since the Wolverines had gone to the Rose Bowl the previous year, they were not eligible this time, although the tie game gave them a share of the Big Ten title.

Close games, a 27 to 0 loss to Minnesota and a tie game with Southern California, in which several Buckeye players were injured, marked the season. Minnesota was the only team to shut out the Buckeyes, and Wisconsin was the only team that did not tally against Ohio State.

The tie game with Michigan was attained after it looked like a 7-6 loss, but the Wolverines were offside on an extra point

126

and had two ties, one of which was against Michigan, enabling the Buckeyes to gain the Rose Bowl invitation. Vic Janowicz, Heisman award winner, and all-American a year later, was a member of the team.

try that failed, and on the second attempt Jimmy Hague made it good.

Had Ohio State not gotten a clean shot at the Rose Bowl, it might have been a ticklish situation. Minnesota, next in line and in third place with a 4-2 record, had always opposed the postseason game and likely would have turned down a bid. That would have made Wisconsin, a fourth-place finisher, the choice to play. Fortunately this likely complication was eliminated.

Although the Buckeyes got off well offensively against the California Bears, they trailed at the half, 7 to 0. A 55-yard pass took the Bears to the Ohio 19, and they scored in 4 plays.

On a fourth and five situation in the third period and the ball on the California thirteen, Jerry Krall jump-passed to Ralph Armstrong for a first down on the six, and then Fred (Curly) Morrison, who put on an all-American performance that day, blasted over to tie the score. A moment later Bill Trautwein blocked a Bob Celeri punt, recovered by Jack Lininger, and Krall scored from two yards out.

Sportswriters voted Morrison the "player of the game."

Just before the third quarter ended, Bob Celeri lateraled

127

wide to Jim Monachino, who got away for a 44-yard touchdown run, and when the extra point was good the score was tied at 14.

Then came another big play by Jimmy Hague, whose extra point, after a miss, had tied Michigan to put the Buckeyes in the Rose Bowl. When Celeri was rushed on a punt try, he kicked left-footed, and it went out-of-bounds on the California thirteen. Three plays gained seven yards, but the Buckeyes were penalized five yards for delay of game trying to get Hague into the game. With the ball placed on the seventeen the kick was good for a 17-14 victory, and Ohio State had its biggest day in a long, long time.

The kick, briefly, avenged Ohio State's 28-0 loss to California 29 years earlier and ended the Bears' winning streak

Fullback and punter Fred (Curly) Morrison was named the most valuable player in the Rose Bowl game of January 1, 1950, when Ohio State defeated California, 17 to 14.

Ohio State's thrilling 17-14 victory over California in the 1950 Rose Bowl game came on this field goal by Jimmy Hague late in the fourth quarter. Several players of both teams forgot their blocking assignments and watched the ball clear the cross bar.

of 10. The boot also continued the Big Ten's domination of the bowl, this having been the fourth success in as many starts against the Pacific Coast under the new pact at that time.

The victory prompted the late Russ Needham, sports editor of the *Columbus Dispatch* who often quarreled with Fesler's coaching tactics, to write:

"Ohio State has known many glorious moments in its football life, but none to compare with this. This was the wow of all time and it came, as all will attest, when it could do the most good."

In appreciation of Wes Fesler's successful season in 1949 the Athletic Board commended the head coach and his staff in a letter, which read:

> "The Athletic Board of The Ohio State University joins with a host of others in congratulating you and your associates upon a successful football season, climaxed by the great victory in the Rose Bowl. Because you and your staff exemplify so fully the type of coaching leadership under which we desire the young men of this university to train in competitive sport, the board is deeply gratified at your decision to remain as a part of the university community.
>
> "That you would remain as head football coach, has, as you know, at all times been our earnest hope; in this hope the board had at no time authorized and consequently the director of athletics had not undertaken any consideration whatsoever of a possible successor.
>
> "You may rest assured that you will have in the future, as you have had in the past, the respect and wholehearted support of the athletic board. We re-affirm our confidence in you as a leader in the field of sports, not alone because of the successes of your teams but even more because of your outstanding contribution to good character and citizenship through the development in those teams of fine sportsmanship and indomitable courage.

> "Yours in loyalty to Ohio State"
> (Signed) Ralph Paffenbarger,
>   (secretary)
> Frank R. Strong, (chairman)

The Blizzard Bowl —
November 25, 1950

"...And the snow came down horizontally."

That was the late John McNulty's "lead" in the *New Yorker* magazine following the Ohio State-Michigan game of November 25, 1950.

You had to be there to believe it. Even then, some were not so sure they were viewing reality.

The game has been called the "blizzard bowl," "snow bowl," "ice bowl," and other names less complimentary.

"Blizzard" probably is the most appropriate. It almost obliterated vision between the field and stands. More than 82,000 tickets were sold, but only 50,503 fans showed up. Some of these hardy souls might not have come except that Ohio State was playing Michigan, with the Rose Bowl on the line for the Wolverines. Some fans may have been fooled at first by the weatherman. Because the weatherman, in turn, was completely fooled by the sudden polar conditions that hit Columbus Saturday morning. Weather conditions on Friday had been normal, cool, with no precipitation.

But by 10:00 a.m. Saturday the stadium looked like a scene from Admiral Byrd's expedition. Stadium seats were ice-covered and getting thicker by the minute as snow, accompanied by a biting wind, froze as it landed.

Nearly all of the spectators present were huddled in "B" deck, sheltered from the snow by the top deck. They were not protected from the wind, however, which swept in from the open end of the horseshoe and circled them like a giant lasso.

131

Fans were wearing all of the clothes they could use, some weighted down so much they could scarcely move. Some clear-thinkers covered their heads with cardboard boxes as a shield against the wind, now blowing 40 miles an hour. Slits, carefully cut on one side, allowed for what vision was available. The temperature, in the thirties early Saturday morning, dropped to five above zero during the game.

Scheduled to start at 2:00 p.m., the game was 20 minutes late getting under way, largely due to the ground crew having great difficulty removing the tarpaulin, which had been left on the field until nearly noon. The snow-covered tarp, valued at $3,000, was then cut to shreds to facilitate removal. Boy Scouts, spectators, and game officials joined the ground crew which was forced to use a road grader with little success.

Meanwhile rival athletic directors, Richard Larkins of Ohio State and Fritz Crisler of Michigan, debated what to do: cancel, postpone, or play.

No Big Ten football game had ever been postponed, and

while weather conditions were bad at all other conference sites that day no thought was given to calling off the contests, rumors to the contrary.

Thousands of fans thought the game should not have been played, but they did not have any answers for the problems of refunding money. A postponement would have carried the game into December, and later events proved that the following Saturday was almost as bad, weather-wise.

A glance at the Big Ten standing prior to the game posed a few problems, too, and both athletic directors were aware of them. Ohio State was leading, 5-1, followed by Illinois, 4-1, and Michigan, 3-1-1, with Wisconsin also in contention with 4-2.

The Buckeyes were not Rose Bowl candidates but the other three were. Ohio State could have "backed into" the title by not playing and could cop the crown by winning. Later events proved that Illinois "blew" the Rose Bowl trip by losing to underdog Northwestern, and the Badgers were eliminated when Ohio State lost.

It was an incredible turn of circumstances that put Michigan on top as well as in the Rose Bowl.

Since Larkins was the home boss, it was his decision to make, and when he and Crisler were unable to contact commissioner Kenneth L. (Tug) Wilson relative to what action to take, the Ohio State athletic director said, "Let's play." For some time Larkins took a lot of "guff" from people who never would have said a word if Ohio State had won.

It was a great day for the second-guessers.

The play-by-play and statistics of the game were as bizarre as the weather.

The first scoring play not only put Ohio State ahead 3 to 0 but proved to be, in the judgement of veteran press box observers, the greatest field goal and single effort they had ever seen on a football field—if indeed the stadium ground could have been called a field that day.

With wind, snow, sleet, and numb hands as handicaps, Vic Janowicz kicked a field goal from the 28-yard line that had to have a lot of leg power to split the uprights. People are still talking about that one. Many writers said they would vote for Janowicz' effort as the biggest single achievement of the 1950 football season.

134

Shortly afterward, also in the first period, Janowicz cleared a spot in the end zone in an effort to punt out, but the kick was blocked and rolled out-of-bounds for a safety.

Then the game-breaker occurred, a play that has caused nearly a quarter century of discussion. With the ball in possession of the Buckeyes on their own 12-yard line and 40 seconds left to play in the half, Janowicz attempted to punt. It was blocked by Michigan's Tony Momsen, and he recovered for a touchdown. The extra point was good. It had been a third down punting attempt, and Fesler was roundly criticized for not stalling out the clock, a decision which reasonably could have accounted for a 3 to 2 Ohio State victory.

Desperation passing occupied the second half, and neither team came close to scoring.

The statistics defied reason. Michigan had won without making a first down and gained only 27 yards on the ground. Ohio State gained 16. Michigan threw 9 passes and did not complete 1. Ohio State threw 18 and completed 3 for 25 yards. There were 2 interceptions. Ohio State had 3 first downs, 2 by rushing and 1 by passing. Michigan fumbled 6 times and lost the ball once, while Ohio State fumbled 4 times, and likewise gave up the ball once.

There were 45 punts in the game, a Big Ten record. Janowicz kicked 21 times for a 32-yard average, but 2 blocked punts cost Ohio State 9 points. "Chuck" Ortmann of Michigan kicked 24 times for a 30-yard average. His only blocked punt gave Ohio State field position for Janowicz' first quarter field goal.

The Momsen brothers, Bob playing for Ohio State and Tony for Michigan, were big factors in the outcome. Bob blocked the first period kick, and Tony got the big one in the second period as well as the touchdown.

So the game that many said should not have been played was played, and the Buckeyes again lost to Michigan. Fesler, who objected to starting the game in the first place, had failed to beat the Wolverines in four tries. Once more it was the pressure of losing to Michigan that discouraged another Ohio State coach.

Wesley Fesler Resigns

When Fesler resigned in Chicago during the Big Ten meetings December 9, 1950, it created a precedent in Ohio State coaching circles. Never before had a coach resigned while outside Columbus. However President Howard Bevis, Athletic Director Richard Larkins and Faculty Representative Wendell Postle, who also were in Chicago, wanted Fesler to make up his mind. He had said that he "would not coach again for a million dollars," yet there seemed to be some doubt that he could be serious.

When, late Saturday night, it was determined that Fesler meant what he said, it created quite a stir in Chicago newspaper circles. The late Arch Ward, sports editor of the *Tribune,* who had departed for home, returned to the office to direct activities which resulted in a page one story. Newspapermen from other cities in the Big Ten bombarded the Ohio State headquarters in the LaSalle Hotel until early hours Sunday morning seeking details.

The athletic board accepted Fesler's resignation January 17, 1951, which was to become effective February 28. Immediately Fesler accepted the head coaching job at Minnesota, and two assistant coaches, Dick Fisher and Lyal Clark, went with him.

It became necessary to reorganize the football coaching staff, and president Bevis requested the chairman to appoint a screening committee to survey the field of eligible candidates and report to the athletic board.

After Fesler's coaching career ended at Ohio State, he told the author, "My entre into Ohio State football in 1947 was an experience I would not have missed for anything—but I would not want to repeat it for the world.

"It came at a really rough time. The records will show that the 1946 season, before I arrived, was a tough one, finishing with that horrendous loss to Michigan. Then the Cleveland Browns went to work, taking what was left. First went captain-elect Tommy James, then Adamle, Cline, and others.

"The 1947 spring practice was anything but hopeful, yet on the other hand was exciting. Even though our immediate future looked dismal, we all became sincerely dedicated to a goal. Every thought, every movement was pledged to that goal. In three years we were going to be in the Rose Bowl and have fun doing it.

"Football, by its very nature, means hard, brutally hard, work. Yet I know from my own undergraduate experience it can, and should be fun. There is plenty of room for laughter on a football field, and, as a coach, I have tried desperately hard to encourage it.

"I sincerely hope that the 1947, 1948, 1949, and 1950 men look back on those days with the fond memories I do."

Chairman Frank Strong presented the following resolution as an expression of the athletic board to Wesley E. Fesler:

"The athletic board keenly regrets, Wes, your decision to give up the position of head football coach at the university. You have exemplified fully the type of coaching leadership under which we desire the young men of this university to participate in competitive sport. It has ever been, as you know, the board's earnest hope that you would remain in this capacity as a part of the university community.

"Although you have now determined to sever this connection, you continue to hold our respect and sincere regard. Firmly assured that you will, in the years that lie ahead, retain for your alma mater that same outstanding loyalty which you have shown in the past, the board joins thousands of other well-wishers in hoping for you satisfying success and happiness."

The athletic council, at the suggestion of director of athletics Richard C. Larkins, should have a screening committee to study the backgrounds of all candidates interested in succeeding Wesley E. Fesler as head football coach.

Chairman Frank Strong then appointed Larkins; vice-president, registrar Bland Stradley, professor Hermann C. Miller, Fred C. Mackey, alumni member, and Walter Donham, student member. Strong also served on the committee.

The function of this committee, the board minutes said, will be to survey the entire range of possible candidates for the position of head football coach at the Ohio State University and to screen the names of those considered for presentation by the director of athletics to the athletic board.

The athletic board, after consideration, will transmit its nomination to the president of the university, who, in turn, will present it to the board of trustees for its final action.

It was the sentiment of the board that "much care should be exercised before giving statements to the press regarding the new head coach."

No information should be divulged to anyone, the board ruled, unless official approval was given through the proper channels.

Woody Hayes Selected

After Wes Fesler's resignation was accepted by the athletic board on January 17, 1951, to become effective February 28, forty candidates applied for the head coaching position. Included were five from the professional ranks, twenty-six from colleges, six from high schools, and three who were inactive at the time. Only eight were screened.

Inasmuch as four head coaches had been on the job since Paul Brown's last year in 1943, the screening committee established elaborate qualifications. They wanted the man selected to stick around awhile and remove Ohio State from the label of "graveyard of coaches."

The committee declared that the man "should be a person of both intellectual and moral integrity, a gentleman in the best sense of the word: that he be suited by temperament, interest, and background for productive work with young men, for cooperative advancement of the present sports program of the department of physical education and athletics, and for professorial membership in the university faculty. He is to be, by proven capacity and experience, skilled in football technique, in the effective teaching of the game, and in the organization and direction of a staff of coaching and administrative assistants."

There was more!

Personal qualifications included headings of personality,

character, conduct, and family. (He was to have a wife). Personal qualifications included headings of coaching ability, coaching attitude, and coaching reputation.

University qualifications came under three categories: departmental, all-university, and the public. Departmental included acceptability, cooperativeness, accountability to superiors, and genuineness of interest in the total sports program. The all-university was acceptability, cooperativeness in general university objectives, undivided loyalty to the university, attitude on football in total educational pattern, and educational background.

In regard to the public he was to have good press relations, be of ambassadorial capacity and, in general, have a good reputation.

It was evident that the committee had not forgotten anything.

Two candidates from the professional ranks wished their names to be held confidential, and their desires were respected. Paul Brown, Buckeye coach for three years, 1941, 1942, and 1943, and for five years after the war with the Cleveland professional team bearing his name, made an earnest bid to regain his old job.

Richard C. Larkins, director of athletics, stated flatly that he would resign if Brown was selected. This seemed to seal Brown out of contention, despite strong support of the *Columbus Dispatch* and other groups.

Larkins then offered the following proposal to the board: "That the athletic board recommend to the board of trustees, the appointment of Wayne Woodrow Hayes as head football coach for one year, at a salary of $12,500, with the possibility of advancement of $500 a year in succeeding years, until the maximum of $15,000 is reached."

A motion was made, seconded, and passed unanimously.

The late Lew Byrer, former sports editor of the *Columbus Citizen*, once told a cub reporter that information regarding Ohio State football, particularly the coaching staff, was the most important news in the city.

"We do not care," he said, "what happens in the statehouse, courthouse, city hall, or any place else by comparison. Ohio State football comes first."

Woody Hayes

There was evidence on Monday, February 12, 1951, to support Mr. Byrer's position. At least the board of trustees felt that the appointment of a new football coach required greater attention than had been focused on appointments of college deans.

A meeting of the athletic board had been called for 9:00 a.m. in the office of Vice-President Bland Stradley. It was for the purpose of relaying word to the trustees that Woody Hayes had been approved as head coach.

Word came back that "Because three members of the board of trustees have found it impossible to be present at today's meeting, and feeling that a matter of this importance should have the consideration of a larger representation of the board, a special meeting has been called for Sunday, February 18, at 4:00 p.m."

Thus, at an unprecedented Sunday meeting, Hayes was approved after considerable discussion, much of it still centering on Paul Brown.

Once more, Buckeye football was Page One news.

When Hayes was being screened for the head coaching job, he did not wait for members of the committee to ask questions. He started right in telling why he wanted the position, how he considered it his greatest opportunity and challenge, and expressing confidence he could handle all facets of the job.

He explained that since both his father and mother had been school teachers he was accustomed to the educational side of life. Hard work, sound fundamentals, and well-conditioned athletes would be adhered to, Woody seriously explained. He said he would pick assistants who would be willing to work at a fast pace or they would not be working at all. In recruiting, he said, education would be stressed above everything else.

Someone asked Hayes, "How about practice on Friday afternoons?"

Hayes replied, "There will be no practice on Friday. By that time, the hay is in the barn."

Vice-President Bland Stradley, an influential member of the committee, and a farming educator, seemed impressed by this homespun remark.

Hayes later said he felt he had the job won, judging from the expression on Stradley's face.

142

He was right.

Hayes came to Ohio State with an all-Ohio coaching career behind him, having started as an assistant at Mingo Junction, Ohio, High School. His first head coaching job came at New Philadelphia, Ohio, High. At this point he enlisted in the navy and served five years. Following his discharge he received his first opportunity to become a head college coach, and it was at his alma mater, Denison University, at Granville, Ohio, in 1946.

He coached for three years at Denison and two at Miami University, at Oxford, before coming to Ohio State. His Denison teams won 19 and lost six, and the 1947 and 1948 teams were undefeated after a 1-6 season in 1946. At Miami his 1949 team was 5-4, and in 1950 the team won nine of 10 games.

A 1935 graduate of Denison, Hayes majored in English and history. He played tackle for three years and was an outfielder in baseball. He holds a master's degree in education administration from Ohio State University.

Hayes, who has made four trips to Vietnam to discuss football with the United States military personnel, was a tireless worker in behalf of his job. He likewise was a fluent speaker, an outstanding recruiter, and a meticulous planner.

Only two Big Ten football coaches were on the job longer than Hayes...Amos Alonzo Stagg at Chicago, 41 seasons, and Robert C. Zuppke at Illinois, 29.

Never one to downgrade his team, or the opposition either, Woody Hayes was always an optimist. While some coaches have been known to build up the opponents to the point of making their own team an underdog and soliciting sympathy for the "down-trodden" home forces, Hayes always gave Buckeye fans a favorable trend.

"We figure to win," was his favorite, almost offhand prediction.

Hayes has been described as a man of many moods and contrasts.

He was often the first to say that he was difficult to work with, but he also would add, "I think I am fair."

Esco Sarkkinen, veteran end coach who joined the Ohio State staff in 1946, five years before Hayes arrived, said, "You do not describe Hayes in one word, one sentence, or even one paragraph, but in chapter after chapter."

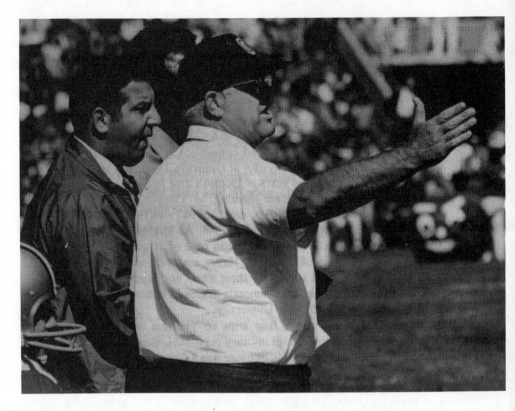

Woody Hayes on the sidelines.

Hayes did not lose his poise too often during a game, probably less than the average head coach on the sidelines. During practice, however, it was another story. He broke countless watches and eyeglasses when a play went wrong. He wore a baseball cap at all times, that is while it still was in one piece. The caps joined the watches and glasses in being shredded. Once Woody had the equipment man slit the seams with a razor blade, making the cap easier to rip.

Hayes laughed off cold weather, usually wearing only a T-shirt at practice and games.

One player contends that it was always possible to tell when trouble was brewing. "He will whip off his cap with his right hand, shoot his hair back with his left (Woody is left-handed), and slam his cap back on. Then you know a play has gone haywire."

Hayes' many antics made the headlines. Unfortunately his humanitarian deeds did not receive as much exposure.

He, in order, loaned money to players, which cost Ohio State a year of probation; evicted Big Ten writers and officials from pre-season practice; had locker room battles with California sports-writers; ripped down sideline markers; and had an altercation with a Los Angeles photographer.

Woody had no trouble enlisting jeers and boos from the stands as his biggest cut-ups came when the Buckeyes have played on the road. This was particularly true at Iowa and Michigan where he threw his coat, kicked folding chairs, and booted a sideline marker which he thought was rubber. It turned out to be concrete, which must have pained him considerably, but he never limped to show it.

Woody's wife Ann, his best friend and severest critic, is proudest of his four Vietnam trips, and his role in campus riots a few years ago. "He came back with several notebooks filled with names of parents, wives, and girlfriends. If he could not contact them by phone, he wrote to them. He did not overlook one person," says Anne.

Woody turned down a fifth opportunity to visit Vietnam in an effort to quell campus disturbances. According to Mrs. Hayes, Woody was on the campus every day and every night making speeches in dormitories in an effort to steer certain people in the right direction. He usually made his point.

Hayes was held in high regard by his fellow coaches, many of whom have wanted to join the Ohio State staff whenever there was an opening.

Players as well as the assistant coaches knew that he had their best interests at heart. He drove the players academically as well as physically. His irritation, call it temper, came to the surface quickly when he detected a loafer, on or off the field. Someone asked what made Woody fly off the handle quicker than anything else. The answer was simple: when he saw someone not performing up to his potential.

Woody worked seven days a week, 12 to 14 hours, and he could not understand why everyone else could not do the same.

145

But returning to Woody's practice of not offering an alibi. Webster defines optimism as: (1) "The doctrine that the world is the best possible world; (2) The doctrine that reality is essentially good; (3) The doctrine that the good of life overbalances the pain and evil of it; (4) An inclination to put the most favorable construction upon actions and happenings, or anticipate the best possible outcome."

With an English major behind him, as well as one in history, it has been said Woody knew the meaning of every word in the dictionary.

The above defines his outlook.

Woody Wins First One

As soon as Woody Hayes was hired as football coach, he went right to work preparing for his first opponent, Southern Methodist, a highly-regarded team with forward passing ace Fred Benners leading the attack. The Mustangs had a winning streak going, during which they had scored handily on all opponents, so it was with considerable surprise that the Buckeyes not only won but shut out the Texans 7 to 0. Benners completed 21 of 29 passes but never connected on a long one. Ohio State intercepted 5 passes, and, while Woody's T-formation was hit-and-miss, 1 touchdown stood up. A pass from Tony Curcillo to Bob Joslin accounted for the touchdown, and Vic Janowicz added the extra point.

The Buckeye victory prompted Wilfrid Smith, former sports editor of the *Chicago Tribune*, who covered the game, to say afterward, "Woody must have worked all summer on that game. He was really out to win the first one."

The next foe, Michigan State, had been admitted to the Big Ten, but its games were not to count in the standings until 1953. It was a rugged, high-scoring game, the Buckeyes losing 24 to 20 when the Spartans came from behind with a last-minute touchdown. While the outcome did not handicap Ohio State in the standings, fans groaned over losing to a team not yet a Big Ten neophyte. Later events proved that the Buckeyes had little to be ashamed of, as the Spartans finished the season undefeated, as they also did in 1952.

Hayes was far from satisfied with his first season of 4-3-2,

147

the same that Paul Bixler had had in 1946. Woody later said he feared that he might be asked to step down since he was on a one-year contract. "Fortunately, Director Larkins stuck with me, and I was determined to work all the harder to justify his confidence," Hayes said later.

The team lost to Indiana and Michigan, in addition to Michigan State, and the tie games were with Wisconsin, 6-6, and Illinois, 0-0. Woody was disappointed in the tie with Wisconsin as the team failed to move the ball as it had the previous week against Michigan State. The tie game with Illinois was the only contest the Illini did not win in an undefeated season that included a Rose Bowl victory over Stanford, 40-7. Wisconsin also had a great year of 7-1-1. On the other hand the one-sided loss to underdog Indiana was a shocker. The Hoosiers did not win another conference game and finished 2-7.

The second season saw a big improvement, a 6-3 year and 5-2 in the league. The big victory was over Michigan 27-7, the first one since 1944. Following on the heels of a 27-7 victory over Illinois the previous week, fans were inclined to forget annoying losses to Purdue, Iowa, and Pittsburgh, games that could have been won as easily as they were lost. The team featured a dazzling freshman named Howard (Hopalong) Cassady and one of Ohio State's most admired quarterbacks, John Borton.

The same record, 6-3, was repeated in 1953, and the three losses were no flukes. Illinois' halfback combination of J. C. Caroline and Mickey Bates ran the Buckeyes dizzy in front of the home folks, 41 to 20. Ray Eliot, Illini coach at the time, said it was one of his greatest victories.

Michigan State, now having its games counted in the standings, defeated the Buckeyes 28 to 13 to tie Illinois for the championship and represent the Big Ten in the Rose Bowl, where it defeated UCLA, 28 to 20. The other loss was to nemesis Michigan, 20 to 0.

This was the year of elimination of the platoon system and of offensive and defensive specialists, at least for the time being. Hayes made numerous shifts to get the best football players in the game for the greatest length of time. His linemen, Dick Hilinski, George Jacoby, Jerry Krisher, Mike Takacs, and Jim Reichenbach, were strong and durable. Often the Buckeyes played with the fewest substitutions in the Big Ten. Backfield men Borton, Bobby Watkins, Dave Leggett, and Cassady, were just as rugged.

Despite fair success with the new rules Hayes was angry about the necessity of playing "one-way" football. He insisted that the rule was ill-advised and made effective too quickly. The players agreed with him, as a vote revealed a 40 to 2 count in favor of the two-platoon system.

But, in spite of "one-way" football, Hayes was working hard toward developing a championship team. Writing in his column, "Letters From Home," Jack Fullen, editor of the *Alumni Monthly*, said "While other coaches are hunting, fishing, playing cards or golf, Woody Hayes is running off pictures and plotting strategy...He is one of the most persuasive and forceful recruiters of talent we have ever had."

Later, Hayes and Fullen were to feud violently, but there was no indication of that here.

National Championship: 1954

The Buckeyes hit the jackpot in 1954. An improvement had been expected over the previous season, but just how much had been anybody's guess. The 1953 team had given up 164 points with all opponents scoring from 6 to 41 points. The Buckeyes had totaled 182. Obviously the defense had to be improved.

An important addition to the offense was Hubert Bobo, a tough sophomore, who could run, block, and play defense. He fitted in well with Cassady, Leggett, Borton, and Watkins.

The Buckeyes swept by Indiana 28-0, California 21-13, and Illinois 40-7 before being pushed to the hilt to stop Iowa, 20-14. The Buckeyes had to stop the Hawkeyes on the five-yard line to preserve the decision.

That brought Wisconsin to Ohio Stadium in a showdown between two of the nation's leading teams. Little Tad Weed kicked a field goal for the Buckeyes for a 3 to 0 lead, but before the half the Badgers scored on a 35-yard pass and kicked the extra point for a 7-3 lead at intermission.

Toward the end of the third period a play occurred that turned the game around, sky-rocketed Cassady toward all-American fame, and started the Buckeyes to the 1954 pinnacle. With Wisconsin on the Ohio State 20, "Hopalong" intercepted Bob Miller's pass on the 12 and returned 88 yards in one of the most thrilling runs in stadium history. He zig-zagged, feinted and, with what Woody called "down field vision," left a flock of would-be Badger tackles scattered all over the field.

Anticipating a great game, the press box was loaded with the nation's leading writers. Cassady made the all-American team right then and there.

With the Buckeyes leading 10-7 at the end of three periods, the Badgers folded to the extent of giving up three touchdowns, the first of which was set up by another long run by Cassady, one of 39 yards. Bobo, Jerry Harkrader, and Leggett added touchdowns before Wisconsin scored with four minutes left. The 31 to 14 decision came right in the middle of the season, and now there was no looking back.

There was a natural letdown the following week at Northwestern, and injuries to Bobo, guard Jim Parker, and end Dick Brubaker added to the difficulties. Cassady played the entire game with a bruised leg. With the score 7-7 going into the final period the Buckeyes pulled out the decision on a pass from Leggett to Watkins, and the latter kicked the extra point for a hard-fought 14-7 verdict.

Pittsburgh was blanked 26 to 0, the first shutout since the opener with Indiana, and Purdue was jolted 28 to 6. The Boilermakers were beaten with long runs by Cassady and Watkins, a 79-yard scoring march, and a pass from Leggett to Brubaker, one of just nine thrown that afternoon.

That brought on the showdown with Michigan in Ohio Stadium, where all tickets had been sold for several weeks. The Buckeyes were leading the Big Ten with a 6-0 record, and the Wolverines were 5-1 with a chance to tie for the title, if they could win. All other contenders had been eliminated.

The Associated Press rated Ohio State No. 1 in the country, followed by UCLA and Oklahoma. The UPI had UCLA first, followed by Ohio State, with Oklahoma third.

As is so often the case, bad weather haunted the game, and rain fell during the morning hours. Hayes wanted the bands kept off the field to preserve the turf, but he was overruled by the university presidents, Dr. Howard Bevis of Ohio State and Dr. Harlan Hatcher of Michigan.

When Michigan took the opening kickoff and scored without losing the ball in 6 minutes and 28 seconds, Buckeye fans were stunned. Nothing like this had happened to their favorites in a long time.

An intercepted pass by Jack Gibbs put the Buckeyes back

151

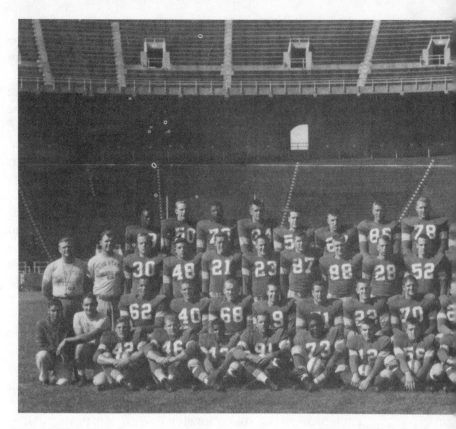

The 1954 team was a national champion contender following seven conference victories and intersectional triumphs over California and Pittsburgh. Led by all-American and Heisman

in business with less than 3 minutes left in the half. Gibbs caught the ball on Ohio's 43 and returned to Michigan's 10 before he· was caught. After a penalty for delay of game, Leggett passed to Fred Kriss for a touchdown, and Weed kicked the tying point. Both Gibbs and Kriss were third stringers going into the game, but at half time they were real heroes.

Neither team scored in the third quarter, but momentum was going Michigan's way and when the final period opened, Michigan had a first down on Ohio's four-yard line. It looked like bad news for the Buckeyes, but four cracks at the line left the Wolverines one foot shy of the goal line, big Jim Parker leading the stonewall defense.

The events which followed have caused Hayes to describe

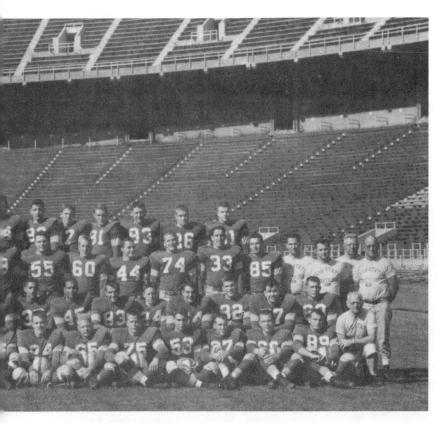

award winner Howard (Hopalong) Cassady, the team defeated Southern California in the Rose Bowl 20 to 7.

them many times as "the greatest thing that has happened in my coaching experience."

What did happen was a march of 99 yards and 2 feet for a touchdown. As usual Cassady supplied the important punch, a 61-yard run from the Ohio 2 to the Michigan 37. After 2 first downs worked the ball to the Michigan 8, Leggett passed to Brubaker for a touchdown and Weed again made the extra point.

The Wolverines suffered a case of jitters at this point and not only fumbled but were penalized for offside. In addition passers slipped while throwing, and Cassady intercepted one, returning it 13 yards. That was the clincher. The Buckeyes never gave up the ball until Cassady scored from the one-yard line. Again Weed split the uprights.

Thus the Buckeyes had their first undefeated, untied team since 1944 and became the second Big Ten team to go through a seven-game conference schedule without defeat. The other was the Chicago team of 1913, the year Ohio State entered the conference.

After the game Hayes not only was carried off the field but was dunked, fully clothed, in the shower. Once in a dry suit Hayes told the press that Cassady had been the big difference with his long runs and pass interception while Parker had supplied the defensive strength.

"Michigan won the first half," Hayes pointed out, "but the second was the reverse. You have to be lucky to go through a season undefeated, and luck came our way. Cassady is a true all-American. He should get the Heisman award."

Statistics showed that Michigan made 15 first downs to 13 for Ohio State and outgained the Buckeyes 303 yards to 254. But, as Hayes said in the post-game conference, Ohio State's defense was geared to stop touchdowns. There was no question about it, stopping Michigan at the one-foot mark turned the game around.

Michigan out-punted the Buckeyes by an average of 42 yards to 24, but 3 pass interceptions were returned for 62 yards, 2 leading to touchdowns. Michigan also lost the ball twice on fumbles. Cassady was the leading ground gainer, netting 94 yards in 14 carries for an average of 6.7. Bobo netted 52 in 7 tries for 7.3. The Buckeyes again played it "close to the vest" personnel-wise. With fullback Watkins out of the game with an injury, only 5 backs were used, compared to 8 by Michigan.

After four years both Hayes and Ohio State football were "tops."

Rose Bowl — January 1, 1955

Never before had it rained on a Rose Bowl crowd, but the first day of January, 1955, spiked the record with a vengeance. Not only did it pour all day, but fog and cool weather added to the woes of the players and fans alike. The miserable conditions were more depressing to Trojan followers, however, as the Buckeyes won the mud battle, 20 to 7.

Whereas Ohio State was undefeated over a nine-game schedule, the Trojans had played 11 games, winning 8. Two of their three losses came in the last two games of the season against UCLA and Notre Dame. UCLA, ranked No. 1 nationally but ineligible to play in the Rose Bowl, had trounced the Trojans 34 to 0, and many west coast fans were annoyed with the rule that prevented the Uclans from tackling the Buckeyes. They had appeared in the bowl the year before, losing to Michigan State. The late "Red" Sanders, UCLA coach, was named coach of the year, Hayes being runnerup. Woody did not complain about playing second fiddle to Sanders, but he was disturbed about the Uclans being No. 1 in the polls. He was positive he had a point that Ohio State had played a stronger schedule than UCLA. Even some of the west coast critics agreed with him.

After both teams oozed around in a scoreless first period, the Buckeyes, thanks to a recovered fumble by Jim Parker, went 69 yards without giving up the ball. On the second play of the second quarter Leggett sneaked over from the three. The Trojans were offside, but the penalty was declined and Tad

Rain, fog, mud, and cool weather met Rose Bowl fans on January 1, 1955. Here quarterback Dave Leggett of the Buckeyes is scoring on a line smash 35 seconds into the second quarter. Leggett was named the most valuable player in the game, won by Ohio State over USC 20 to 7.

Weed booted the extra point.

Following the ensuing kickoff Joe Contratto's slippery pitchout to Jon Arnett went wild, and Leggett recovered on the Trojan 35.

Bobby Watkins smashed through tackle for 14 yards and on the next play caught a pass from Leggett for a touchdown. He grabbed the ball on the 7 while running at full speed and carried a couple of Trojans over the goal with him. Weed kicked the 14th point, and the Buckeyes had gotten all of their points in 1 minute and 20 seconds.

With 9 minutes left in the half Bobo punted to Aramis Dandoy on the Trojan 14 and, with fine blocking ahead of him, went 86 yards for a touchdown. When Sam Tsagalakis kicked the extra point the Trojans were back in the game, they thought.

The field, now muddier than in the first half, held the offenses down in the third quarter, neither team scoring. With 2 minutes and 10 seconds gone in the fourth quarter, Leggett took charge and directed the team for 77 yards, passing to Jerry Harkrader from the 9-yard line for a touchdown. This time Weed's kick was blocked.

The Buckeyes again were knocking at the door with three minutes left, but Leggett's pass was intercepted on the USC 10-yard line. It was the only time during the game that a Trojan had stepped in front of a Buckeye receiver.

Statistics were top-heavy in favor of the winners, who piled up 22 first downs to 6 for USC. Total yards gained

Dave Leggett

favored the Buckeyes 360 to 206, and Leggett, who was named "player of the game," completed 6 of 11 passes for 65 yards. The Trojans were able to complete only 3 of 8 for 29 yards. Ohio State lost the slippery ball only once, but the Trojans gave up 3 fumbles. Punting was outstanding considering the playing conditions, and the Trojans had this average edge, 46 to 38.

Ohio State rushed the ball 69 times compared to the

Coach Woody Hayes (left) does not seem to be as happy as he should be. His Buckeyes have just defeated Southern California 20 to 7 in the rain-drenched Rose Bowl game of January 1, 1955. However Hayes is telling reporters that the bands should not have been permitted on the field at half-time because playing conditions then became intolerable.

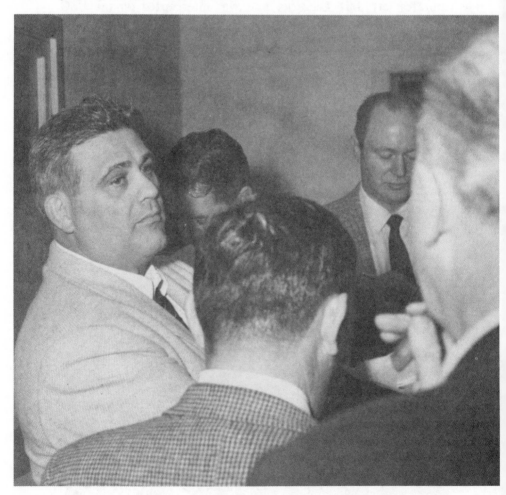

Trojans' 28, with Cassady carrying 21 times for a net of 92. Leggett carried 16 for 67, gaining every time he handled the ball. It was his perfect ball-handling that earned him the "most valuable" award and was a tremendous factor in the victory. Watkins was right behind with 64 yards in 15 tries. Bobby was a ball of fire all afternoon and seemed oblivious to the hazardous running conditions. Harkrader had the highest average of 7 yards, with 49 gained in 7 trips.

After the game Hayes had the first of many controversies with the west coast writers. He said that at least five teams in the Big Ten could have defeated the Trojans, and this was taken in some quarters as an insult to west coast football. He was merely giving an honest answer to an honest question, but it was not accepted in that light.

Hayes also criticized the bands being on the field at half time. He made it clear that he thought that the musicians chopped up the grass too much for second half play. Since the university had gone to great expense and much trouble to get the 120-piece marching band to Pasadena, this even back-fired on the home front.

Ohio State fans went back to the Huntington Hotel wet but happy. Many of them never dried out until they returned to Columbus where the cleaners made extra revenue trying to get coats, suits, and dresses back in shape.

The date of January 2 dawned warm and clear with no sign of the previous day's disturbance. The day was made even brighter when word was received just before the squad left for the depot that the Football Writers' Association, ignoring the opinion of wire service polls, had voted Ohio State No. 1 for 1954.

1955 — Another Big Ten Championship

Many of the stars of 1954 were back again, so it was with great optimism and fanfare that the 1955 campaign was welcomed. Cassady was ready to go again and so was Don Vicic, a powerful fullback, who made people scatter when he barged into them. All-American Jim Parker was set to anchor the forward wall; Fred Kriss was available for place-kicking chores; and some good-looking sophomores were considered to have enough talent to start.

After a 28 to 20 win over Nebraska, Stanford stopped the Buckeyes cold at Palo Alto, 6 to 0. It was just the second time the Buckeyes had been shut out since the Iowa game of 1952. The Cardinals trained on Cassady, who was held to 37 yards in 11 carries. Stanford took the opening kickoff and went 69 yards for the touchdown, something few teams had done to the Buckeyes in recent games. The score came on a 2-yard pass, breaking Ohio State's 11-game winning streak.

The Buckeyes were ready for Illinois at home the following Saturday, stopping the Illini 27 to 12, with Cassady scoring 2 touchdowns.

It was a real oddity that this powerful team should lose another non-conference game, but Duke took the measure of the Buckeyes, 20 to 14. It was the first showing of the Blue Devils in Ohio Stadium, and they made the most of their opportunity. Hayes was disappointed after the game but praised Duke and said that the visitors deserved to win.

Getting back on the Big Ten winning streak again, the

Buckeyes rolled over Wisconsin, Northwestern, Indiana, and Iowa to make it 12 league victories in a row. The Badgers and Wildcats did not present too many problems, but Indiana and Iowa applied the pressure, striving for an upset. The Hoosiers finally bowed 20-13, and Iowa was out-lasted 20 to 10.

Both Michigan and Michigan State were in the running to go to the Rose Bowl when Ohio State invaded Ann Arbor for the season's finale. The Buckeyes were in front with 5-0, followed by Michigan with 5-1, and Michigan State at 4-1. The Spartans, who had plenty of fans in Ann Arbor that day, needed an Ohio State victory to send their favorites to Pasadena for the second time in three years.

Hayes had said that the 1954 game with Michigan was his favorite victory, but the 1955 battle with the Wolverines must have given it a run for the money. The first game featured offense and this one defense, for Michigan was to cross the midfield stripe only once this afternoon, that on a penalty.

Wearers of the Maize and Blue seemed completely frustrated, particularly in the fourth quarter when they were penalized three times for unsportsmanlike conduct and once for unnecessary roughness. One player was expelled from the game and near fist-fights occurred on the field. Meanwhile, Michigan State fans in the stands were gleeful and shouting "unpack," just in case Wolverine followers had ideas of preparing for a Rose Bowl trip.

With 5:10 left in the half Kriss kicked a 24-yard field goal that was the only scoring before intermission. The Buckeyes put on a sustained drive midway in the third period, and Cassady scored from 2 yards out. The point was missed by Don Sutherin. With only 2:20 on the clock Bob Barr was thrown for a safety by Bill Michael, running the score up to 11-0. The real clincher came with only 1:15 remaining on the clock. Penalties moved the ball to the 1-yard line, and Vicic dove into the end zone. It mattered not that Sutherin again missed the extra point, as the score now was 17 to 0.

Fans flooded the field, and the Michigan goalposts came down.

Statistics were overwhelming in support of the Buckeyes except for punting, a category in which the Wolverines always have excelled. First downs were 20 to 5, and the net yards gained were 333 to 95. The Buckeyes attempted only 3 passes, completing 1 and intercepting 2. The Wolverines completed 3 of 9 attempts.

Cassady, with 146 yards, outgained the entire Michigan team by 51 yards, and hard-running Vicic averaged just under 5 yards with 81 in 17 tries. Sophomore Don Sutherin, who later was to be a big factor in Ohio State's kicking game, averaged better than 4 yards per try with 75 in 18 trips.

With two successive championships behind them, the players were as happy as any group of college players could be—and the happiest of all was Woody Hayes, who has said many times that the 1955 victory over Michigan comes close to being a "perfect game."

As usual Hayes did not flood the field with substitutions, only 21 players seeing action. Sutherin and Michael played the entire 60 minutes; Cassady missed only 30 seconds, the same as tackle Francis Machinsky; and Ellwood played 59. This was quite in contrast to the way 1955 had started, as 43 out of 44 players saw action in the Rose Bowl. Quarterback and co-captain John Borton voluntarily declined to play due to an injured finger on his right hand. Although Hayes wanted him to play, so that all members of the traveling squad would make an appearance, Borton said that he might make a ball-handling mistake which could prove costly. Besides, he said, Leggett was playing too well to be removed.

Such an attitude reflected the quality, dignity, and leadership of the 1955 team.

Howard Cassady —
An Inspiration

Howard (Hopalong) Cassady, described by coach Woody Hayes as "the most inspirational player I have ever seen," came to Ohio State as a 150-pound freshman in 1952. He wound up being an all-American in successive years as well as the Big Ten's most valuable player in 1955.

In making the *Chicago Tribune's* Most Valuable Award to Cassady in January of 1956, Wilfrid Smith, former sports editor of that newspaper, said that "Howard Cassady is the greatest college football player I have ever watched."

Cassady scored three touchdowns in his first varsity game against Indiana and then gained 113 yards against Wisconsin in an upset victory over the Badgers. Avoiding injury during nearly all his varsity career, Cassady played in 36 of 37 games. During Cassady's four years on the varsity, Ohio State won 29 games and lost 8.

In Cassady's freshman season he rushed for 293 yards in 65 tries for an average of 4.5. Scoring 6 touchdowns he caught 13 passes for 192 yards, his total yardage being 485.

His sophomore year indicated what was to come later. He rushed for 514 yards in 86 carries for an average of 5.9, scored 8 touchdowns, caught 16 passes for 273 yards, and had a total yardage of 787.

When Cassady first made all-American in 1954 (a unanimous choice), he had total yardage of 849, based on 701 yards in rushing, 13 pass receptions for 148 yards, 8 touchdowns, and an average of 5.7. The 1954 team was undefeated in 10 games,

Howard (Hopalong) Cassady, described by Coach Woody Hayes as the most inspirational player, as well as the greatest Ohio State player he has had, twice was named all-American and was the Heisman Award winner in 1955. Cassady excelled in the art of "downfield vision."

including a 20-7 decision over USC in the Rose Bowl and was named No. 1 in several polls.

In Cassady's 1955 season, when he repeated as all-American and won the Heisman award, he starred in all games and helped the Buckeyes gain a 13-game winning streak in the Big Ten, later stretched to 17, a conference record. Cassady's 1955 yardage was his greatest—964 yards total, when he ran his

TD count to 15, bettering by one his combined freshman-sophomore total.

In addition to playing football Cassady was a shortstop-outfielder on the Ohio State baseball team for three years. He came to Ohio State from Columbus Central high school where he starred in basketball as well as baseball and football. After graduation Cassady played professional football with the Detroit Lions, Cleveland Browns, and Philadelphia Eagles.

CASSADY'S FOUR-YEAR STATISTICS

Year	Games	No. Of Rushes	Yds.	Ave.	TD	Passes Caught	Yds.	Total Yds.
1952	9	65	293	4.5	6	13	192	485
1953	9	86	514	5.9	8	16	273	787
1954	9	123	701	5.7	8	13	148	849
1955	9	161	958	5.9	15	1	6	964
4 Yr. Total	36	435	2466	5.6	37	43	619	3085

An amusing incident occurred toward the end of the 1955 season when the Buckeyes won their second straight Big Ten title and Howard (Hopalong) Cassady again was everybody's all-American. A long distance call came to the sports information office and the young lady on the phone introduced herself as being identified with a Catholic newspaper in Chicago.

"I thought you would like to know," she explained, "that your Mr. Howard Cassady has been named on the all-Catholic all-American team."

"I regret to tell you," a publicist informed her, "but Cassady is a Lutheran."

"Oh my God," the girl exclaimed, "that makes him ineligible."

It was the only time during Cassady's career that he was ineligible.

The following week he won the Heisman Trophy.

165

Probation In 1956

Probation came in 1956. It followed an investigation by Commissioner K. L. (Tug) Wilson into alleged irregularities by Ohio State football players and the "job program."

At a special meeting on January 22, 1956, the Ohio University athletic board met with Director Larkins and Coach Hayes for a discussion of plans, procedures, and problems of administering the intercollegiate football program. No action was taken, it was reported by Dr. James Pollard in his book, *Ohio State Athletics*.

Part of the difficulty, it was pointed out by Dr. Pollard, arose from the fact that Hayes had personally advanced small sums of money to individual players for immediate needs. The coach insisted it was a personal matter, freely admitting what he had done. It also was charged that varsity players received pay for jobs they did not do, in some cases merely appearing for their pay check. About 30 players were involved.

The matter was cleared up before the 1956 football season began by having the players do the work they were supposed to have completed. Meanwhile, the conference placed the Buckeyes on probation and made them ineligible to participate in the Rose Bowl, even if the team did win the title. Under the terms of the probation, all athletes who were involved in irregularities in the work program of 1955 had to repay fully in services the wages they had received. All of them did so before fall practice began.

The university accepted the punishment without protest,

but many felt that the infraction had been minor. Hayes, at the time, did not see any harm in giving some needy players a few dollars for essentials.

Writing in his book, *Hot Line to Victory*, Hayes devoted a paragraph to discipline. "Football," he wrote, "is discipline, discipline which starts with the coach, but must become the player's own discipline. Discipline is more than merely imposing plays, tactics, and techniques upon a player. For us discipline implies disciple, for the player will first believe in the coach as a person before he will fully accept the teachings of that coach. Obviously, the player-coach relationship is of paramount importance."

Hayes proved to be a good example of a man who not only demands discipline, but one who can accept it.

Jim Parker, one of Ohio State's all-time great guards and an all-American in 1955 and 1956, won the Outland trophy as a senior. He was all-pro nine years with the Baltimore Colts and recently was enshrined in the National Professional Football Hall of Fame at Canton, Ohio. Coach Woody Hayes credits Parker with having much to do with the Buckeyes' dynamic offense of that period. Parker was picked on the all-time team for the first 100 years of college football.

For the third time in a five-year period the Buckeyes were heading for a 6-3 season, this one coming in 1956. Despite the probation penalty hanging over their heads, the players were experiencing a great campaign, and at the end of seven games the only loss had been 7-6 to pesky Penn State, whom the Buckeyes never have defeated. The last two games, however, resulted in white-washings from Iowa 6 to 0 and Michigan 19 to 0. For many players the loss to Iowa was the first Big Ten defeat they had ever experienced.

Guard Jim Parker repeated as all-American just as Cassady had in 1954-55. With end Dean Dugger having been selected in 1954 the Buckeyes were represented for three consecutive years on the mythical team.

With probation lifted and an opportunity to play in the Rose Bowl possible, the Buckeyes went to work in 1957. This year proved to be an even greater season than 1954 in that Woody Hayes was named coach of the year. Only Carroll Widdoes, in 1944, had brought such an honor to Ohio State.

A fine Texas Christian team stung the Buckeyes in the opener, 18 to 14, and many thought the absence of Parker, Michael, Ellwood, Dick Guy, and Jim Roseboro might be felt more than met the eye. Eighteen lettermen were back, but only

The 1957 team, which lost only the opening game to Texas Christian 18 to 14, went on to win another Big Ten title. This led to the Rose Bowl and a 10-7 victory over a fine Oregon

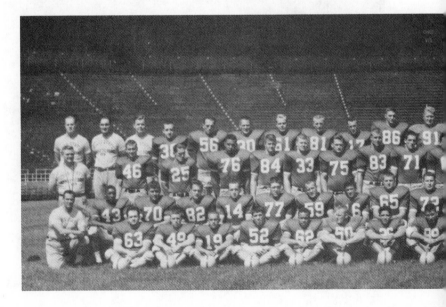

three linemen and two backs, Don Clark and Galen Cisco, were considered regulars. It was Ohio State's first opening game loss since 1950 and the first for Hayes. This extended the losing streak to three.

It was not long, however, before Hayes and his aides had the right men in the right places. Russ Bowermaster was paired at end with little Leo Brown; John Martin and Dick Schafrath formed the tackles; and Aurelius Thomas, who was named all-American, was one of the guards along with Bill Jobko. Dan James was the center, the biggest man on the squad at 258 pounds. Frank Kremblas won the quarterbacking job; Dick LeBeau and Clark were the halfbacks; and Cisco, now the pitching coach for the Kansas City Royals, was the fullback.

After defeating the Buckeyes, coach Abe Martin of Texas Christian said, "Don't worry about Ohio State this season. They'll be OK."

Any thought that Ohio State would be a "patsy" as a result of the opening game loss was a misnomer. A trip to Seattle resulted in a 35 to 7 victory over the University of Washington. A punt return for a touchdown by Don Sutherin broke the game open, and Hayes later said that the play gave everyone a big lift.

team. Guard Aurelius Thomas was named on the all-American team.

When the Big Ten season opened, Illinois and Indiana were defeated handily 21 to 7 and 56 to 0, but Wisconsin posed a different problem. Both teams scored 13 points in the first period, and it was a field goal by Sutherin in the third quarter that won the game, 16-13. Northwestern was beaten soundly, 47 to 6, but Purdue was more of a problem, 20 to 7. The Buckeyes scored all of their points before intermission, and then Purdue dominated the second half completely.

This brought on a showdown with Iowa at home. The Hawkeyes had broken the Ohio State 17-game winning streak over conference foes the year before, and the Buckeyes were eyeing revenge. They got it, 17 to 13, after a long afternoon with fullback Bob White the hero. Carrying the ball seven times out of eight midway in the final period, White gained 65 of the 68 yards needed to cross the goal line. LeBeau gained the other three yards.

Iowa coach Forest Evashevski was dumbfounded after the game. "That's the first time I ever saw one player gain so much ground in such a short period of time," he said. "And we knew what he was going to do, too."

For one of the few times in recent years the Big Ten title was won regardless of the final week's outcome. The Buckeyes still had Michigan to play at Ann Arbor, but they were the only undefeated team. They had one more game in the victory column than Michigan State, the leading contender after Iowa had been removed. The Buckeyes played seven games that year, and all others playing that number lost at least three times.

Rose Bowl — January 1, 1958

The season's-ending game with Michigan was somewhat of an anticlimax with the title already in the bag, but nonetheless Hayes and the players were elated with the 31 to 14 victory. Though Michigan led at the half 14 to 10, the Buckeyes dominated the play from then on, scoring twice in the third period and again in the fourth. It was the eighth straight win of the season and enabled Hayes to take the "rubber" game of seven from the Wolverines since he had become head coach.

After the season there was quite a division of opinion as to the No. 1 team in the national rankings. Auburn had won 14 straight games and got the nod from the AP, but UP and INS (before it merged with UP to form UPI) favored Ohio State. Guard Aurelius Thomas, who played his high school football at Columbus East, was named on four major all-American teams.

Woody was loud in his praise of the team as a unit. "We have had more stars before (obviously referring to the 1954-55 group), but all of these fellows have worked hard, not only on the playing field but in their attitude toward training."

Hayes was rewarded himself by being named coach of the year by his colleagues, members of the American Football Coaches Association. The speaker at the coaches' banquet in Philadelphia was none other than Richard M. Nixon, who was vice president of the United States at the time. He and Hayes since have become close friends.

In an off-to-the-side remark, Nixon said to one of Hayes' co-workers from Ohio State, "You have a good product, one of

The Ohio State football team of 1957 was given an enthusiastic welcome by the Tournament of Roses queen and her court upon arrival at the Los Angeles Airport. The Buckeyes defeated Oregon in the Rose Bowl game, 10 to 7.

the best. Stay with it."

When the Buckeyes reached Pasadena to play Oregon in the Rose Bowl, they read about a team that was being downgraded about as badly as any they had ever faced. They also were about to meet a group of players, mostly seniors, who were fighting mad about their image. Oregon, in a preseason rating, had been ranked seventh in the conference, and apparently many writers and fans thought they really belonged there.

Oregon was eager and aggressive from the start, but the Buckeyes moved right in with a first-quarter touchdown, Frank Kremblas going over on a one-yard quarterback sneak. Oregon tied the score in the second quarter on a five-yard run following a pitchout to Jim Shanley. That is the way the score stood until late in the fourth period when Sutherin place-kicked from the 24 yard line—a 34 yard boot.

Sutherin, whose only punt in the game had gone only 14 yards, said after the game, "I was sure I would make it good. I kept my head down, but I did not know it was good until Kremblas, who was holding the ball, told me."

Oddly, from that very same spot on the field, Jack Morris of Oregon had missed earlier in the game.

Oregon coach Len Casanova admitted that the pre-game ballyhoo in favor of the Buckeyes had irritated his players. "Nobody can be humiliated like our boys and take it. I think we have the best team in the country."

Coach Hayes praised Sutherin as the Ohio State star, adding that his kicker had been bothered by a bad back and leg for some time. "He had not kicked for a long time until a week before the game," Hayes said.

"We intercepted two passes and recovered two fumbles. Whenever we can get the ball four times on turnovers we figure we can win," Hayes added in a post-game chat.

Statistics were interesting. Ohio State gained 283 yards running to Oregon's 95, but the Webfoots led in first downs, 21 to 19. Ohio State, as usual, threw only 6 passes, 2 being completed for 59 yards. Both were caught by Jim Houston. Oregon, on the other hand, threw 21, completing 13 for 191 yards. Jack Crabtree threw 17 of Oregon's passes, completing 10 for 135 yards, but he threw the 2 interceptions. Oregon did

174

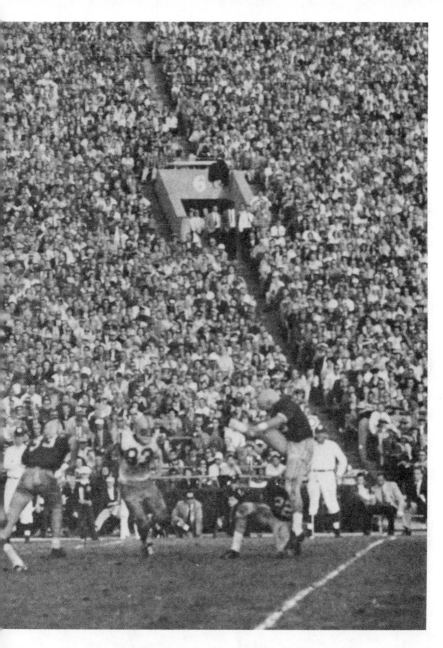

For the second time in three Rose Bowl appearances, covering just an eight-year period, Ohio State won the Pasadena Classic by the margin of a field goal. Here Don Sutherin, right, is kicking a 34-yarder to edge Oregon 10 to 7 in the 1958 game. In the 1950 game the Buckeyes had defeated California 17 to 14.

not have to punt once, and neither of Ohio State's 2 punts was returned, both going out-of-bounds.

Although the game was hard-fought from start to finish, it was one of the cleanest in Rose Bowl annals. Each team was penalized three times, but total yardage assessed was 15 against Ohio State and 25 against Oregon.

One sportswriter following the Buckeyes said that Oregon had won everything but the score, but the fact remained that Ohio State held onto the ball. The Buckeye backs, headed by Kremblas, were sticky-fingered as they had been in the 1955 Rose Bowl game against Southern California.

Bob White carried the ball 25 times, well over one-third of the team's 61, and was the game's leading ground-gainer with 93 yards. Don Clark carried 14 for a net of 82. Shanley led Oregon with 59, followed closely by Morris with 57.

Ohio State used only 23 players in the game, and 4 of them, Kremblas, Thomas, Jobko, and Houston, played all but one-half minute.

Sutherin remarked after the game that Ohio State simply could not "get up" for it. Yet the Buckeyes held on long enough to win.

High Ranking In The Classroom

Since 1953, sports information directors of the Big Ten have been sponsoring all-conference academic teams, thus calling attention to achievements in the classroom as well as on the gridiron. In this category the Buckeyes have ranked high, indeed, with 34 representatives, many being chosen for more than one year. By positions, quarterbacks and fullbacks have led the group, but linemen and defensive players also have claimed their share of prestige.

Heading the list is fullback Bob White, who was selected 3 times—the seasons of 1957-58-59. As a sophomore White is well remembered for his ball-carrying exploits against Iowa. Lugging the ball 7 times, all but once in a march of 68 yards, White was largely responsible for a 17-13 victory which eventually put the Buckeyes in the Rose Bowl. His gains ranged from 3 to 29 yards.

Two-time honorees on the scholastic teams have been quarterbacks John Borton and Frank Ellwood; center Ray Pryor; guard Dave Cheney; linebacker Mark Stier; tackles Dave Foley and Dick Himes; safety Rick Seifert; end guard Bill Lukens; wingback Brian Baschnagel; linebacker Ken Kuhn; defensive back Bruce Ruhl; and defensive end Pat Curto.

White, Pryor, and Foley achieved all-American recognition on the field, as did defensive back Arnie Chonko, who also was an all-American baseball player. A first baseman of tremendous agility, Chonko had numerous offers from professional clubs in both sports but spurned all to enter medical school, where he promptly became the No. 1 man scholastically in his class.

Two other football players, quarterbacks Don Unverferth

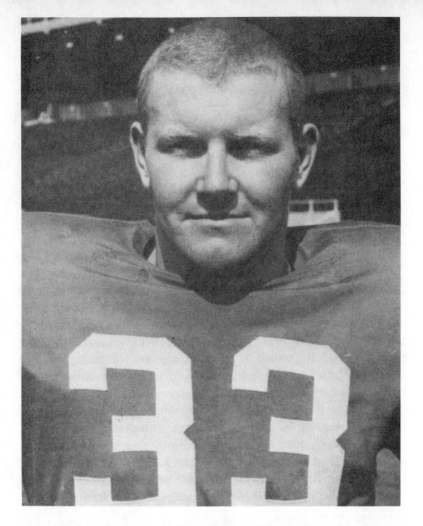

Bob White, Ohio State's fullback in 1957-58-59, was selected those years on the Big Ten's first all-scholastic football team. White came to Ohio State from Lexington, Kentucky.

and John Darbyshire, matched Chonko's feat. Darbyshire was prevented from playing when a physical examination revealed that he had developed a heart murmur.

Coach Woody Hayes, who always was justifiably proud of these men heading their respective classes, likewise has been embittered that such a fine story, although released through proper university channels, failed to receive the exposure he felt it deserved.

Two outstanding athletes, Arnie Chonko and Don Unverferth, became No. 1 students in their respective medical college classes. Chonko was an all-American in both football (1964) and baseball (1965), while Unverferth quarterbacked the Buckeyes in 1963-64-65.

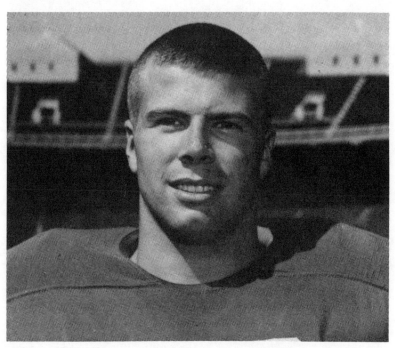

"The dope addicts make page one but these fine young men get little or nothing," he complained.

One-time selections have included Fred Kriss, quarterback, 1955; Billy Wentz, halfback, 1961; Tom Perdue, end, 1961; Dave Katterhenrich, fullback, 1962; Arnie Chonko, halfback, 1964; Bill Ridder, guard, 1965; Tom Portsmouth, safety, 1966; Dick Himes, tackle, 1967; John Muhlbach, center, 1968; Bill Urbanik, tackle, 1969; Doug Adams, linebacker, 1969; Rex Kern, quarterback, 1970; Mike Sensibaugh, safety, 1970; Rick Simon, tackle, 1971; Randy Gradishar, linebacker, 1973; Chris Ward, offensive tackle, 1975; Pete Johnson, fullback, 1976; Jeff Logan, tailback 1977; Greg Castignola, quarterback, 1978; Jim Laughlin, linebacker, 1979; Joe Lukens, offensive guard, 1980; Marcus Marek, linebacker 1980; and Joe Smith, offensive guard, 1981.

Time Out: Matte, Warfield, Ferguson, Snell

One of Ohio State's most underrated players of the 1958-60 era was Tom Matte, described by coach Woody Hayes as a "winner." Hayes says that Ohio State never had a better man when it came to running the option. Matte was a little-used sophomore, carrying the ball only once, but he did intercept a pass for a 36-yard return and brought back 4 punts for 30 yards.

In the 1959 season as a junior, Matte moved up fast, carrying the ball 92 times for a net of 190 yards. He completed 28 of 51 passes for 439 yards and had only 2 intercepted, scoring 4 touchdowns. He led the team in total offense with 629 yards, punted 5 times, intercepted a pass, had 1 punt return of 15 yards, and returned 4 kickoffs for 66 yards.

Matte's versatility was solidified in 1960 when he again performed triple threat duties. Rushing 161 times he netted 682 yards, averaging 4.2 yards per carry and scoring 2 touchdowns. He passed 95 times, completing 50 for 737 yards, and having only 4 intercepted as he threw for 8 touchdowns. He led the team in total offense with 1,419 yards and 10 touchdowns, punting 29 times for an average of 35.2.

Matte starred for the Baltimore Colts for 10 years, retiring last year.

Tom Matte, Option Expert

A superb athlete, and a gentleman on and off the field. This was the reputation of Paul Warfield, Ohio State's all-around performer in 1961-62-63. Always ready and always in condition, Warfield played in every game for three years and went on to become the ace pass receiver for the world champion Miami Dolphins.

As a sophomore Warfield played 300 minutes and netted

Paul Warfield: Athlete and Gentleman

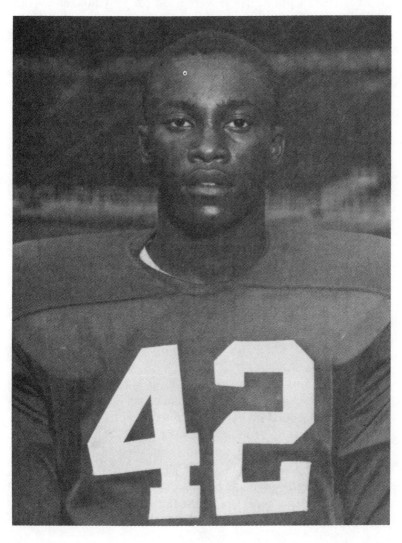

183

420 yards in 77 carries, averaging 5.4 yards and scoring 5 touchdowns. Showing the all-around ability which he has carried to the heights as a professional player, Warfield caught 9 passes for 120 yards and 1 TD; returned 10 kickoffs for 196 yards; and returned 11 punts for 88 yards.

As a junior Warfield led the team in playing time with 373 minutes, netted 367 yards in 57 tries for an average of 6.4; and scored 2 TD's. He caught 8 passes for 139 yards and 2 more touchdowns and returned 4 kickoffs for 123 yards, an average of 30.7. His 14 punt returns were good for 99 yards, an average of 7.1.

Warfield again led the team in playing time as a senior, seeing action for 376 minutes. Maintaining his art of catching passes, he received 22 for 266 yards and 3 touchdowns. His kickoff returns totaled 15 for 383 yards, an average of 25.5, while his punt returns added up to 10 for 101. He intercepted 2 passes for 23 yards, and carried the ball 62 times for a net of 260, an average of 4.2.

Despite playing both offense and defense and doing everything on a football field except carry water, according to many observers, Warfield failed to make any of the leading all-American selections. However, he was named to the all-Big Ten team in his junior and senior seasons.

Outstanding defensive players say that it was impossible to play Warfield "one on one."

Coach Woody Hayes describes Warfield as "the most graceful athlete I have ever seen."

Bob Ferguson, a real bulldozer of a fullback, moved into Coach Hayes' offense as a sophomore. Carrying the ball 61 times, he gained 374 yards, losing only 3, for a net of 371, an average of 6.1.

Scoring only 2 touchdowns as a sophomore, Ferguson hiked this category to 13 in his junior year. Carrying the ball 160 times, he gained on every occasion except 1, when he lost 1 yard. His net was 853 for an average of 5.3.

Ferguson was a real workhorse in 1961, carrying the ball 202 times for a net of 938 yards. His average per try was 4.6, and he crossed the goal line 11 times.

Matt Snell, a super star with the New York Jets until his recent retirement, was one of Ohio State's most versatile

Bob Ferguson: A Bulldozer

Matt Snell: Versatile Star

football players. As a sophomore he was a running halfback and a year later was playing defensive end, despite a weakened knee. As a senior he was an outstanding fullback.

Snell, who played with the Buckeyes in 1961, '62, and '63, wanted to get a degree in dentistry, but the financial lure from pro football was too great for him to turn down. Since retiring from the Jets, Snell has been identified with a Wall Street brokerage house.

Eleven Years
Between Bowl Games

In the 61 years of Big Ten membership, Ohio State has become a football power. Most of the non-championship seasons have been winning ones, and every coach—eight of them—has had moments of glory and satisfaction.

Although 11 years went by between the Rose Bowl appearances of 1958 and 1969, many successful seasons and many all-Americans dotted the Buckeye football map.

After the 10 to 7 victory over Oregon by the 1957 group, the holdovers from the championship team, and another promising group of sophomores, went through a 6-1-2 season in 1958. The only loss was to Northwestern, 21 to 0, and tie games were played with Purdue, 14-14, and Wisconsin, 7-7.

A real novelty occurred in the Purdue game when tackle Jim Marshall scored both touchdowns, first by blocking a punt and running it over and then by deflecting a pass which he held onto again running the play into the end zone.

Iowa won the title, but Ohio State inflicted the only loss on the Hawkeyes, 38 to 28, in the season's highest-scoring game.

This was the year, September 11 was the exact date, when Hayes ordered Commissioner Kenneth L. "Tug" Wilson and a group of touring sportswriters from the Buckeye practice field. His explanation was that he wanted to criticize his players for a poor drill and that he did not want to do this in front of outsiders.

"It would not be fair to the boys," he explained.

He granted a lengthy post-practice interview in which he apologized many times for his actions, but many of the writers never forgave him. Nearly all of the stories involving Ohio State's 1958 prospects, to be exposed in print during the following week, dealt with Hayes' order instead of an outline of the players' abilities.

Three all-Americans heaped prestige on the team and themselves—tackle Marshall, fullback Bob White, and end Jim Houston, with Houston repeating in 1959.

The season of 1959 was to be Ohio State's poorest under Hayes up to that point. It was the first time any of his teams had lost as many as 5 games. Only Michigan State and Purdue were defeated in the conference, and Wisconsin beat the Buckeyes for the first time since 1946. Other losses were to Southern California, Illinois, Iowa, and Michigan. Indiana, which had been defeated 7 straight years, held the Buckeyes to a scoreless tie. As it turned out, there was a second tie, as these 2 teams finished in a deadlock for eighth place with a 2-4-1 record.

For the first time in the modern era (1939–) a team won the Big Ten title with two defeats against its record. Wisconsin was the champion with a 5-2 mark, nosing out Michigan State's 4-2. The Badgers also were unimpressive in the Rose Bowl, losing to the University of Washington, 44 to 8.

The 1960 season saw Iowa and Minnesota tie for the title with 5-1 marks, the Buckeyes finishing third at 4-2. Since Iowa had been in the Rose Bowl two years earlier, Minnesota got the bid and had the same fate as Wisconsin, losing to Washington 17-7. Ohio State won 7 games decisively due largely to pile-driving Bob Ferguson, who won the all-American fullback spot, repeating in 1961.

Hayes regarded his "forgotten" squad of 1961 as a team as dedicated as the championship teams of 1954 and 1957. After a 7-7 tie with Texas Christian, UCLA was topped 13 to 3, after which both Illinois and Northwestern were blanked, 44 to 0 and 10 to 0. Wisconsin, showing the best offense the Buckeyes were to face all season, ran up 21 points, but Ohio State tallied 30. Iowa was the next victim, 29 to 13, followed by Indiana 16-7. The Hoosiers did not win a conference game and finished with a 2-7 record, yet gave the Buckeyes a stubborn battle. Oregon,

189

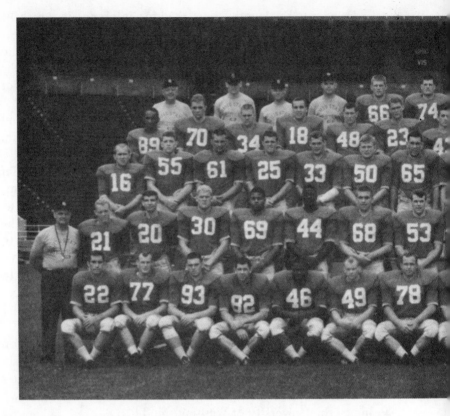

*The 1961 squad won the Big Ten title and wound up the season
with a 50-20 victory over arch-rival Michigan but was denied the
opportunity to go to the Rose Bowl. The Ohio State faculty*

which had been scheduled because of the congenial Rose Bowl
meeting 4 years before, was defeated, 22 to 12.

The windup against Michigan at Ann Arbor saw the
Buckeyes score 50 points, highest number in history against the
Wolverines who wound up with 20. Bob Ferguson finished his
career with 4 touchdowns; sophomore quarterback Joe Sparms
passed for 200 yards; and Paul Warfield made a dazzling 69-yard
run, longest of the day among many big gains.

After the Buckeyes were turned down by the Ohio State
faculty to appear in the Rose Bowl, Minnesota represented the
Big Ten for the second straight year. It had better luck this
time, defeating UCLA, 21-3. The Gophers provided the confer-

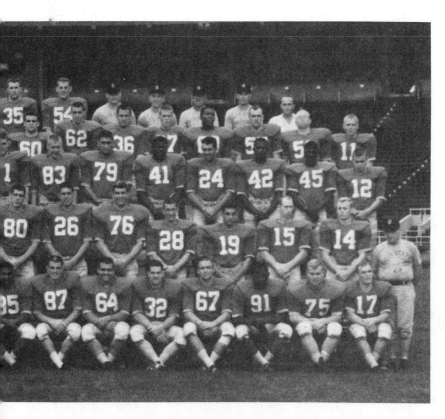

council voted 28 to 25 against participation. No formal pact existed between the Big Ten and Pacific Coast rivals.

ence oddity during the long Rose Bowl negotiations. Always voting against the postseason game, Minnesota not only wound up going to Pasadena twice but in successive years at that.

The ramifications of the 1961 football season never had been experienced in the Big Ten, nor were they likely to be repeated. It was a story of Ohio State winning the conference title and being denied permission to play in the Rose Bowl.

The winning team was not without its detractors, however, even at Ohio State. John B. (Jack) Fullen, editor of the *Alumni Monthly*, blasted the Buckeye football program editorially. Also Woody Hayes was standing in the line of fire as he and Fullen had been feuding ever since the editor had asked, editorially, "for a balance on the campus."

"We have small-time support for the true mission of the university and big-time support for athletics," Fullen wrote in the *Monthly*. "You are not going to have a very good house if you put all your money in the game room and ignore the rest."

Fullen also accused the football players of being a "bunch of pros," to which Hayes objected strenuously.

Since there was no contract binding the Big Ten to supply a team in the Rose Bowl, it was not known whether Ohio State's faculty committee would approve the Rose Bowl trip, even if the Buckeyes did win the title. The faculty council took the final vote in a meeting said to have attracted a record attendance of 53 out of a possible 57.

The bid was turned down, 28 to 25. If 2 voters had changed their minds, the bowl trip would have won by 1 ballot. Hayes was bitter, and so were the players, but the coach said that he respected the integrity of the faculty men and that there would be no demonstrations by squad members. In fact, co-captains Tom Perdue and Mike Ingram addressed protesting groups, urging them to accept the verdict peacefully.

The athletic board carried the decision to the trustees who determined that the decision of the council should be final, otherwise Ohio State's status in the Big Ten might be in jeopardy.

Athletic Director Dick Larkins was chagrined but realized that there was no use pressing the point any further. "We have no recourse now," he said.

The issue was the subject of editorial comment in newspapers of Ohio and other midwest points. Opinion was divided, some attacking the outcome as being an injustice to the team while others said it was a wise academic decision.

In rebuttal Fullen said that he was opposed to the Rose Bowl venture because of the high rental fee charged for the facilities and for the manner in which tickets, both complimentary and saleable, were allotted.

Professor Roy A. Larmee, later a faculty representative, told a story which reflects an attitude of many of the off-campus people regarding the "turndown." Larmee joined the faculty in 1962, the year after the bowl refusal. Going to one of the neighborhood banks, he informed the teller that he was

192

from out of the city, wished to open an account, and that he was going to be a member of the faculty.

The teller gave him an evil eye and said, "The faculty, eh? Do you know what those so-and-so's did last fall? Voted down the Rose Bowl game. I hope you're not going to be like one of them."

Wisconsin regained the pedestal in 1962 with a 6-1 record, nosing out Minnesota that was completing a fine three-year record during which the Gophers won 16 conference games and lost only 4. The Buckeyes tied Northwestern for third place with 4-2, losses being to Iowa, 28-14, and Northwestern, 18-14. A non-conference game was lost to UCLA, 9 to 7.

The 1963 season found the Buckeyes tying Michigan State for second place with a 4-1-1 mark, Illinois winning with 5-1-1, the extra victory paying off. After shutout victories over Texas A&M, 17 to 0, and Indiana, 21 to 0, the Buckeyes had a sensational 20-20 tie with Illinois. Former Illini coach Ray Eliot has always regarded this game as one of his personal highlights.

Southern California gave the Buckeyes one of their worst defeats in years, a 32-3 decision, so the team was hard-pressed the following week to edge Wisconsin, 13-10. The same was true against Iowa, a 7-3 squeaker. Another close game followed, but this time the Buckeyes were on the short end, as usual, against Penn State, 10-7. Northwestern, returning to the Buckeye schedule, won 17 to 8, but Michigan was defeated in the finale, 14 to 10, resulting in a 5-3-1 mark for the year.

President Kennedy's assassination had delayed all Big Ten games, and the Ohio State-Michigan contest was played after Thanksgiving. With gloom covering the nation, coupled with the fact that the game's outcome had no bearing on the title picture, the usual Buckeye-Wolverine excitement was missing. To complicate matters further, the postponement was not announced until shortly before noon on Saturday. Consequently, special trains and motorists arrived in Ann Arbor not knowing that the game had been called off.

With the team and followers making another round trip the next weekend in inclement weather, a listless game was no surprise. Attendance fell off and so did enthusiasm. Everyone seemed to wish that the season could have ended the week before.

Michigan returned to the top in 1964 for the first time since 1950 when it won the title by taking the famous "blizzard bowl" game 9 to 3. The record was 6-1, with the Buckeyes second with 5-1.

Three all-Americans dotted the Ohio State scene, those honored being tackle Jim Davidson, center Ike Kelley, and defensive halfback Arnold Chonko, who scored a double by being named to the all-American baseball team as well. Chonko was an outstanding first baseman.

The overall record was 7-2, losses being to Penn State (again), 27 to 0, and Michigan, 10 to 0.

The intersectional loss to Penn State was offset somewhat by two victories in the same category, 27-8 over Southern Methodist and 17-0 against Southern California. Biggest victory of the year was a 26-0 triumph over Illinois.

The season of 1965 was another of those 7-2 seasons, the fourth in 10 years. When North Carolina won the opening game 14 to 3, and Washington was barely nosed out 23 to 21 by virtue of a last-minute field goal by Bob Funk, it looked like the Buckeyes were in trouble.

The first-game loss was the first since 1957, when the 18-14 decision was dropped to Texas Christian. Illinois was defeated 28 to 14, but the following Saturday at East Lansing, Coach Duffy Daugherty was going to present one of his better teams.

The Spartans led only 7-0 at the half, but with all-American Ike Kelley injured in the second half the home team went to work offensively and won going away 32-7. Led by "Bubba" Smith, the Spartans stopped the Buckeyes cold as they showed a minus 22 yards on the ground.

It was the first time in Hayes' coaching career that his fullback offense did not move.

The next three games resulted in 10 points for each of the opponents, but the Buckeyes won all: 20-10 over Wisconsin, 11-10 over Minnesota by virtue of a 2-point conversion, and 17-10 over Indiana. Iowa was defeated for the third straight year 38 to 0, and Michigan was shaded 9 to 7 on another winning field goal effort by Funk. Ike Kelley repeated as all-American, and he was joined by tackle Doug Van Horn.

The 1966 campaign was another long season, five losses

being suffered for the second time in eight years. Ray Pryor was honored as all-American center but there was little else to cheer about. Although Michigan State had lost the Rose Bowl game to UCLA 14 to 12 in what was termed an upset, the Spartans were on top again with a second straight undefeated conference season.

Three consecutive Ohio State defeats occurred early in the year to Washington, 38-22, Illinois, 10-9, and Michigan State, 11-8. Although considerably outmanned the Buckeyes gave the Spartans their toughest game of the season. Point-after-touchdown plays had much to do with the outcome. Michigan State connected on a two-pointer after the Buckeyes missed a conversion attempt. This was the only time in Hayes' career that the Buckeyes had lost three straight in one season.

After Wisconsin was defeated 24 to 13, Minnesota inflicted a 17-7 loss in a disappointing showing at Minneapolis. Indiana was defeated in the rain 7 to 0, and Iowa was shaded 14 to 10 at Iowa City, a sputtering pass attack failing for the Hawkeyes in the final minute when they had a chance to put over the winning tally.

After Michigan won the finale 17-3 before a jam-packed Ohio Stadium crowd, the old challenge, "Wait 'til next year," was heard once more.

Purdue, with a 6-1 record, represented the Big Ten in the Rose Bowl and nosed out Southern California 14 to 13. It was the 15th victory in 20 games for the mid-westerners at Pasadena.

It had been six years since the "forgotten" title season of 1961, and Hayes and his staff were determined to do something about moving toward the top again. The overall record during that time was 29-15-1, not exactly shabby, but still well below the pace to which the Buckeyes had been accustomed.

The policy had been to concentrate on Ohio boys in recruiting, as the "crop" had been good, and likewise the kind of disciplined athletes Hayes desired. Now it was evident that too many were leaving the state. So, in an effort to point to the immediate future, the Buckeye staff went out of the state, too.

While the varsity was going through a 6-3 season in 1967, a talent-laden freshman team was defeating Indiana's frosh 26 to 7 and Pittsburgh 36 to 20. A few boys from "far-a-way" places

195

were getting to be pretty well-known before the snow fell. These included Jack Tatum of Passaic, New Jersey, Jan White of Harrisburg, Pennsylvania, Bruce Jankowski of Fair Lawn, New Jersey, John Brockington of Brooklyn, New York, and Tim Anderson of Follansbee, West Virginia.

Headed by Rex Kern from nearby Lancaster, the Ohio contingent was both large and dripping with ability. Soon 17 sophomores would be starting for Ohio State. Blood pressures were moving up to the point that 1967 losses to Arizona, Purdue, and Illinois were almost forgotten, not entirely, however, as all three defeats occurred in Ohio Stadium and fans really could not believe what they had been seeing in the 14-7 setback to Arizona and the 41-6 trouncing by a powerful Purdue team.

Ernie Godfrey: Kicking Coach

No story of Ohio State football would be complete without including Ernest R. (Ernie) Godfrey, supreme teacher of place-kicking and line coach.

"Keep your head down" and "Keep your eyes on the ball" may sound like instructions from a golf pro, but on the Ohio State practice field it was Ernie working patiently with a kicking prospect. Godfrey joined the Buckeye staff in 1929, following an enviable coaching record at Wittenberg College. He retired in 1962.

Immediately games were won by the margin of a successful extra point or field goal, largely through Godfrey's tutoring. During the next decade 6 decisions were gained in this manner, and before he retired in 1962, 17 more kicking triumphs were recorded, including 2 Rose classics. These were 17 to 14 over California, January 1, 1950, and 10-7 over Oregon, January 1, 1958.

Godfrey continued to coach the kickers on his own time after retirement, and all of them were credited with university records. Gary Cairns kicked three against Illinois in 1966, one of them being 55 yards, a Big Ten record. Dick Van Raaphorst kicked eight in 1963, a school mark which was tied by Bob Funk in 1965. Stan White kicked a former season's record total of thirty-nine in 1969, and Fred Schram set a record for most consecutive extra points with forty in 1970-71.

Two of Godfrey's pupils were little fellows, Dave Kilgore and Tad Weed weighing less than 150 pounds, but another one,

E. R. (Ernie) Godfrey was a member of the Ohio State football staff from 1929 until his retirement in 1962.

Lou Groza, was not so small. The all-pro star played freshman football at Ohio State, then entered the service before joining the Cleveland Browns. He became the greatest kicker in NFL history, and always gave Godfrey credit for his success.

"I want to see the ground give and the grass fly." These were the stern commands of Godfrey as he instructed his linemen in preparation for a game.

Ernie also had some expressions which puzzled his listeners. When he was coaching at Wittenberg, he told the players to "pair off in threes," and on another occasion urged them to "line up alphabetically and according to size."

In neither case could they accommodate him.

After coming to Ohio State, he was known to have said, "The best way to fly is by plane" and "Never advance the ball backward."

When it came to turning out all-American guards and tackles, however, his candidates knew exactly what he was talking about.

Four tackles and eleven guards fall into this exclusive category.

The tackles included Charles Csuri, 1942; William Willis 1944; Warren Amling, 1946; and Jim Marshall, 1958.

Guards started with Joe Gailus, 1932, and followed with Regis Monahan, 1934; Inwood Smith, 1935; Gust Zarnas, 1937; Lindell Houston, 1942; William Hackett, 1944; Warren Amling, 1945 (Amling made all-American in successive years at two positions); Bob Momsen, 1950; Mike Takacs, 1952; Jim Parker, 1955-56; and Aurelius Thomas, 1957.

Godfrey was inducted into the National Football Hall of Fame for coaches, joining two previous Ohio State selections, Dr. John W. Wilce and Francis A. Schmidt.

1968 — "Best College Team Of The Sixties"

Perhaps the best way to describe the strength and versatility of the 1967 freshmen would be to say that 19 earned letters as sophomores. Another way would be to write that Jack Tatum, twice an all-American in 1969 and 1970, could not earn a special award as a frosh player. In any event football talent was solid at every position and, in most instances, the backup man was capable of starting on nearly every other team in the Big Ten.

This 1968 squad was not all sophomoric, however. Co-captains Dave Foley, tackle, and Dirk Worden, linebacker, were outstanding football players, as were 1967 holdover tackles Rufus Mayes, Chuck Hutchison, Paul Schmidlin, Brad Nielsen, and Bill Urbanik; ends Nick Roman and Dave Whitfield; guards Alan Jack, Vic Stottlemyer, and Tom Backhus; and centers John Muhlbach and Jim Roman, who also was a place-kicker.

In the backfield from the 1967 squad were quarterbacks Bill Long and Kevin Rusnak; halfbacks Dave Brungard and Ray Gillian; fullback Jim Otis; and defensive players Ted Provost, Mike Polaski, Mike Radtke, and Mark Stier. In all, 28 lettermen returned, 15 from offense and 13 defense.

This, indeed, was a formidable group. Otis was the leading ground-gainer in 1967 with 530 yards, followed closely by Brungard with 515. Gillian showed promise with an average of 4.1 yards per carry. While the 1967 team scored on all opponents, it tallied only one touchdown against Arizona,

Northwestern, and Purdue for 155 points in 9 games. All teams scored against the Buckeyes, except Oregon, for a total of 120—not too much spread. It was obvious that more punch must be sought. The defense might be adequate.

Some concern was expressed whether quarterback Rex Kern, one of the prize sophomores, would be available early in the season as he had submitted to a spinal disc operation in mid-June. However he was ready and played 26 minutes with the offensive unit against Southern Methodist in the opener. The Buckeyes won, 35 to 7, quite a reversal from the first game of the year before when Arizona won, 14-7. Twenty sophomores played, the tip-off on what was to come. Nine of them, including Kern, played more than 25 minutes. Sophomore safety Mike Sensibaugh played 30, one less than the game leader, Dirk Worden.

Hayes and his assistants liked what they saw from their young newcomers, and 12 of them had as much game time or more in the second game with Oregon, defeated 20 to 6. The Buckeyes watched SMU attempt the amazing number of 76 passes, a stadium record, and Oregon contributed 21, yet only 3 touchdowns were scored. Seven of the aerials were intercepted. Ohio State was conceding short gains both on the ground and in the air as the opposition showed 33 first downs in 2 games. However, the Buckeyes had 40.

The biggest game of the season was about to be played in Ohio Stadium. Purdue, which had scalped the Ohioans 41 to 6 the year before, figured to roll over the younger Buckeyes. After all, the Boilermakers had Heisman award candidate, Leroy Keyes, and a big veteran line. They were a 13-point favorite.

When the game was over, they were 13 points behind and whitewashed at that.

Tom Keys, sports editor of the *Columbus Citizen Journal*, writing in his column following the game, said: "Beautiful is the only way to tag Saturday's super, super special upset registered by Woody Hayes' young Buckeyes over No. 1 Purdue. It has to gain a place with all-time classics spanning 79 seasons at Ohio State."

He wrote on: "If Keyes has been knocked out of the Heisman box in this one, his first regrets should be forwarded to sophomore Jack Tatum, who seemed to wear numbers 32 and

201

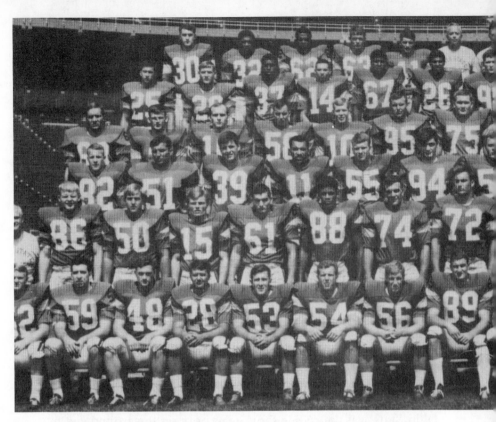

The 1968 Ohio State team was voted the "outstanding college football team of the sixties." Led by all-American tackles Dave Foley and Rufus Mayes and directed by fabulous ball-handling

23 all afternoon...his and Leroy's."

A 35-yard run, following a pass interception by defensive back Ted Provost, proved to be the game-breaker, but a second touchdown was added by senior quarterback Bill Long who, not finding a receiver, darted into the end zone. The point after touchdown, which was missed after the first score, causing great concern, was good this time.

Many regarded the Purdue victory as the turning point in the season. One player who felt so was sophomore end Jan White, who said: "We had to win that one to keep going, and after we did win, we felt we could beat any team we had to play. Both the offense and defense had complete confidence in what we could do."

Ohio State outgained Purdue in total yardage, 411 to 186.

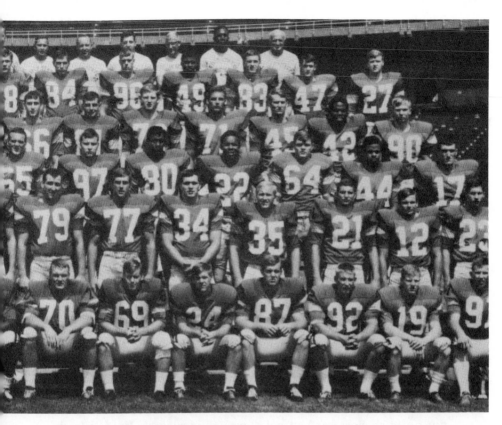

Rex Kern, the Buckeyes rolled over nine opponents before upsetting Southern California in the Rose Bowl, 27 to 16. The Trojans were led by all-American O. J. Simpson.

Northwestern was defeated 45 to 21 in a free-scoring game in which the Buckeyes rolled up their biggest yardage total of the season—565. The Wildcats totaled 288.

Illinois was the next victim, but it was not easy. The Buckeyes led at the half 24 to 0 and it looked like a romp, but by midway in the third period the score was tied at 24 all. Three Illini touchdowns had been accompanied by as many incredible 2-point conversions. Each was a rushing play, and there was no doubt about any of them. With less than 3 minutes left, a Buckeye drive of 74 yards was good for the deciding touchdown in a 31-24 thriller. Again the Illini charged back, but Mike Sensibaugh intercepted a pass to end the threat.

Illinois finished the season 1-6 in the conference and 1-9 overall, but for 30 minutes they gave every indication of scoring the upset of the year.

Michigan State, always a tough nut for the Buckeyes to crack, was edged, 25 to 20. Bruce Jankowski, sophomore end, caught 8 passes to highlight the game. The Buckeye scouting report showed that the Spartans could be passed against so a season's high of 26 were thrown, 16 being completed for 215 yards and 10 first downs. Only 214 yards were gained rushing. It was the first time since the opening game of 1967 that passing yardage was greater than rushing.

The statistic of 26 passes thrown stood out like a beacon, too. In the early days of Hayes' coaching career there were entire seasons when 26 passes were not thrown. Mediocre passers and fumbling receivers did not make for a good passing attack, Hayes correctly figured.

Wisconsin was defeated for the ninth straight year, 43 to 8. With Kern injured, Ron Maciejowski, who had directed the winning touchdown against Illinois, was at the throttle. The Badgers were held to 88 yards on the ground and 99 in the air. "Mace," the "super sub," completed 15 of 25 passes as the Buckeyes continued to put the ball in the air.

Iowa was troublesome on its home field, but the game was not quite as close as the final score would suggest. Jim Otis and John Brockington carried the offensive brunt in the 33-27 victory, and Jack Tatum keyed on Ed Podolak, Iowa's fine runner, at critical times. Iowa scored in the last few seconds to narrow the gap to 6 points.

For the second time in 7 years the Buckeyes scored 50 points on Michigan, the last being the championship team of 1961. Tatum and Tim Anderson took care of the defense while Otis powered the offense. Hard tackling led to 9 fumbles, 5 by Michigan, as the Buckeyes matched their season's high with 28 first downs. Kern connected on 6 of 9 passes for 46 yards while the rushing yardage of 421 was the highest of the season, surpassing the gains against Northwestern by 74.

Considering that this was a championship game between two previously undefeated teams, it seems amazing that the Wolverines were so outclassed. But Kern's passing, team direction, pitch-outs, and hand-offs, coupled with Brockington's long gainers and Otis's terrifying line smashes, kept Michigan off-balance all afternoon.

Ohio State's national champions of 1968 were voted the "Outstanding College Football Team Of The Sixties." Many Buckeye fans have said that the two all-American tackles, Dave Foley and Rufus Mayes, "put the show on the road." Few have disputed the assertion.

Tackle Rufus Mayes, Brockington, and Kern played 31 minutes, while Otis was only one minute behind. Coach Hayes used all 48 members of the traveling squad, who not only were smelling roses but holding a large bouquet, it was said. It was just like Jan White had said. "We think we can beat anyone we play."

So, this young team, now being watched nationwide, had scored 44 touchdowns, gaining 4,402 yards, representing 2½ miles of ground. Offensive tackles Dave Foley and Mayes were named on several all-American teams. They paved the way for the Buckeye backs, Otis in particular. As veteran coach Ernie Godfrey often said, "Show me a squad with good offensive tackles and I will show you a winning team."

Now for the first time in 11 years the Buckeyes had earned the right to return to Pasadena. There they could give Ohio State a fourth straight victory over coast elevens.

Trojan Coach Is Impressed

By the time the Buckeyes reached the Rose Bowl, the word had gotten around that Ohio State had a defense, particularly against passing, as well as an offense. Twelve different players had figured in 23 interceptions, and Jack Tatum, with three of them, was feared the most. The Trojans reasoned that with Tatum's blinding speed (9.5 for the 100 in high school), he could return one for the distance any time.

When John McKay, USC coach, was asked what he felt was most impressive about Ohio State, he replied, "Nine wins and no losses." He then went on to say: "Ohio State has fine balance on offense and an excellent defense. The team has excellent personnel and is extremely well-coached. We are impressed with the quarterback-fullback type of offense they use."

Woody Hayes was equally as complimentary about the Trojans.

"I think John McKay uses the tailback offense better than any coach in the country. He has gotten a lot of mileage out of his tailbacks ever since he began coaching."

The Buckeyes' season record was beginning to impress coast scribes. Writing in the *Pasadena Star-News*, sports editor Joe Hendrickson said: "A strategic phase to the game will center around the defensive tactics which USC will employ to check the Ohio State 'moving' offense. The Buckeye quarterbacks like to work the option. When a team has good bolting power straight ahead to keep a defense honest, such as Ohio

207

Jack Tatum was Ohio State's star defensive halfback in the 1968-70 era when the Buckeyes lost only two games in three years. An all-American in 1969 and 1970, Tatum's great speed and ability to diagnose opponents' plays kept the Ohioans in many a game.

State has with fullback Jim Otis, the quarterback-pass-run stuff is difficult to handle."

"Kern loves to roll outside," Hendrickson wrote on. "Whether an injured left shoulder will prevent this remains to be seen. It would seem probable that Rex would be handicapped, especially going to his left. But USC will have to figure on Kern, Ron Maciejowski, or Bill Long high-tailing it to the

Jim Otis was an all-American fullback in 1969 and a powerful factor in the Buckeyes' 1968 Big Ten and national championships. Otis, described by Coach Woody Hayes, as the quickest-starting fullback he has ever seen, was a regular as a sophomore in 1967. He led the team in rushing with 530 yards for a 3.7 average, his total offense was 622 yards, and his average was 3.9. As a junior on the team that was termed the "best college eleven of the Sixties," Otis again led the team in rushing with 985 yards, an average of 4.5, and scored 17 touchdowns, which made him the leading scorer with 102 points. He was second to Rex Kern in total offense and caught 10 passes in his fullback role for 82 yards. In his senior year Otis went over the 1,000 mark with 1,027 yards rushing for an average of 4.5, scored 16 touchdowns to again head the scoring with 96 points, and once more was second to Kern in total offense. He caught 5 passes for 36 yards, one good for a touchdown.

outside."

Tatum gave one of his rare interviews, brief as it was, to Hendrickson, saying: "I am looking forward to playing against O. J. Simpson, and I am also looking toward our victory party afterwards. I started thinking about O. J. after our win over Purdue. I figured we would make it here after we beat the Boilermakers."

For Tatum, this was a long speech.

Tatum's concentration on Leroy Keyes had been largely responsible for the Buckeye victory, and the Purdue star said afterward, "Tatum is a monster."

The word also had arrived from the east that Tatum, after being knocked down in the Northwestern and Michigan games, had gotten up and caught ball-carriers from behind. Bob Olsen and Ron Johnson were the respective victims as they appeared headed for touchdowns.

This prompted Hendrickson to write, "Tatum is Jack-be-tough, Jack-be-quick."

Comparison of the passing statistics of Kern and the Trojans' Steve Sogge revealed an amazing fact. Both had completed 57 percent of their tosses during the season, Sogge with 103 of 177 and Kern, throwing less, 75 of 131. Sogge connected for 8 touchdowns; Kern for 7. Sogge had 8 interceptions; Kern 6.

Though playing 2,500 miles apart, it was obvious that the 2 quarterbacks had learned their lessons equally well.

With 102,063 watching, the first quarter was a punting duel between Trojan John Young and Ohio State's Mike Sensibaugh. The Buckeye had an edge, two kicks going for 41 and 47 yards while Young, kicking three times, booted 47, 38, and 34.

When the second period opened, Bill Long held the ball on the USC 17-yard line for an attempted place-kick by Larry Zelina, but the ball sailed wide. The Trojans then put on a march that carried to the Buckeye three-yard line and a first down. Three plays lost a yard and, with Sogge holding, Ron Ayala kicked from the 11-yard line for a 3-0 lead.

Ohio State came back to midfield and Sensibaugh, forced to punt, booted one for 51 yards. However, it mattered little, as Simpson took a pitchout to his left, cut back to his right, and

Mike Sensibaugh, weighing only 187 pounds, has been regarded as Ohio State's premier safety man, a position he played during the amazing three-year winning period of 1968-70. Missing only one game in three years, that because of an injury, Sensibaugh intercepted 22 passes to establish a school career record. On six occasions he played the entire game on defense. His playing time ranged from 217 to 231 minutes, and, as the team's punter, he had the amazing consistency of a 37-yard average each season.

went 80 yards for a touchdown. When Ayala's kick was good, the Buckeyes were in the hole, 10 to 0. Leo Hayden returned the Trojan kickoff 18 yards, and the Buckeyes did not quit until Otis barged over from the one. Five first downs were made in succession with Kern's pass to Ray Gillian for 18 yards being the longest gain. Jim Roman's place-kick made it 10-7.

When Polaski made a fair catch of Young's ensuing punt, the Buckeyes were off again. Taking the ball on their own 40, they went right down to the Trojan 10, the longest gain again being Kern's pass to Gillian for 19 yards. With Long holding on the 16, Roman's field goal made the score 10-10 at the half. Only three seconds were left to play.

Someone called it a Roman holiday. This was not far from the truth as all of the players and coaches felt better about starting all even again instead of being three points behind.

Half-time statistics showed that Kern and Sogge were maintaining their usual pace and staying close together. Each completed five of ten passes, Kern's for 61 yards, Sogge's for 65. Simpson, as expected, netted 137 yards to lead both teams, an average of 7.61. Otis gained 68 to lead Ohio State, but Hayden had the best average of 7.58. The Buckeyes seldom have an edge in punting, but this time Sensibaugh's average was 46.3 to 37.7 for the Trojans and it was a factor in keeping Ohio State even at half-time.

In the third quarter a drive started on the Ohio 46, and after three first downs Roman booted another field goal from the 15 for a 13-10 lead. The Buckeyes were on fire now, and Kern passed to Hayden for a touchdown. When Roman again converted it was 20 to 10.

After Simpson fumbled Sogge's pass, Polaski recovered, and again the Trojans could not cover Gillian as a pass receiver. He caught another for 16 yards, this time for a touchdown, and when Roman converted it was 27 to 10 and out of the Trojan's reach.

With 45 seconds left, a disputed pass reception was ruled good for a Southern Cal touchdown. Officials decided that Trojan Sam Dickerson had more of the ball than interceptor Polaski. The game ended after Ohio State was penalized 15 yards for having unauthorized personnel on the field.

To nobody's surprise Kern was named the most valuable player in the game, the third such honor for an Ohio Stater, following selection of Fred (Curly) Morrison in 1950 and Dave Leggett in 1955.

National syndicated columnist Jim Murray wrote: "Rex Kern missed his calling. He should have been a pick-pocket."

This seemed to sum up how well the Buckeyes were directed in a sleight-of-hand performance.

Now the Buckeyes were national champions, and Woody Hayes was coach of the year.

1969 — Another Awesome Team

At the conclusion of the 1969 season coach Woody Hayes, who dislikes making comparisons, was asked which team he regarded the better, the undefeated team of 1968 or the high-scoring unit of 1969 which often decided the outcome of a game in the first quarter.

Hayes' reply was, "Even though the 1969 team scored a lot of points and only lost one game (to Michigan) I guess you would have to say that an undefeated team is better than one that loses a game."

The average fan accepted this solution, yet the fact remained that the predominately junior squad was awesome in its accomplishments.

Rewriting the record book by scoring 383 points in 9 games, breaking the 10-game record of 337, this explosive outfit scored 121 points in the first quarter to a mere 14 by opponents. Fourteen players figured in scoring a record 56 touchdowns. A total offense record was set of 4,438 yards, and fullback Jim Otis hit a single season mark of 1,027.

Hayes' former conservative passing offense blossomed to the point that 14 players figured in receptions, 17 resulting in touchdowns. Of the first downs 74 were by passing, and the 250 total first downs were school records.

The Big Ten winning streak, which had started with the Michigan State victory in 1967, reached 17 before being snapped in the season's finale at Michigan when the Wolverines won, 24 to 12. The streak matched the 17-game string of the

Jim Stillwagon is regarded as one of Ohio State's all-time great middle defensive linemen. He won both the Lombardi and Outland awards in 1970. He was all-American in both 1969 and 1970.

1954-56 era.

The team boasted four all-Americans in guard Jim Stillwagon, fullback Jim Otis, and defensive backs Ted Provost and Jack Tatum.

The least number of first downs made by the Buckeyes was 20 against Michigan, when a pregame injury to Rex Kern not only handicapped him but the team as well. He played only 22 minutes, smallest time of the year. With Michigan putting

214

pressure on the defense, linebacker Doug Adams, defensive back Tim Anderson, safety Mike Sensibaugh, defensive end Dave Whitfield, and cornerback Jack Tatum played the entire game.

In prior games the Buckeyes had held the ball an unbelieveable number of times against their opponents. Whereas total plays against Michigan numbered only 79 (more than an average number for a team), ball control numbered 101 against both Illinois and Texas Christian; 99 against Wisconsin; 95, Northwestern; 93, Michigan State; and 91, Purdue.

Michigan not only spoiled a second undefeated season but hurt the Buckeyes statistically. The 24 points represented the greatest scored against the team, and the 12 total was the poorest offense.

Probably the biggest setback of all was a tremendous opportunity to be national champions for the second straight year.

Seniors Take A Vow

After Michigan put an end to a 22-game winning streak, which included 17 straight in the Big Ten, a senior group that had played together since freshman days vowed to close out their college careers with another undisputed championship. They were to succeed, including the Rose Bowl, where the venture was not as enjoyable as two years previously.

With virtually the same key men in their respective positions, the team scored 273 points during the conference season compared to 383 the year before. Defense also slipped from 93 points surrendered in 1969 to 120 in 1970. However there were two prominent absentees on offense, Jim Otis and Ray Gillian. Missing from the defense were Dave Whitfield on the line and Ted Provost and Mike Polaski from the backfield.

Michigan State was the only team shut out, 29 to 0, but five teams, Minnesota, Northwestern, Wisconsin, Purdue, and Michigan, were held to one touchdown. Only the Purdue game was close, and the Buckeyes were fortunate to win in the snow, 10 to 7 on Fred Schram's field goal.

As was the case in 1968, Illinois reached a season's high in effort and dedication. This time the team rallied for and around coach Jim Valek, whose dismissal had been sought for some time by certain factions.

In a most unusual announcement made just before the game, Valek's resignation was demanded. The players countered by declaring they would not finish the season unless Valek did too. The reaction scared the daylights out of the Buckeyes (48

J. Edward Weaver was only the third man to serve as director of athletics at the Ohio State University. He assumed the duties October 14, 1970, succeeding Richard C. Larkins. As head of the department, Weaver made a move to increase revenue rather than cut the budget. The first accomplishment was to schedule a 10th football game, and in addition a professional game was played in the stadium in both 1972 and 1973. Permission later was granted to play an 11th game, and this was scheduled for the 1974 season. Artificial turf was installed in the stadium and on the practice field in 1971. Two projects were finalized in 1973—a new varsity tennis court complex and installation of fiberglass covering for 53,805 stadium seats.

to 29), and it carried over to the following Saturday when the Illini upset a heavily-favored Purdue team.

Against Michigan it was a case of ball control again. The Wolverines had only 56 plays, smallest number by an opponent during the season. Ohio State had 77 and more than doubled the net gain in yardage, 329 to 155. Michigan had only 37 yards on the ground. Even Texas A&M, walloped 56 to 13, showed 50.

The Buckeyes were heavily-favored over Stanford in the Rose Bowl, January 1, 1971. Undefeated, compared to a Stanford record that showed three losses, Ohio State followers were confident of the outcome and another victory celebration to go along with that of two years before when Southern Cal was downed, 27 to 16.

Just as the Trojans had done, Stanford took an early lead when Eric Cross got away for 41 yards, setting up a touchdown by Jackie Brown on a four-yard smash. Steve Horowitz kicked the first of two field goals, and now the Indians, now known as the Cardinals, had done exactly what the Trojans did on January 1, 1969—they took a 10-0 lead. Then Ohio State put the ground power in action, and Rex Kern pitched, John Brockington and Leo Hayden smashed, and the Buckeyes took a 17-13 lead. Nearly all press box occupants thought that the lead would be increased and that the Buckeyes would be home free despite a Rose Bowl record field goal by Horowitz of 48 yards.

One play seemed to turn the game around and give Stanford the momentum it needed. With fourth down and inches to go on Stanford's 19 Brockington attempted the first down, but instead of making inches he lost a yard when he was met head-on by linebacker Ron Kadziel.

Then Jim Plunkett, Stanford's Heisman trophy winner, went to work with a dazzling display of passing. Up to that point Kern had been overshadowing his quarterback opponent and actually was the No. 1 candidate for "player of the game," an award he had received in 1969.

Connecting to Randy Vataha and Bob Moore, Plunkett passed for two fourth-quarter touchdowns that spelled doom for the Buckeyes. Moore seemed to make an "impossible" catch between two defenders on the four-yard line that set up another

John Brockington gained a mile and 100 yards while playing with the Buckeyes in 1968, 1969 and 1970. His 378 carries, 261 of which were in his senior year, netted 1,663 yards, and his 37 pass receptions were good for 197 yards. The sum totaled 1,860 yards, 100 beyond the mile mark. As a senior, when he was named All-American, Brockington returned six kickoffs for 160 yards, an average of 26.4. His three-year per-carry average was 4.4. Brockington scored 24 touchdowns during his career, 17 of them as a senior, which was a Buckeye record until another fullback, Harold Henson, scored 20 in 1972 and led the nation in both touchdowns and point-making. Brockington was the fifth Buckeye fullback to be named All-American.

219

John Brockington scores for the Buckeyes against Stanford in the 1971 Rose Bowl, but Ohio State lost, 27 to 17.

touchdown by Brown.

The Buckeyes outgained their opponents 439 to 408, but poor pass defense hurt as Stanford picked up 265 yards in the air.

Time Out: Rex Kern

Why Rex Kern was not a consensus all-American in at least one of his three years as an Ohio State quarterback is a question often asked. Kern directed, ran, passed, and inspired the Buckeye offense to 27 victories in 29 games, including a Rose Bowl victory over USC on January 1, 1969, in which he was named the most valuable player. Rated as one of the finest quarterbacks in Buckeye history, Kern had the intangible quality of leadership which aroused his mates to superior heights.

A master in taking advantage of broken plays, Kern also often concealed the ball so well that opponents despaired of finding it until the play had been completed. Always imaginative, his ball-handling likewise was faultless.

In addition to his exploits on the field, Kern was one of 12 scholar-athletes honored by the National Football Foundation. He received a graduate fellowship and has earned a master's degree in athletic administration. Just recently he joined the Ohio State athletic department on a parttime basis to learn all facets of the operation.

As a youngster Kern's first interest in athletics leaned toward baseball, then basketball, and finally football. Although Kern did not play varsity baseball at Ohio State, he was drafted in an early round by a major league club, an opportunity he did not pursue.

A native of Lancaster, Ohio, Kern had the rare distinction of winning all-Ohio honors in football, basketball, and baseball.

Rex Kern, the Buckeyes' multi-talented quarterback

At the same time he turned toward religion which led to his leadership in work for the Fellowship of Christian Athletes. In this he had joined Bart Starr, Bill Glass, Bobby Richardson, Don Shinnick, Carroll Dale, Willie Richardson, Bobby Mitchell, and two of his own Buckeye teammates, John Muhlbach and Mark Stier.

Kern gives numerous speeches in behalf of the movement. He says that he has three approaches: "My main one is how I compare athletics with the Christian way of life, how in athletics we have to have faith in our teammates, and we have to have desire and dedication and enthusiasm. Then I tie it in with the Christian way of life, how we need faith in the Supreme Being as we have faith in our teammates and coaches, and have to be dedicated in the summer to work and strive and sweat for our goal, just as we have to be dedicated Christians, and then I try to bring in some of the Bible verses with Paul on the road to Damascus and the conversion there. Then I draw symbols, with the goal line being the gate to Heaven, first down being rebirth, loss of game, loss of life, faith in God, faith in the coach."

When Kern was 19 he was the speaker at a high school commencement, his audience being only a year or two younger than himself. He pointed out four principles as being basic in athletics: having a goal, sacrifice, dedication, and unity. His audience was attentive and responsive.

"Toward the end of my freshman year I was not certain that fall I would even be in shape to try out for the squad," Kern relates. "I was having trouble with my back, and one doctor said I would have to have a spinal disc operation. But another specialist refused to recommend it. I had to decide, knowing full well that my playing career might hang in the balance. I prayed about it, then made up my mind to go ahead with the operation. I put myself in the hands of the Almighty and stopped worrying.

"As it turned out the surgery was successful, and I got my chance. Prayer such as this is an indispensable part of my life. So is Bible reading. And I do not hesitate to let people know it."

Kern's yardstick is more than remarkable. He is the single-season total offense leader with 1,585 yards (1969) and is the career total offense leader with 4,158 yards during his three varsity seasons.

Kern's table:

Year	Carries	Net Yds.	TD's	Passes Att.	Comp.	Yds.	TD's
1968	131	534	8	131	75	972	7
1969	109	583	9	135	68	1,002	9
1970	112	597	7	98	45	470	3
Career	352	1,714	24	364	188	2,444	19

Rushing - 1,714
Passing - 2,444
Total Offense - 4,158

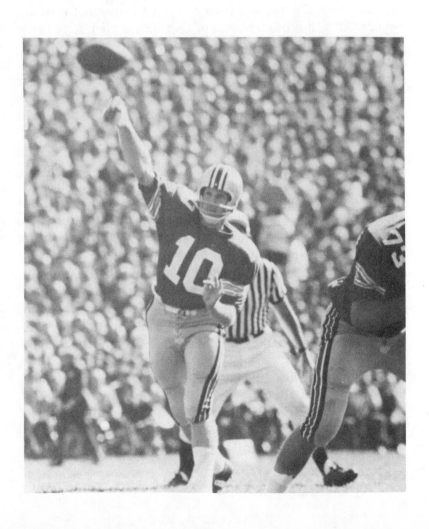

1971 — Poorest In Six Years

The 1971 season was the poorest, won-lost-wise, since 1966, four losses being sustained against six victories—a winning season, yet a disappointment.

After a 52-21 victory over Iowa in the season's opener, which represented the biggest scoring punch of the season, the Buckeyes lost an intersectional game to Colorado, 20 to 14. Ohio State won everything but the long end of the score. First downs favored Ohio 24 to 19; total yardage was 444 to 382 and the Buckeyes had the ball for 90 plays compared to 59 for the winners. Ohio State also completed a season's high of 21 passes in 34 attempts and had none intercepted, while Colorado completed four of nine and had two snatched away. The Buckeyes did not fumble while Colorado erred twice, recovering once. Even in yards penalized, Ohio State had an edge of 59 to 47. Only in punting did Colorado have an advantage, and it was a mere 39.7 to 38.5. The answer was that the Buffaloes made their wishbone offense move at strategic times, the 285 yards rushing almost doubling the Buckeyes' 145.

Intersectional-wise, the Buckeyes lost no time in getting even as the California Bears were defeated the following week 35 to 3. The sunshine of the west was over-matched by the Columbus humidity, and the Bears seemed to suffer more from the 90-plus temperature than did the Ohioans, who rolled up a season's high first downs of 28. For the third straight game the Buckeyes totaled more than 400 yards in net gain rushing. However, it was the last time during the season that the team was to achieve this figure in moving the ball.

A four-game winning streak followed against Illinois, Indiana, Wisconsin, and Minnesota. Only the Gophers provided trouble. They piled up 14 first downs to 11 for the Buckeyes and outrushed Ohio State 273 to 198. A two-point conversion try following a last-minute Minnesota touchdown missed by inches, preserving a 14-12 victory.

In the next two games the Buckeyes could get only 10 points from their offense and bowed to Michigan State 17-10 and Northwestern 14-10. The Michigan State loss was the first to the Spartans since 1966, while Northwestern had been defeated every season since 1963.

This brought the season to the closing game with Michigan at Ann Arbor where Woody Hayes made his widely-publicized

Woody Hayes invades playing field.

invasion of the playing field to protest a "call" by an official that was "not called."

With the fourth quarter rapidly ticking away, the Buckeyes had the ball in midfield. A pass was thrown to Dick Wakefield who was so completely interfered with that Woody could not restrain himself from dashing onto the field. While there he smashed the yard markers to dramatize what he considered an injustice to his team which was trailing 10 to 7 at the time. That is the way the game ended, too.

Hayes admitted later that he probably should not have gone onto the field but he said, "After seeing the pictures, I would have been ashamed of myself if I had not registered a protest."

The Buckeyes were a decided underdog prior to the game and were making a tremendous effort to score an upset. Woody never said that his team would win or tie, but he felt that an opportunity had been denied his players.

Michigan coach "Bo" Schembechler, when asked to comment about Woody's action, said: "That's a personal thing with him. On occasion, I have been aroused, too."

Don Canham, Michigan athletic director, said: "If Woody ever stops his antics our games will draw 30,000 fewer people. We need his showmanship."

No criticism of Woody's actions was ever released from the Big Ten office. Buckeye adherents assumed from this that the commissioner agreed with the movies and that Hayes had made his point.

Michigan won the title with an 8-0 record and 11-0 overall, the first undefeated, untied season for the Wolverines since 1902. Stanford, however, won the Rose Bowl game, 13 to 12.

The Buckeyes finished in a three-way tie for third place with Illinois and Michigan State with a 5-3 mark. Center Tom DeLeone was chosen on the all-American team, the fifth Buckeye to be honored at the pivot position.

Halfback Don Lamka had an outstanding year. He led the team in touchdowns with eight; passing, with 54 completions in 107 attempts for 718 yards; total offense with 1,026 yards; and tied for first in scoring with 48 points. On defense he tied for the lead in recovered fumbles with three.

227

Ohio — Michigan:
A Ping-Pong Match

Until Iowa went to the 1982 Rose Bowl, Ohio State and Michigan had made a ping-pong match of winning the Big Ten title and going to Pasadena since the 1967 season.

The Buckeyes defeated USC three times and lost to them three times and lost to Stanford and UCLA. Michigan lost five straight until it beat Washington in 1981.

Two-team domination has been the name of the game.

Until 1973 Ohio State and Michigan had not played a tie game since 1949, but Wolverine fans thought there should have been one in 1972. A field goal in Michigan's 14 to 11 defeat would have given the Maize and Blue an undefeated season as well as an undisputed Big Ten title, but the Buckeye victory created a two-way tie at 7-1.

Three magnificent goal line stands inside the five-yard line prevented Michigan from scoring. A Wolverine touchdown appeared to be within easy reach so often that coach "Bo" Schembechler gave no thought of going for a tie. Coaches have been criticized for playing for a deadlock. In this case an 11-11 tie would have been very pleasing to Michigan followers. The final standing then would have appeared:

	Won	Lost	Tie
Michigan	7	0	1
Ohio State	6	1	1

It was obvious before the 1972 season opened that Buckeye fans could count on another winner. Fourteen lettermen had been lost from the previous year, including eight regulars, four from each unit, but thirty-six veterans were available. There was

228

an extra incentive, too, as historic Ohio Stadium was about to have its golden anniversary, covering 50 years of exciting football since its dedication in 1922.

Seven offensive regulars and the same number of defensive veterans were ready to go. The group included offensive stars Rick Middleton, Merv Teague, Jim Kregel, Chuck Bonica, Rick Galbos, Morris Bradshaw, and John Bledsoe. In addition there was all-American John Hicks, who missed the 1971 season due to surgery. From the defense were Tom Marendt (later ruled out due to a knee injury), George Hasenohrl, Shad Williams, Vic Koegel, Randy Gradishar (a concensus all-American), Jeff Davis, and Rick Seifert.

The team staged a seven-game winning streak, and there were no threats to victory as the offense rolled up 210 points and the defense yielded only 85. However the margin of triumph tightened in games six and seven (28-20 versus Wisconsin and 27-10 versus Minnesota).

Perhaps this was a tip-off on what was to follow the next Saturday when the Michigan State Spartans, emotionally keyed by the announced resignation of Coach Duffy Daugherty, upset the Buckeyes 19 to 12. A walk-on place-kicker from the Netherlands, no less, stole the spotlight. Kirk Krijt, who never had participated in a varsity game, kicked four field goals, all in the first half, matching Ohio State's game total. This tied a Big Ten record, oddly enough established only one month before by Chris Gartner of Indiana. Krijt since has dropped out of school and returned to Holland, one year too late to please Ohioans.

Daugherty likes to tell about his soccer-style kicker, the favorite story being Krijt's query as to whether the ball should go under or over the crossbar. When informed that the ball should go over the bar, Krijt went to work on his specialty. His fourth field goal, which came seconds before the end of the half, struck the bar after traveling 22 yards and toppled over for three points. It tied the score and enabled the Spartans to enter the dressing room all even at 12-12. Krijt, who never had seen a football game until he came to America, was successful on earlier kicks of 40, 31, and 24 yards.

Some of the doldroms carried over to the next week as Northwestern's undermanned squad gave the Buckeyes all they

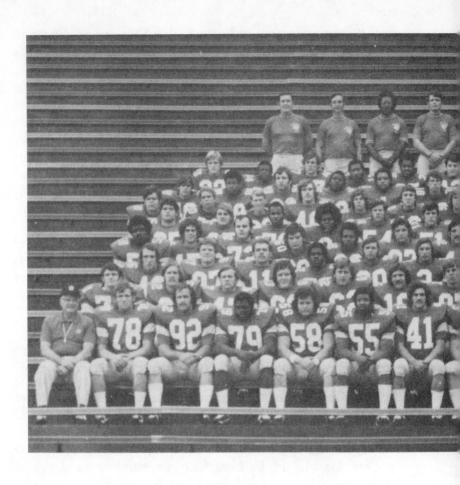

could handle before losing, 27 to 14. Fullback Harold Henson established a new Ohio State rushing record of 44 carries, good for 4 touchdowns and 153 yards. This surpassed by 2 tries John Brockington's 42 of 1970, also against Northwestern.

Henson led the nation in scoring with 20 touchdowns, an Ohio State single-season record, breaking the previous mark of 17, held jointly by Brockington and Jim Otis. For the seventeenth time more than one Buckeye made the all-American. They were linebacker Randy Gradishar and offensive tackle John Hicks.

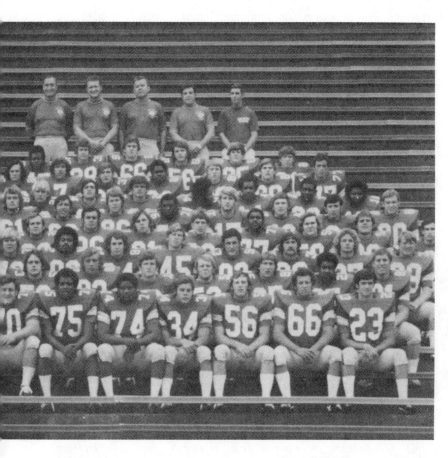

Ohio State's 1972 squad won the Big Ten title by defeating Michigan in the season's finale 11 to 8 but lost to USC's national champions in the Rose Bowl, 42 to 17.

When the first half of the 1973 Rose Bowl game ended 7 to 7 after the Trojans got a break in recovering a fumble to help them score, it seemed that the Buckeyes were in the tilt as much as their opponents. But tailback Anthony Davis shredded Ohio's defense with his brilliant running and quarterback Mike Rae passed with precision as the Trojans broke the tie with three touchdowns in the third period and won going away. Two more were added in the fourth quarter while the best the Buckeyes could do after intermission was a field goal in the third period by Blair Conway and a last-minute score in the

Seniors Randy Gradishar, left, and John Hicks joined Ohio State's two-time all-American group in 1973. The 6-3 236-pound Gradishar, showing speed, strength, and consistency from his linebacking spot was a unanimous choice for the second straight year. He also was runnerup in the "Player of the Year" sweepstakes. Hicks, 6-3, 258, has been described by Coach Woody Hayes as the "best interior lineman I have ever had." Hicks won both the Outland and Lombardi trophies and was named the UPI Lineman of the Year in 1973. When the Associated Press all-Americans met at the season's end, Gradishar was named captain of the defensive squad and Hicks received the same honor from the offense.

fourth stanza on a five-yard run by John Bledsoe.

Coach Hayes used all 48 eligible players in the game with Rich Parsons, Rick Middleton, and Van DeCree leading in **playing time with 31 minutes each. Merv Teague was next with**

29. The Trojans won 42 to 17.

The Buckeyes actually had one more play than the Trojans, 73 to 72, and out-rushed the winners 285 to 207, but the passing difference was shocking, 244 to 81. The west coast aerial game hurt the Buckeyes as it did two years before when Stanford cut the Ohioans down. Completing 19 of 27 passes, with none intercepted, the Trojans kept on the move despite 48 yards in penalties to only 7 by Ohio State. The Buckeyes gave the ball twice on interceptions and conceded a 5-yard edge in punting, 41 to 36.

The Buckeyes were rated third nationally behind the Trojans and Oklahoma.

A Truly Magnificent Team

There were some great ones that went before, a half dozen claiming a piece of the mythical national championship, but perhaps the best-of-all in 84 years of football materialized with the 1973 team.

It really was not until January 1, 1974, however, that Woody Hayes would admit that his swashbuckling 23rd team was his best despite that frustrating knot at Michigan, which was the only blemish in 11 games. The only blemish, that is, if you discount the verbal beating the Buckeyes and others in the Big Ten took from Michigan mentor Glenn E. (Bo) Schembechler.

Like a bad case of indigestion was that 10-10 Bo-tie, but it was relieved almost majestically in the Rose Bowl where the Buckeyes came back full bloom, to manhandle Southern California 42-21. There were 105,267 live fans and the biggest TV audience this side of the Super Bowl on New Year's Day to obliterate the bad taste of both Michigan and the 1973 mis-adventure with virtually the same Southern Cal team.

That was the frosting on the cake, making amends for the misery in Ann Arbor where some said Woody's conservatism almost "did in" a truly magnificent team.

In the beginning 1973 was particularly impressive, in fact awesomely ominous because this team started with much the same perfection it displayed at the uproarious conclusion in Pasadena, California. What the Buckeyes did for openers was annihilate a reviving Minnesota Gopher team that was supposed to have new teeth ready to sink into the whole league. They did it with astonishing ease, 56-7, and second-year Minnesota Coach Cal Stoll paraphrased an old Hayes trademark when he solemnly noted after the carnage, "They are no longer three yards and a cloud of dust—now they are twelve yards and a mass of humanity."

Stoll, unquestionably, was shell-shocked in terms of the game because he had spent the entire spring, summer, and early fall building for this revenge shot at a Buckeye team his first Gopher gang nearly caught before bowing, 28-20. This time, however, Ohio State had 14 points on the board before Minnesota's touted offense ever touched the football, and it soon became a track meet. A crowd of 86,005 watched as the Buckeyes rolled to 383 rushing yards and 25 first downs. They put the ball in the air only 5 times.

Saying it even better than Stoll was his predecessor, crusty Murray Warmath, a Minnesota administrator and advance man who had come to bury an old adversary but wound up praising Woody. He said, "Never have I seen a team execute better so early in the season."

There were some old reliables leading the way, like junior fullback "Champ" Henson, the 1972 national scoring champion with 20 touchdowns, starting strongly in 1973 with 3 touchdowns and 81 yards. And the incredible sophomore tailback Archie Griffin, picking up where he left off after a dazzling freshman year.

With almost equal dispatch, but certainly more consistent defense than offense, did the Buckeyes handle the non-conference part of their 10-game schedule—a 37-3 rout of Texas Christian before 87,439 and nearly a carbon copy 27-3 job on Washington State with 87,425 witnesses.

The record crowd at the TCU Horned Frog game added their own tears to the worst rainstorm to hit Ohio Stadium in history when the 228-pound block-buster from Teays Valley, "Champ" Henson, was felled with a damaged knee midway in the second quarter. It was shortly after his fourth TD of the young season had given his mates a 14-0 edge. The Bucks went on to score 17 more the second quarter, then buttoned things up, still piling up 433 yards and 20 first downs to 151 yards and 8 first downs for the Frogs.

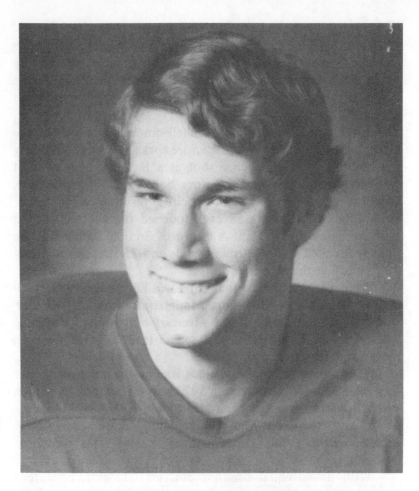

Harold (Champ) Henson, Ohio State's brilliant fullback, suffered a knee injury in the second game of the season against TCU and was lost for the season. Henson led the nation in scoring in 1972 with 20 touchdowns, a new Buckeye scoring record. His 44 carries against Northwestern set a school record and his 4 touchdowns in the same game tied a university mark.

It was a bit tougher doing in Coach Jim Sweeney's Washington State Cougars in a game that launched linebacker Bruce Elia's fullbacking career with a pair of touchdowns and 57 yards in 11 carries. But once again it was indomitable Archie Griffin who carved up the Cougars with 128 yards in just

When fullback Harold Henson was lost for the 1973 season with a knee injury, Bruce Elia, another junior, moved into the position. Elia started the 1972 season as a reserve fullback, but was shifted to linebacker. Although preferring to play defense, Elia took full advantage of the opportunity to succeed Henson and scored 6 touchdowns in his first 3 appearances, finishing the season with 14. Elia's success at the position indicated the depth of the Ohio State squad.

15 trips, one a 26-yard dart in the third quarter to make a tense situation relaxed. And like Woody acknowledged, "Having Archie around is a pretty good thing."

Archie also nabbed a six-yard pass from Cornelius Greene for a touchdown on a broken play that dumbfounded Sweeney.

237

*Halfback Archie Griffin proved to be Mr. Spectacular for the Buckeyes. Not only was he the first sophomore ever to win the Big Ten's "most valuable" award (*Chicago Tribune*), but he rushed to a new conference record of 1,695 yards in 1974. Named on several all-American teams he amassed a total of 5,589 yards for Ohio State, making him the Buckeyes' all-time rushing leader. Archie Griffin won the Heisman Trophy in 1974 and 1975 and was all-American at Ohio State in 1973, 1974, and 1975. He earned Ohio State's top three single-season rushing honors and is the only two-time winner of the Heisman Trophy in the award's long history. Archie's younger brother Ray later became an all-American defensive back at Ohio State.*

"That is the stuff that beat us—a busted play," he moaned. But only in the mid-section of the game, when they scored all 27 points, were the Bucks impressive, leading Woody to comment "we did not play as well as we did in the first two," though he left unsaid his paramount point—he saves everything for the Big Ten.

Now the Buckeyes were back to the real business at hand, the Big Ten, and the Badgers of Wisconsin. Camp Randall stadium was overflowing with 77,413 fans dreaming of an upset of the then No. 1-ranked Buckeyes. They became downright rabid at the outset when they took it to the visitors, and at the conclusion when the Bucks had done them in 24-0. Sticks, stones, marbles, eggs, bottles, tennis balls, ice-filled towels, and verbal insults were hurled at the Bucks and their coach by part of the fifth largest crowd in Camp Randall history, but none of it deterred the Ohioans.

The Buckeyes forced yet another team to change courses in the middle of its screams when it made a second straight road trip, this one to Bloomington where it convinced Indiana Coach Lee Corso, if not an over-loaded Memorial Stadium collection of 53,183 sun-bathers.

Corso, the rookie coach who quickly became the king of gimmickery because of a curious string of weird innovations, played it totally straight, noting on Friday: "I admire Coach Hayes too much. He has a great team and I do not want to get him mad. I even think I will have my wife go down and give him a big kiss before the game because I do not want him mad at her either."

The Bucks did a workmanlike job on Corso's troops, jumping out front 24-0 at halftime, then coasting home as they took the opportunity to re-establish their fullback attack for a final score of 37-7.

The 60-0 homecoming rout of Northwestern was shattering to Woody's old Miami player and aid John Pont, in his first year with the Wildcats, as well as to a record crowd of 87,453 fans who saw a record 82 players gather another record 87 Buckeye leafs (citations for outstanding play).

Pont was solemn—"It was just one of those games when everything went right for Ohio, everything we did was wrong; you cannot explain them; you just try to pull yourself together

239

for next week."

Ohio State scored nine touchdowns on just seven possessions, a strange statistic brought about when the remarkable Neal Colzie intercepted and raced 19 yards for a touchdown the second straight week and when sophomore cornerback Tim Fox blocked a Wildcat punt, then covered it for a 12-yard touchdown play.

Maybe they were looking ahead, maybe the hometown inspiration of Ray Eliot Day (honoring Illini grid coach of 1942-59), or maybe just the midseason "blahs" caught up with them, but the Bucks had a real hassle initiating a 30-0 win over Illinois at Champaign for their seventh victory.

Hayes admitted that his offense "lacked consistency early," credited a "sticky" Illini defense for doing "the best job of any team yet on our option," and cited a "tough break on the opening kickoff" (a touchdown called back) for the sluggish early performance that saw Ohio State held to a 3-0 advantage on Conway's first-quarter, 35-yard field goal.

Hayes became convinced that "this is the best defense I have had in 23 years" after his Bucks squared a lot of accounts with Michigan State in front of another record crowd of 87,600.

The 35-0 shiner dished to rookie Coach Denny Stolz' Spartans was the Bucks' third straight shutout, squared the all-time series with the Spartans at 7-7 (leaving Michigan the only Big Ten team with an edge on the Bucks), and atoned for 19-12 and 17-10 Spartan victories in the two previous years. It also was the widest margin of victory in the series, surpassing Ohio State's 54-21 win in 1969.

After having their two-game victory streak snapped and being held to just four first downs and 94 total yards, five Spartan players, who also had lost to Michigan in a rainstorm, put their heads together and agreed that Ohio State's remarkable offensive line gave it a decided edge over the Wolverines.

Hayes saluted Colzie as "the greatest punt return man I have ever seen," but took the occasion to single out 255-pound senior John Hicks as "the best lineman I have ever had—and that includes Jim Parker. Hicks has NEVER had a bad game."

Iowa certainly took nothing away from the Buckeyes in their home finale before 87,447 fans, least of all terrific tailback

Griffin, who ripped them for a school record of 246 yards in 30 carries which wiped out the 239 he had set as a freshman.

The Hawks, folding 55-13 in a game that was the forerunner of Coach Frank Lauterbur's departure from the school, did succeed in getting Woody's goat and causing him to take some wrath out on the reserves. Iowa scored two late touchdowns that matched the total scoring output of Ohio State's first eight victims.

"I had a notion to make the Bombers (reserves) shower in the back room for lousing up a good effort by the first defensive unit," Hayes said.

All of this, though, as everybody knows, was just so much trimming for the real thing—that season windup at Ann Arbor.

And what a windup!

Both teams unbeaten, Ohio State in nine games, Bo Schembechler's Wolverines in ten. It was strangely, for Ann Arbor, a mild day, 50 degrees, overcast and a touch of wind—but still wild as an all-time record crowd of 105,223 jammed into the Wolverine bowl, largest gathering ever to see a regular season game under NCAA auspices.

Then came the most talked-about 10-10 tie since the 1966 Michigan State-Notre Dame knot, a game in which Ohio State dominated the first half with a 10-0 lead, and threatened to run the Wolverines out of their own orchard, and Michigan coming back to dominate the last two quarters.

And Schembechler making a bigger scene in the post-game hullabaloo than Hayes ever dreamed in his best yard-line-shredding form.

If you did not care who won—and the nation's television audience may have felt that way—it was a slam-bang performance by both teams.

The teams thus tied for the conference title, and the decision as to which went to the Rose Bowl was up to a Sunday morning vote of the league's athletic directors. This eventually brought critical remarks from the disappointed Schembechler.

When the directors' vote went to the Buckeyes, rumored 6-4, Schembechler made comments for the better part of a week in a manner, to say the least, not complimentary to the directors of the league.

Both coaches had made impeccable preparations for the

championship, sealing off practice areas for a week, and Hayes had said he had never had a team better-prepared mechanically and emotionally. Woody was criticized for his conservative offense but stated after the game, "Now it can be told....our passing is no good....has not been good all season. We can't pass." He explained that Greene did not pass because of a sore finger.

But between that game in Ann Arbor and the brilliant one in Pasadena six weeks later, the passing game made a miraculous recovery because the Buckeyes came out throwing against Southern California and quite effectively, at that.

For the first time all season the Buckeyes fell behind in their Rose Bowl rematch with John McKay's vaunted Southern Cal Trojans. In fact they lagged twice, 3-0 on Chris Limahelu's 47-yard field goal in the first period, and again 14-7 midway in the second quarter when rifle-armed junior quarterback Pat Haden pitched to tailback Anthony Davis on an apparent sweep, only to have Davis drop back and loft a 10-yard scoring pass to flanker J. D. McKay. To complete the trickery, the Trojans then went for a two-point conversion pass from Haden to McKay, and the Buckeyes sagged, 14-7.

Freshman Pete Johnson, that 244-pound fullback, softened the Trojans plenty with a one-yard touchdown burst that set up a 14-14 halftime tie, and when Davis dove a yard for a touchdown, capping an 84-yard march early in the third period, the 105,267 fans and a national TV audience of 128 million might have sensed another Trojan rout, similar to the 1973 game that was tied 7-7 at half.

They were half right. It was a rout, but that was USC's last gasp as the Buckeyes then exploded for 27 points while holding McKay's men at bay.

McKay's worst fears were realized because before the game he had said, "If anybody makes a rout of the game, I'm afraid it might be Ohio State." He also said that "Nobody can outrun us, of this I am sure." And then he had to swallow those words painfully as the Buckeyes rolled up the third highest total by a Big Ten team in this series when the incomparable Griffin snaked through his team, faked four of the Trojans out of position, out-ran three others, and carried two more into the end zone on a 47-yard touchdown scamper that put the nail in the Trojan coffin.

It was a remarkably good game offensively, the Trojans doing it mostly through the air with Haden's bombs, the Buckeyes surprising by traveling all routes, including that familiar game-breaker Colzie, who lit the fuse for the explosion once again with a daring 56-yard punt return late in the third quarter that carried to the USC nine. This set up the go-ahead touchdown on a one-yard keeper by Greene on fourth down after he handed off to Pete Johnson the first three times.

Griffin was worth 149 of Ohio State's 320 rushing yards in only 22 turns; Johnson hammered 94 in 21 trips; Greene added 45 in 7; and Elia 27 in 8. More surprising was Greene hitting the Trojans with six completions in eight passes for 129 yards, four of them to senior tight end Fred Pagac, who had caught only five in ten previous games.

The Trojans' 27 first downs were 7 more than the Bucks, but came primarily as Haden threaded 21 of 39 passes for 229 yards. On the ground USC settled for 167 yards, 74 by the touted Davis in 16 trips.

Strangely, if Woody was to be criticized for not putting the ball in the air enough in early games, McKay might be cited for throwing it too much because eventually the Buckeye defense absorbed all of Haden's shots.

Hayes was ecstatic and cordially greeted the press after the game with a thank you, adding that "I have great respect for you, you know. ....this is the greatest victory I have ever had....the greatest we have ever had."

McKay was subdued but gracious and said, "I will not get into that argument about who is No. 1. I will just say Ohio State is the best team we played."

Most of his players concurred, and in a post-game survey they generally agreed that Ohio State was the toughest, Oklahoma second, and that both Ohio and Oklahoma were tougher than Notre Dame.

Hayes said he thought that the biggest play was Colzie's 56-yard punt return, and after that he figured victory was in sight.

Hayes was impressed with the appearance of the Trojans' Haden, Lynn Swann, linebacker Dale Mitchell, and defensive tackle Art Riley in the Buckeye locker room after the

243

Junior Pete Cusick (6-2, 244) and senior Fred Pagac (6-1, 210) played countless positions since their high school days. Cusick played five positions in high school—fullback, tight end, guard, linebacker, and defensive end—just about everything except defensive tackle, where he starred for the Buckeyes. Tackle coach Chuck Clausen, who said defensive tackle is not a glamorous position, said that Cusick, "has the ability to over-power anybody and has super techniques." Pagac (pronounced

Pugitch, as in Polish-Lithuanian), came to Ohio State hopeful of being a running back. He became a defensive end as a freshman and then was switched to fullback. During spring practice he moved to tight end, and, while he had some tough opposition, became the No. 1 man. In high school, he was a fullback and linebacker. Pagac was regarded as the top blocker among the tight ends and is today an Ohio State assistant coach.

game—"One of the most sportsmanlike acts I have seen." But he was just as impressed with his entire offensive line that eventually out-toughed the Trojans, blew them so far off the scrimmage line that you could have pushed the Rose Bowl press box through a couple of the holes.

Maybe the toughest, most overlooked was 252-pound junior center Steve Myers, who played Trojan all-American linebacker Richard Wood off his feet.

Just about as devastating was the Buck defense, though coordinator George Hill sheepishly confessed that the unrealistic shutout he had set as the team goal "was a bit egotistical."

It was the finest hour, for certain, for what many say is the greatest Buckeye squad of all.

Heisman Celebrations
Championship Frustrations

There was no mistaking the slant of the offense as 1974 dawned—Ohio State was rushing into the next season on a dead run.

The previous season's tie with Michigan, although the only blemish on the Buckeye record, had kept Ohio State from the national championship honors that many thought it deserved, but the new squad was so talented that some thought the championship might be even easier to come by this time. Four first or second-team All-Americans returned, and the returning backfield was already being hailed as possibly the greatest in the school's history.

Two of the players, junior quarterback Cornelius Greene and junior tailback Archie Griffin, entered the season with outstanding tags. The others, junior wingback Brian Baschnagel and sophomore fullback Pete Johnson, did not have the past statistics of Griffin and Greene, but were expected to produce big numbers nonetheless. Additionally, senior fullback Harold "Champ" Henson, the nation's leading scorer as a sophomore, returned to challenge Johnson for the starting job after a knee injury had cost him practically all of his junior season.

With that kind of backfield, eight returning starters on offense; eight more on defense; returning All-Americans Van DeCree, a defensive end; and Pete Cusick, a defensive tackle, the Buckeyes were favorites to win their third straight Big Ten title. And Griffin, an All-American as a sophomore, was the favorite to win the Heisman Trophy as a junior.

"All that publicity that we get, we can't believe that," said

Griffin, trying to remain level-headed about the situation. "I believe that we have a better team than last year. I think we can win the Big Ten championship if we take them one at a time. If we keep our heads straight, it will work out."

It certainly worked out the first week, anyway. Although Archie Griffin played the second half with strained knee ligaments, the quick junior managed to grind out 133 yards for a new Ohio State career rushing record in a 34-19 win over Minnesota in Minneapolis.

The game marked the return of Woody Hayes from a heart attack suffered only 13 weeks before.

"I was tired, but no more than usual after a game," said Hayes, as reporters pressed the issue about the 61-year-old coach's health. "I always get excited during a game, but it's when they print things that aren't true in national magazines that can give a man a heart attack."

It was the same old Woody, and for over two months, the Buckeyes looked like the same powerful Ohio State team. Week after week, Archie Griffin continued to pile up 100-yard-plus rushing games, and the Buckeyes continue to pile up lopsided win after lopsided win. Griffin etched his name into NCAA record books with his eighteenth consecutive regular season 100-yard game in a 49-7 romp over Illinois, and all appeared perfect for the Ohio State footballers as they took their No. 1 national ranking to Michigan State the following week. And although their win streak and national championship hopes did not end until almost an hour after the game was over, both ended nonetheless.

Ohio State appeared to have the game in hand when Henson bulled over right tackle for a touchdown with 9:03 remaining in the game and Tom Klaban added the extra point for a 13-3 lead. But Michigan State quarterback Charlie Baggett fired a 44-yard touchdown pass to Mike Jones with 5:30 left to cut the margin to four. A Levi Jackson touchdown and Hans Nielsen conversion kick with 3:17 remaining gave the Spartans a three-point lead, and Ohio State began a drive to retain its national championship hopes that ended, apparently, a couple of seconds short.

The final seconds were shrouded in confusion. Henson plunged six yards to within inches of the goal line with 29 seconds remaining.

As expected, the Michigan State players were slow in getting off the pileup. The Buckeyes then attempted to line up and get a play started before the clock ran out and the ball squirted through Greene's legs to Baschnagel, who picked it up and ran into the end zone for an apparent touchdown. The head linesman signaled touchdown, invoking a celebration among the Ohio State fans, but both the back judge and the field judge ruled that time had run out before the play had started. Big Ten Commissioner Wayne Duke huddled with the officials after the game to sort out what had happened, and 46 minutes after the game, with half of the 78,533 fans still waiting for word in the stadium, the announcement was made that Michigan State indeed had won.

Hayes reacted bitterly.

"The officials were obviously remiss; they made a mistake," said Hayes. "There were 26 seconds left in the huddle when we called two plays. Normally we can run four or five plays in 26 seconds in practice. The officials did not untangle the mess. They layed on top of the pileup and wouldn't let us run the play, and the referee wouldn't call a time out. He should have stopped the clock, but he let time run out."

As far as national championship hopes were concerned, time also ran out on the Buckeyes in East Lansing. Ohio State rallied for an easy victory over Iowa the following week, then used four Tom Klaban field goals to beat Michigan in a 12-10 classic in Ohio Stadium the last week of the regular season. The win left OSU and Michigan in a tie for the league crown, but the conference athletic directors voted to send the Buckeyes to the Rose Bowl for a third straight season, where the team still clung to the hope that an Ohio State win over USC and the right set of circumstances would somehow drop the national championship in its lap.

In the weeks between the end of the regular season and the Rose Bowl, Ohio State scored one stunning victory over Southern Cal, when junior Archie Griffin became the fourth Buckeye player to win the Heisman Trophy by a wide margin over the Trojans' Anthony Davis. But the Rose Bowl game result was considerably closer and just the reverse. Despite the fact that Griffin had his overall 100-yard rushing games record of 22 snapped when he picked up just 75 yards against the tough Trojans, Ohio State still led 17-10 as the game wound down to its final moments. That was when USC quarterback Pat Haden took the Trojans on a late game drive, capped by a 38-yard touchdown pass to J.T. McKay with 2:03 remaining. A subsequent conversion pass from Haden to Sherman Diggs gave USC an 18-17 win. When Notre Dame upset Alabama a few hours later in the Orange Bowl, meaning that the Buckeyes could have won the national title had they hung on for the win, it also added to an acute case of heartache.

The Ohio State team that had dedicated itself to a dream of national championship had finished but 10-2, a couple of seconds and a couple of points away from the title.

But, like the heartaches of the previous season, the Buckeyes' wounds were quickly salved by the return of a nucleus of players whom most expected to compete for championship honors again.

Champ Henson was gone, but the rest of the backfield returned intact. Archie Griffin's overall streak of 22 games over 100 yards rushing had been snapped, but the Heisman Trophy winner's NCAA record of 21 straight remained, because the NCAA does not count bowl games in its record keeping. Griffin's 1,695 rushing yards, an OSU season record, and Corny Greene's 842 were a formidable starting point for an offense that still featured Baschnagel (335 yards) and Johnson (320). Losses were heavy on defense, where only three regulars returned, but one, safety Tim Fox, was destined to be an All-American. Hayes and his staff were confident of the replacements, and once the season started, it was easy to see why.

The Buckeyes took revenge on Michigan State in the opener, winning 21-0, and then showed Penn State the depth of its backfield in a 17-9 home victory. Although Griffin continued his regular season streak with 128 yards on the ground, Pete Johnson gained 112 and Brian Baschnagel burned the Lions with a 49-yard sprint on a reverse during OSU's first touchdown drive. Penn State's Joe Paterno was impressed.

"I didn't realize that Johnson was quite that strong," said Paterno. "But any one of the Ohio State backs can beat you, including Baschnagel, who did it today."

250

After a romp of North Carolina, UCLA was the next big-name football power on the Buckeye schedule, and the game was on the West Coast. It turned out to be no problem. The Buckeyes jumped out to a 31-7 lead and coasted to a 41-20 win.

From there, it was clear sailing to Michigan, by which time, it was becoming increasingly obvious that the Buckeyes were within striking distance of the slippery national title again. For a while it looked like the dream might end in Ann Arbor when a series of miscues and a below-average day for Archie Griffin—he had his streak snapped at 31 games when he gained just 46 yards—helped Michigan carry a 14-7 lead into the final seven minutes of the game. After Greene took the Buckeyes on an 80-yard game tying drive, Ray Griffin made the play that set up OSU's victory and fourth consecutive Rose Bowl appearance.

Ray Griffin followed his older brother Archie to Ohio State and switched from tailback to defense on his way to All-American honors.

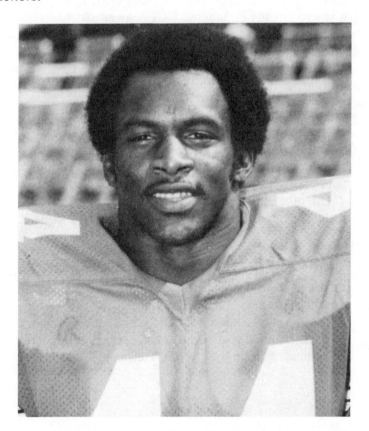

From the Michigan 33, Wolverine quarterback Rick Leach cut loose of a third-and-19 pass, and Ray grabbed it from his defensive backfield position and streaked to the Michigan three. Pete Johnson then plunged in for his third touchdown of the day and the Buckeyes, 21-14 winners, were again en route to Pasadena.

It was Griffin's first interception of his first season at safety, after he had switched to that spot from the more glamorous tailback position.

"I've been waiting so long," said Ray Griffin. "But I got it at the right time."

His older brother was happy for his brother and his teammates and not down in the mouth about having his rushing streak snapped.

"I couldn't be happier," said Archie. "We won the game and that's the most important thing. I feel great. The streak has to end sometime and as long as we won, man, that's all that counts."

What also counted was the fact that Ohio State now carried an 11-0 record and the nation's No. 1 ranking into the Rose Bowl, where already-conquered UCLA awaited.

In the meantime, Heisman Trophy voting came to an end, and Archie Griffin, with 1,327 yards in 245 rushes (a 5.5 average), seemed like a good bet to become the first two-time winner ever. Although many argued that his credentials were not as good as they had been when he won the previous season, and some thought that California's Chuck Muncie, USC's Ricky Bell, or Pittsburgh's Tony Dorsett should have won it this time, he garnered two and a half times the votes of any of the others to make Heisman history with his second straight award.

"The other players fretted and stewed more than Archie about the Heisman and about the 100 yards every game," said Woody Hayes. "He epitomizes everything you want in an athlete."

Griffin proved that when he downplayed the second Heisman and instead concentrated on the January 1 goal that lay ahead in Pasadena's Rose Bowl.

"I've never played on a national championship team," said Griffin. "I want that badder than ever. It's one thing I've always wanted. People look at the Heisman Trophy as an individual award, which it's not. It's a team thing at Ohio State.

"If you win a national championship, you know it's a team and not an individual thing. That's the reason I want that national championship."

Unfortunately for Griffin and his teammates, the championship that seemed so certain after the come-from-behind win over Michigan never came. Although Ohio State thoroughly dominated the first half, the Buckeyes led only 3-0, and OSU's failure to take advantage of its dominance was a portent of doom. UCLA coach Dick Vermeil made some offensive adjustments at halftime and the Bruins' 366 second-half yards indicated that OSU could not handle them. When the smoke cleared, UCLA had a 23-10 upset victory that left the Buckeyes stunned.

Afterwards, a highly disappointed Woody Hayes refused to talk to the press, and the four-year reign of Archie Griffin and a troupe of talented Buckeyes who had come close to the national championship three straight times only to miss out on all three occasions, ended with a three-word comment Hayes made to Vermeil on the field following the game after the Ohio State coach congratulated the winner.

"We blew it," Hayes said.

Few could give him an argument.

Three Years Of Rose Bowl Drought

The Archie Griffin Era had ended, and with it ended the Buckeyes' annual flirtations with a national football championship. No one knew or even suspected it at the time, but Ohio State would not come close to either a national title or the Rose Bowl for the next three years. And, ironically, it was not the graduation of the major part of the backfield that marked the downturn in Buckeye grid fortunes, but a gradually worsening defense.

Junior speedster Jeff Logan, back-up to Archie Griffin the previous season, stepped in and proved a more than adequate replacement in 1976, and sophomore Rod Gerald replaced Cornelius Greene at quarterback and immediately impressed with his quickness and cunning. Pete Johnson was still available at fullback, and the offensive line still had tackle Chris Ward and guard Bill Lukens to allay offensive fears.

The defense, with seven starters, including future All-American defensive end Bob Brudzinski, returning from a unit that allowed only 8½ points per game, looked solid, and two weeks into the season, everything seemed the same.

The Buckeyes exploded offensively and buried Michigan State 49-21 the first week and then outlasted Penn State 12-7 in a defensive duel in University Park. But unranked Missouri slipped into Ohio Stadium the following Saturday and quickly pointed up some Ohio State defensive flaws. In a 22-21 stunner, the Tigers snapped a 25-game OSU home winning streak.

In the process Missouri racked up 211 rushing yards and 113 passing yards against the OSU defense. The most critical of those came in an 80-yard, 13-play drive that was capped by a 31-yard touchdown pass from substitute quarterback Pete

Woods to flanker Joe Stewart with 12 seconds left. The six-pointer left Missouri one point down, but Woods took the snap and lunged left for a two-point conversion run that left the Buckeyes a loser for the first time in Ohio Stadium since Northwestern beat them 14-10 in 1971.

"Going down the field, we knew we were going for two points," said Missouri coach Al Onofrio. "With less than three minutes, you're not likely to get the ball back."

The Buckeyes wanted to get their respect back the following week against UCLA, but for all of the revenge motives remaining from last year's loss in the Rose Bowl and the previous week's loss to Missouri, all they could manage was a 10-10 tie. They needed a 25-yard field goal by Tom Skladany midway in the final quarter to get even that. After four games, the Buckeyes were just 2-1-1.

Spirits picked up when six consecutive Big Ten victories followed, but the wins merely gave OSU false confidence entering the season finale against Michigan. When it was over, the Wolverines were possessors of a 22-0 romp, the first shutout of an Ohio State team since 1964. The Michigan offense, meanwhile, punished OSU's defense to the tune of 366 rushing yards.

"Michigan will get my vote for No. 1," said Hayes, "because any team that can beat us that badly had got to be No. 1!"

Still, Ohio State's offense had not been helped by the loss of quarterback Rod Gerald to a back injury the last four games of the regular season, and although Jim Pacenta had done a credible job of leading the team, many looked toward an Orange Bowl date with Colorado—for the first time Big Ten teams were eligible to accept bids to other bowl games—as an opportunity for Gerald and the Buckeyes to make amends for what had been a frustrating year.

The amends were quickly made. Gerald replaced Pacenta late in the first period with Colorado leading 10-0 and carried the Buckeyes to a 27-10 victory. The offensive surge obviously also inspired the defense. The Buckeye defense, yielder of more Ohio State opponents points than any OSU team since 1971, shut out the Buffaloes the final three quarters.

"We played them like an accordion," said Hayes. "We stretched them in and we stretched them out. We felt we could

255

Oklahoma kicker Uwe von Schamman reacts to his 41-yard field goal with three seconds remaining that sealed the Sooners' 29-28

victory over Ohio State that some called an equal to the famous
1935 OSU-Notre Dame football game in terms of excitement.

intercept them, and we did (twice).''

The game also provided a peek at the future from an offensive standpoint. Although Jeff Logan had been used at tailback all year with junior college transfer Ron Springs as his back-up, Hayes surprised everyone by moving Logan to fullback, where he alternated with Pete Johnson, and giving Springs some time at tailback. Springs responded by carrying the ball 22 carries for 98 yards.

"Doing good in the Orange Bowl," said Springs, "will open some doors for me.''

He admitted that he thought the same doors were closed to him most of the year, and that he, at times, thought he had made the wrong decision in attending Ohio State.

"It crossed my mind a few times during the season," said Springs. "But there is no sense in worrying about that now. I've got something to look forward to next year, knowing that I can do the job. Next year it (the split backfield with Logan) should be a big part of our attack."

It was, too. When 1977 dawned, there was Jeff Logan, a 5-foot-10, 184-pound tailback, in the fullback position in the Buckeyes' "I" attack, while Springs occupied the tailback spot. Logan, for one, was less than thrilled about the switch, and since he had gained 1,248 yards as a tailback the previous year you could not really blame him, but Woody seemed determined to adjust to his personnel and base the team's offense on speed rather than power.

Ironically, Logan and back-up tailback Ricky Johnson, two speed backs supposed to change the Buckeyes' style, were hurt in the opener and the Buckeyes, with Ric Volley and Paul Campbell sharing the fullback position, used power football to beat Miami (Florida) 10-0. Consequently, the defense led by up and coming All-American linebacker Tom Cousineau, picked up the charge.

Minnesota was an easy 38-7 victim the following week, setting up a big showdown with unbeaten Oklahoma the next week in Ohio Stadium. The game took on all the drama of a Michigan game, with Hayes closing practices to the media and public the week before and even going so far as to announce a move of All-American safety Ray Griffin to tailback, because Logan and Johnson were still hurting.

As it turned out, the move was a bust—Griffin gained only 16 yards in seven carries—but the game itself merited all of the Michigan game treatment and more.

The swift Sooners, led by halfback Elvis Peacock, future Heisman Trophy winner Billy Sims, and quarterback Tommy Lott, dazzled the OSU defense early in jumping out to a fast 20-0 lead. Then the game took on a dramatic reversal. Springs dashed 30 yards for a touchdown, and when Lott fumbled, Gerald streaked 19 yards for another. A 52-yard third-period drive was capped by a one-yard plunge by freshman fullback Joel Payton. Vlade Janakievski's third conversion kick made it 21-20, and two minutes later, Kelton Dansler picked off a Sooner pass at the Oklahoma 33.

Rod Gerald suffered a head bump three plays later and had to be removed, but substitute quarterback Greg Castignola promptly fired a 16-yard touchdown pass to Jimmy Moore with 4:44 remaining. The conversion kick made it 28-20, and the Buckeyes appeared safe.

They were not, Oklahoma charged back, with Peacock finally scoring from the one with 1:29 left to leave the Sooners two points short. Peacock's attempt at a game-tying conversion run was spoiled by a Mike Guess tackle, and the Buckeyes again appeared to have the win secure.

They did not. Uwe von Schamann, a German-born soccer-style place-kicker tried an onsides kick attempt, and incredibly, the Sooners recovered. Four plays later, von Schamann re-entered the game with three seconds remaining and booted a 41-yard field goal that resulted in an amazing 29-28 Oklahoma victory.

Immediately, the game was compared to the fabled 1935 Ohio State-Notre Dame football game as one of the greatest in history. Hayes did not think so.

"To heck with the most exciting game," said Hayes. "I'd rather have them drab as heck and win."

The Buckeyes won for eight straight weeks after that, and it began to look as though the one-point loss would keep Ohio State from another shot at the national championship. That theory finally disintegrated in Ann Arbor, where the Buckeyes outplayed Michigan everywhere but on the scoreboard in losing 14-6.

"This is by far the best game we ever played and lost," said a disappointed Hayes after the game. And the stats seem to prove it was so. Seven times Ohio State drove the ball into Michigan territory, five times inside the Wolverine 15, and yet had only two Vlade Janakievski field goals to show for it.

After that kind of showing against Michigan (and with a one-point loss to Oklahoma as the only other blemish), Buckeye fans were thrilled when a Sugar Bowl bid brought the opportunity to match the Buckeyes and Woody Hayes against Alabama and Bear Bryant. But what looked to be an opportunity to atone for two venial sins turned out to be an afternoon of hell-like punishment.

The Buckeye defense stopped the Tide on its first drive, but Alabama rolled over the OSU defense the next two times it had the ball. Consequently, the score was 13-0 Alabama in the second quarter, and when the Buckeyes failed on a fourth-and-four situation at the Alabama five with 30 seconds remaining in the half, the die was cast. Led by fullback Johnny Davis and quarterback Jeff Rutledge, Alabama ran away from the Buckeyes in the second half for a 35-6 rout that surprised even the most ardent Alabama fan. The Buckeyes, in finishing 9-3, no longer seemed as close to the nation's best teams as they had thought they were.

"I thought we had a great team," said Logan. "But great teams should be able to win the big games."

Woody Hayes agreed.

"They beat us with a team that had half the talent we had." he said. "They were the best team we played this season. Our team got about a quarter of the coaching that their team got."

It was a clear reference to all of the pre-game hype that pictured the forty-fourth Sugar Bowl as a game between two great coaches rather than two great teams. After the game, Bryant made a face when the subject arose.

"I don't think winning or losing today has anything to do with how good or bad a coach I am or how good or bad a coach he is," said Bryant. "He's a great coach and he always will be. And I ain't bad."

The theory, at least as far as Hayes was concerned, was tested almost immediately at the beginning of the 1978 season, though, and many fans gave the venerable coach, starting his twenty-eighth year at Ohio State, failing marks.

In the offseason, the Buckeyes had recruited the state's and possibly the nation's best high school quarterback in Miami Trace High School's Art Schlichter, and everyone knew that the pressure was on to use the talented freshman immediately. This posed a problem since two-year starting veteran Rod Gerald was returning for his senior year, although Hayes was given an out by pro scouts who said that Gerald's career as a professional would have to come at a wide receiver spot.

When fall practices started, Hayes slammed the practice doors to the news media and fans, heightening the mystery. Powerful Penn Sate, which opened a week earlier with a win over Rutgers, beckoned in the Ohio State opener, and Hayes did not want to play his hand. Finally, with 88,203 fans in Ohio Stadium reaching for their binoculars, the Buckeyes' offensive starting unit ran out on the field, and when all saw that Schlichter was at quarterback, the crowd erupted in a cheer. Unfortunately, it was the highlight of a dismal afternoon for the home crowd. Although the crowd had what it wanted in passing, rather than a running quarterback, the wisdom of starting an untried freshman against a team of Penn State's caliber was quickly questioned. Five pass interceptions led the Nittany Lions to an easy 19-0 romp.

Even Hayes admitted afterwards that he may have made a mistake.

"I think our new quarterback is probably as fine a passer as there is in college football," he said. "He's going to be real great. I'm sure he'll end up being one of the best quarterbacks we've ever had. But I think we were asking a little too much of him to go in and take over against that team. On some of those interceptions, we didn't help him by getting him rushed in there."

It was a disappointing start to what turned out to be a disappointing year. Although the Buckeyes rolled over Minnesota 27-10 the next week, Baylor quarterback Steve Smith visited Columbus the following Saturday and pointed up serious deficiencies in the Buckeyes' pass defense. Ohio State finally won that 34-28, but the following week, SMU quarterback Mike Ford brought the Mustangs back from a 35-21 deficit by com-

Art Schlichter on his way to earning all Ohio State career passing records and most individual game marks. His career stats would show 951 attempts, 497 completions for 7,547 yards, and 50 touchdowns, all school records. He also would rush for 35 touchdowns and have 8,850 total offensive yards, also a record. He would start all 48 games during his Buckeye career.

pleting 36 of 57 passes for 341 passing yards that gave SMU a 35-35 tie. From an Ohio State standpoint, the result could have been even worse. SMU place-kicker Eddie Garcia missed a 47-yarder with seven seconds remaining that could have won the game for the unheralded underdogs from the Southwest Conference.

"If you like high scoring games and don't care who wins," said Hayes afterward, "then I guess you could enjoy this. But for a coach who gets a 14-point lead and blows it, it's not much. And I feel we blew it too."

Ultimately, Hayes had to deal with the increasingly apparent problem with his team's pass defense.

"We've got a shortage of material in pass defense, deep men in particular," said Hayes. "Injuries have hurt us, but this is no alibi. We're not as agile going to the ball as we were a year ago."

The theory was proven again the following week when Purdue beat Ohio State 27-16 at West Lafayette, and though Ohio State won five straight Big Ten games after that, the squad was well on the way to giving up what was then the high point total in OSU history, 216.

By the time Michigan finally beat the punchless Buckeyes 14-3 in Ohio Stadium for the Buckeyes' third loss (with a tie) in 11 games, OSU had compiled several unimpressive streaks. The Buckeyes had three successive losses to Michigan (the first time in the Hayes era and a negative streak that had not been branded on OSU since the 1945-1948 seasons); 12 consecutive touchdown-less quarters against Michigan, dating back to the fourth quarter of the OSU Michigan game in 1975; and five consecutive losses on national television.

On a sour note, the Buckeyes accepted a post-season bid to the Gator Bowl, where an even more sour note awaited.

The Hayes Era Ends
With A Punch

After six consecutive appearances in New Year's Day bowl games, the 1978 Gator Bowl was something of a step down in class. The Buckeyes, who had grown used to playing post-season games against the likes of USC, UCLA, and Alabama, suddenly found themselves trying to prove their worth against the Atlantic Coast Conference and Clemson.

It was a game that the Buckeyes could not afford to lose. After three losses in their last four bowl appearances, and probably just as important, five consecutive nationally televised losses, Ohio State went to Jacksonville knowing that the team's lustre had begun to fade. A victory over Clemson would not restore the Buckeyes to their earlier glory, but everyone knew that a victory might help the team get back on the positive side on the recruiting trails. Woody Hayes, never one to take defeat lightly, knew that the Buckeyes could absorb no further televised humiliations. Ohio State needed a bowl win, any bowl win, to save face.

For a while it seemed that the Buckeyes might get it. Freshman quarterback Art Schlichter, often maligned throughout the season for his movement into Rod Gerald's starting position when some of the OSU seniors obviously felt that Gerald deserved the call, had the game of his freshman life, completing 16 of 20 passes for 205 yards and rushing for 70 more, establishing an OSU record for single-season total yardage in the process. The 18-year-old freshman also scored twice.

But for all of Schlichter's heroics, the Buckeyes still fell behind 17-9, and they stayed on the short end when Schlichter directed an 88-yard drive, climaxed by a Schlichter touchdown on a keeper play. Unfortunately for Ohio State, a similar Schlichter option keep failed to convert the two-point conversion, and the Buckeyes trailed 17-15 as the game wound down to the final minutes. No one knew it, but time was also running out on Woody Hayes' career.

The Tigers had the ball, but OSU middle guard Tim Sawicki gave the Buckeyes life when he recovered a fumble by Clemson quarterback Steve Fuller on the Tiger 24. Two plays later on third and five, Schlichter dropped back and made one of his few mistakes of the game—he fired a ball easily picked off by Clemson linebacker Charlie Bauman. When Bauman finally ended up out of bounds near the OSU bench, Hayes attacked, punching him in frustration. The game was over for the Buckeyes, and although no one knew it at the time, so was Hayes' 28-year Ohio State career.

"Coach Hayes grabbed him (Bauman) by the helmet and hit the player three times around his face," the *Columbus Dispatch* reported an OSU athletic official as saying. And OSU Athletic Director Hugh Hindman was quoted as saying that firing Hayes was the "toughest decision I have ever had to make."

Precisely how it was made is, to this day, still something of a mystery. Hayes reportedly told *Dispatch* sportswriter Paul Hornung immediately after the game that the end was near and that he was thinking seriously of giving OSU officials his resignation. Meanwhile, Hindman, who had viewed the incident from the Gator Bowl press box, had already come to a decision regarding Hayes' future, as had OSU President Harold Enarson, who viewed the game from the stands.

"We both felt the same way afterwards," said Hindman, who had played for Woody one season at Miami (Ohio) and had coached under him for seven years at Ohio State. "But I still have great admiration for him."

Both Hayes and Hindman reported meeting in Hayes' hotel room in Jacksonville early Saturday morning and addressing the issue. Hindman quoted Hayes as saying "Do I have the opportunity to resign?"

"I said 'Yes, you do have that opportunity,'" Hindman said. Hindman then quoted Hayes as saying that "I'm not going to resign. That would make it too easy for you. You better go ahead and fire me."

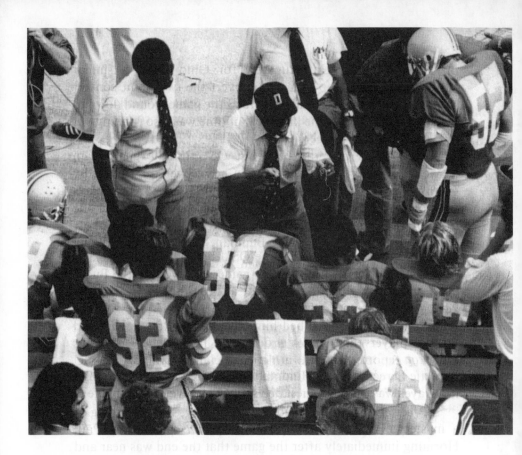

Woody Hayes gives a stern lecture to his offensive unit during 1978's 34-28 "close call" against upset-minded Baylor.

Hayes later called Hornung and announced his decision to resign, although Hindman was already in the process of calling a brief press conference in the hotel to announce Hayes' firing.

"Coach Hayes has been relieved of his duties as head football coach at Ohio State University," said Hindman, in the hastily called press conference. "This decision has the full support of the president of the university."

When the plane carrying the president and a party of 112 university officials and their families was diverted to Pittsburgh because of bad weather in Columbus, OSU president Harold Enarson, in a press conference at the Pittsburgh airport, confirmed that fact.

"It was Hugh Hindman's decision that the services of Mr. Hayes be discontinued," said Enarson. "I concurred in that decision. There was no difficulty in reaching the decision. There is not a university or an athletic conference in the country which would permit a coach to physically assault a college athlete.

"One thing cries to be said. I, along with many, many people feel a great sadness that a coach with such an illustrious record for a quarter century should leave the business in such a tragic fashion."

In that regard, it was easy to be highly sympathetic. Although Hayes' coaching career had been marked by many such incidents, most of which were unprovoked, those close to him were able to ignore his volatile temper and occasional outbursts and see him as a tireless worker who spent a large part of his personal time trying to educate his athletes and caring for fellow human beings. Many fans would miss Hayes because of the 238 victories, two national championships, and 13 Big Ten titles he produced in his 28 years as OSU boss, but some of Hayes' players expressed sentiments that reflected on his off-the-field victories. They were many.

"It's going to be a deep loss," said defensive tackle Bryon Cato. "Newspapers say all the bad things about Hayes...and don't say enough about all the time he spends in hospitals helping the handicapped to believe in themselves."

Other Ohio State players felt similar sentiments.

"I'm very, very sad," said two-time All—American Tom Cousineau. "He was a great coach and a great man. If I had a chance, I would play for him again."

It was the best tribute that any coach could receive.

New Coach, New Look

The new Ohio State football coach was no stranger to his Ohio environment. Earle Bruce, culled by Hugh Hindman from a large group of former Ohio State players and assistant coaches who had succeeded in the head coaching business elsewhere, had just come off three successive 8-3 seasons at Iowa State but had an Ohio coaching background.

Born in Pittsburgh, Bruce's family had moved to Cumberland, Maryland, at age 10. He was star sprinter and halfback in high school, and enrolled at Ohio State under Coach Wes Fesler. A serious knee injury as a freshman interrupted his football career, and when he reinjured it in 1951, he was forced to drop football. The new coach, Woody Hayes, persuaded him to remain in school and earn his degree, which he did in 1953.

The following fall he started his coaching career as an assistant coach at Mansfield Senior High School, and he went on to Ohio head coaching positions at Salem, Sandusky, and Massillon. He was unbeaten in his final two years at Massillon and joined Hayes' Ohio State coaching staff in 1966 as an assistant coach. After six years on the Buckeye staff, Bruce became head coach at the University of Tampa and, after a 10-2 season there, moved on to Iowa State, where he coached six years. While at Ohio State, he served as an assistant with Hindman, also an assistant coach during that period.

"This is like a dream come true for me," said Bruce. "I consider Ohio State the top coaching job in the country and I will do all I can to insure that it stays that way. All my efforts will be to keep Ohio State football at its current level of excellence."

Not everyone was sure, though, that the Buckeyes were the power that they once were. After all, the team had finished fourth in 1978, its worst finish in the league since 1971. The four losses and a tie also represented the most blemishes on a Buckeye football record since 1966.

There were other problems, too. Six regulars were gone on offense, including tailback Ron Springs and tackle Joe Robinson, while the defense, most porous in Ohio State history to that point, now had six more holes to fill, including a huge one at linebacker left by departed All-American Tom Cousineau.

The immediate concern of the fans was whether, with Schlichter at quarterback and a new coach on the field, the run-oriented offense would be scrubbed in favor of a wide-open passing attack. Insiders suspected that Bruce was too much of a Hayes' disciple to make such a radical change, but the new coach refused to make any pre-season commitments either way.

"I am not really interested in the number of times we pass," said Bruce. "Scoring is what counts. Not yardage or numbers of passes. We'll take what the defense gives us. We'll feature our best players and we'll emphasize the things they do best."

It was obvious from the beginning that the nation, after seeing last year's Ohio State loss to Clemson, was not impressed with what the Buckeyes did best. For the first time in several years, Ohio State did not land a spot in the top 20 of either of the national wire service pre-season polls.

Whether the doubts were caused by the new coach, last season's disappointments, or both, the situation wasn't debated long. Looking exactly like the Buckeyes of the Woody Hayes era, Ohio State rolled over Syracuse 31-8 in the opener with (surprise) the rushing attack leading the way. Junior tailback Calvin Murray, stepping in for the departed Springs, carried 19 times for 86 yards and Schlichter ran for 91 yards in 15 carries. The sophomore quarterback's eight of 16 passing for 81 yards might have been a disappointment for some, but the post-game scene was one of happiness.

"I feel a little relieved that the first game was a victory," said Bruce, who had endured nine months of Woody Hayes comparison questions since accepting the job the previous January. "Up until an hour before the game, I was very calm.

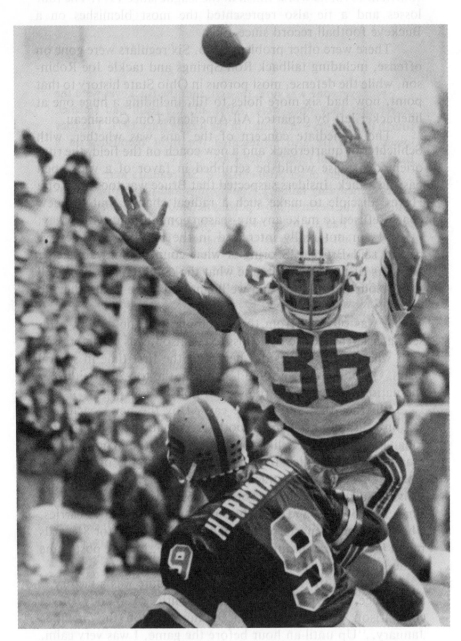

Linebacker Tom Cousineau demonstrates some of the tactics that made him All-American, burying Purdue quarterback Mark Herrmann.

Then the fuse ignited while I was sitting in the motel room. It's a very exciting thing to coach in Ohio Stadium."

It was the beginning of a storybook year. The following week at Minnesota, Joe Salem's Gophers surprised the Buckeyes with a double winged-T offense and scored on their first two possessions for a 14-0 lead. Minnesota connected on 20 of 32 passes for 227 yards and also ran for 278—Garry White rushed for 221 yards himself—against the confused Buckeye defense, but Schlichter brought the Buckeyes charging back and finally won, 21-17, on a 32-yard touchdown run.

The following week Washington State burned the Buckeye defense, but Schlichter, flanker Doug Donley, and tailback Calvin Murray burned the Cougars even more, big-playing the Buckeyes to a 45-29 romp that included a little Schlichter pass over the middle to Murray that went for 86 yards and into the record books as the longest touchdown pass in Ohio State history.

And so it went. The following week in the Los Angeles Coliseum, UCLA led the Buckeyes 13-10 when the Bruins' place-kicker, Peter Boermeester, missed a 23-yard field goal with 2:21 remaining. The Buckeyes took the ball at their own 20, and, before a national television audience, Schlichter became a household name. The sophomore quarterback completed six consecutive passes for 62 yards in the ensuing 80-yard drive, including a 22-yarder to split end Gary Williams and the final two-yard touchdown pass to fullback Paul Campbell with 46 seconds remaining that pulled out a 17-13 Ohio State victory.

"We knew we had to put the ball in the air," said Schlichter. "We didn't want to panic or make a mistake that could knock us out of the game. On that last play, all I had to do was fake the run so that it looked just like the running play that we had just tried from the three. Two of their people came at me, so that meant pass. I knew Paul would catch it. He has great hands."

Suddenly, it looked as though the Buckeyes had not only a great quarterback, but a great football team as well. Although Ohio State struggled a bit the following week against Northwestern (a 16-7 win), the Buckeyes romped their way to the Michigan game with an improving defense, anchored by senior linebacker Jim Laughlin, junior linebacker Al Washington,

271

freshman linebacker Marcus Marek, and a talented backfield of Todd Bell, Ray Ellis, Mike Guess, and Vince Skillings.

With Schlichter passing mostly to Donley and Williams and Schlichter, Murray, Ric Volley, and Campbell providing the run, the offense was expected to dominate Michigan and earn the team's first Rose Bowl trip since 1975, and the offense did dominate everywhere but on the scoreboard. In the end, it took a blocked fourth-quarter punt by Jim Laughlin that was scooped up by Todd Bell and ran 18 yards for the touchdown for an 18-15 win that capped the Buckeyes' Cinderella 11-0 regular season.

"I wasn't touched," said Laughlin. "Nobody touched me. The ball hit both forearms as it came off his (Michigan punter Bryan Virgil's) foot."

"Vince Skillings tried to pick it up," said Bell, "but he fumbled it. I just picked it up and ran it in."

The Buckeyes would have gone to the Rose Bowl anyway—Purdue's 37-21 victory over Indiana the same day assured that—but the Buckeyes were twice as happy because they had earned the trip on their own.

"We're going to the Rose Bowl," said Bruce. "And we're going the right way. This makes it for real."

Unfortunately, though, it turned out to be nothing more than a real trip to another in a succession of West Coast nightmares. They Buckeyes went to the Pasadena with another shot at the national championship that had eluded Woody Hayes' Buckeye teams in recent years, and although Bruce's team came closer to winning it than Hayes' recent teams had, the result was still the same.

Although Ohio State played probably its best game of the season and led 16-10 late in the game, USC charged downfield in a late game scoring drive and won it when Charles White, the 1979 Heisman Trophy winner, scored from the one with 1:32 left. Eric Hipp's conversion kick gave the Trojans the 17-16 victory.

But it was White who ultimately wrote a sad ending to the Buckeye fairy tale. The Trojans' senior tailback carried 39 times for a Rose Bowl record 239 yards and had gains of 32 and 28 yards in USC's game-winning 83-yard scoring drive.

"Charles White is the best football player I've ever seen,"

Earle Bruce, a former assistant coach under Woody Hayes, continued Hayes' winning tradition by compiling an 81-26-1 record in his nine years as OSU coach. He was fired after compiling a 6-4-1 record in 1987.

said USC Coach John Robinson. "If anyone ever doubted that, go back through the fourth quarter. His dominance and control of the fooball game was almost complete."

The Buckeyes were understandably disappointed.

It doesn't go down easy," said Bruce. "We came within two points of what I believed would be a national championship."

Junior cornerback Ray Ellis felt the same way.

"We were so close this time," said Ellis. "Just a little bit more...but we'll just have to pick up the pieces and go on next year."

Two Frustrating Years

Picking up the pieces after a heartbreaking Rose Bowl was not as easy as it looked. While everything had fallen into place just about perfectly during Earle Bruce's first season as football coach, the breaks did not cooperate quite as much the second time around.

On paper, the losses didn't seem to be that great. While the offensive line suffered substantially when All-America guard Ken Fritz, center Tom Waugh, guard Ernie Andria, and tackle Tim Burke departed, the backfield was essentially intact and only two players, Jim Laughlin and Mike Guess, were missing from the entire defensive unit.

On the field, however, the Buckeyes were unable to recapture their 1979 Big Ten championship glory. The opener, though a victory, may have been a portent. The Buckeyes entered the game top-ranked nationally yet fell behind unheralded Syracuse 21-3 before finally kicking it in gear for a 31-21 win.

Minnesota was an easy 47-0 victim the next week as the Buckeyes took revenge on the Gophers for their surprise in Minneapolis the previous season, and Arizona State was beaten 38-21 the following week. But UCLA rolled into town on October 4, and the Buckeyes' line deficiencies were quickly exposed. The Bruins dominated Ohio State on the line all day and coasted to an easy 17-0 win that was Bruce's first loss as Buckeye football coach.

"I don't want to see one of those again in Ohio Stadium," said Bruce. But his other comments seemed to indicate that it was only wishful thinking.

"Our offense was very inept," he said. "When you don't control the line of scrimmage, you don't win. They did a great job on us defensively. They controlled us."

274

Rod Gerald succeeded Cornelius Greene as OSU quarterback and quickly established himself as one of the most dangerous running quarterbacks in college football. He moved to wide receiver when Art Schlichter came to the Buckeyes in 1978 and was a dangerous offensive threat there as well.

That would not happen again for six more weeks, but there were enough defensive lapses to convince even the most ardent OSU supporter that the Buckeyes might have some difficulty against the good teams defensively. The most notable sign of that came on November 8 in Ohio Stadium, when Illinois quarterback David Wilson put on a record passing performance that few would forget. The Buckeyes seemed to have the game well in hand with a 28-7 halftime lead, but the hapless Illini passed their way back into the game with an amazing display. When the smoke cleared, the Buckeyes were on the long end of a 49-42 score, but Wilson had completed 43 of 69 passes for 621 yards and six touchdowns that broke or tied five NCAA records.

"He didn't look too good in the first half," said Bruce, "and I'm glad of that. He might have passed for a thousand."

Wilson was not as impressed. "We lost the game. We could have beaten those guys. They were No. 7 in the nation and we could have beaten them."

Ohio State recovered for an easy 41-7 win over Iowa the following week, giving the Buckeyes an 8-0 conference record and hope of a second straight Rose Bowl berth if they could upset unbeaten Michigan in Ohio Stadium. Ironically, the game turned out to be a defensive struggle, and when Michigan finally won 9-3, many blamed the loss on Bruce's conservative offensive style. Michigan wanted to control the ball on offense to keep it out of the hands of Schlichter and the Buckeyes' offensive machine, but the Buckeyes converted only four of 15 third-down situations in the game, often because of its grind-it-out attack. The usually successful option play virtually disappeared from the Ohio State playbook.

"Right now, I can say I would have liked to option more," said Bruce. "But as the game unfolded, I didn't see it that way...because of the defenses they were playing."

The game was tied 3-3 at halftime, and by the second half, Michigan's ball-control tactics seemed to finally work. By keeping the Buckeye defense on the field, Michigan began to tire the OSU defenders down, and one 14-play, 56-yard second-half drive, culminating in a 13-yard John Wangler pass to Anthony Carter, was all the scoring the Wolverines needed.

Bruce second-guessed his play calling in addition to the option, saying that he probably should have passed more, but Schlichter's eight of 26 passing stats seemed significant. The Michigan defense did not allow a touchdown in its last four games for a reason.

"I never thought we had the game under control," said Bruce. "This is not the kind of game I would like to see Ohio State play, naturally."

But a post-game Fiesta Bowl bid raised hope, if not for a national championship, then at least for a successful conclusion to a successful season.

"We still have a chance to have a pretty fair season," said Bruce. "If we can go to the bowl, play a good game, and beat Penn State, that wouldn't be too bad."

And it wouldn't have been, either, if the Buckeyes had done it. Instead, Ohio State saw its post-season Arizona trip and its season ruined because of a strong dose of overconfidence.

With Schlichter completing 15 of 22 first half passing attempts, mostly to Doug Donley and Gary Williams, the Buckeyes shot out to a 19-10 halftime lead that spelled their doom. The Buckeyes started thinking that the Nittany Lions were easier than they were.

"We were very confident," said Schlichter. "We thought we had their number."

But because of the Buckeyes' cockiness and Penn State Coach Joe Paterno's halftime adjustments, the numbers quickly changed. By the time the Buckeyes figured out what happened, they were on the short end of a 31-19 score and losers of their fourth consecutive bowl game.

"We just didn't execute," said OSU offensive tackle Joe Smith. "The coaches had us prepared, but remember, you're talking about a first-class ball club. They came out to play with a lot of emotion in the second half. They wanted the ball game more than we did."

Nobody wanted a good season more than Earle Bruce did when the team assembled for fall practice in 1981. Although Bruce had led the Buckeyes to a two-year record of 20-4, he was being stung with repeated criticisms for the Michigan and Penn State losses. A 1980 pre-season No. 1 ranking that had evolved into a post-season No. 15 position did not help much either.

"If you're No. 1, everybody's shooting for you, baby," said Bruce, "and if you keep it, you're doggone good."

The 1980 Buckeyes had clearly not been "doggone good," and prospects were no brighter, especially with a squad that was ignored in most pre-season forecasts. Some suggested that there were parallels between the 1981 team and the one that just missed winning the national championship in 1979, but Bruce offered a fast rebuttal.

"We were a lot more experienced in 1979 than we are now," said Bruce. "And it's always a disadvantage going in inexperienced."

Defense was a particularly critical area. Seven of the 11 defensive starters from the season before were gone, including all four from the defensive backfield. There were plenty of good young talents floating around the defensive backfield in pre-season—Shaun Gayle, Garcia Lane, Doug Hill, Jeff Cisco, Mark Eberts, Kelvin Bell, and Rod Gorley to name several—but there still was little game experience. OSU defensive coordinator Dennis Fryzel took a look and immediately projected a trying year.

"I'll bet that at the end of the year," said Fryzel, "people will have averaged throwing the ball 40 times a game against us. You talk about an aerial circus. This year, there will be."

As it was, Fryzel turned out to be a prophet. Opponents launched a season-long assault against the young Ohio State pass defense, and although it withstood the barrage at times, it was primarily because of the leakage that the 1981 season had more ups and downs than any Buckeye season in recent memory.

The opener was a case in point. Inexperienced and unimpressive as Duke was ("Ohio State knew what it was doing, getting us for its first game," said Duke coach Red Wilson), the Blue Devils gave the Buckeyes a scare, trailing OSU only 14-13 at halftime. The first half down eventually turned into an Ohio State up, as the Buckeyes rolled to a 34-13 victory as its depth and strength paid off, but the down-up scenario for the season was set.

The second game was just the opposite of the first. The Buckeyes opened fast with a 17-0 halftime lead, then watched as the Spartans came charging back. Ohio State finally won 27-13,

Quarterback Art Schlichter and flanker Doug Donley celebrate in the end zone following a Schlichter-to-Donley touchdown pass against Iowa in 1978. When Donley departed, his 106 catches made him the second leading pass receiver in OSU history behind Billy Anders, who had 108. Cris Carter (168), Gary Williams (154) and John Frank (121) have since passed both of them. Donley's 2,252 in reception yardage trails only Williams (2,792) and Carter (2,725).

giving it a 2-0 record to take to the West Coast for a long-awaited meeting between Art Schlichter and Stanford quarterback John Elway. A Stanford loss the previous week to San Jose State dulled the match-up a bit, but there seemed little question that the Buckeyes needed a win on the West Coast to restore their credibility. When Ohio State jumped out to a 24-6 lead constructed mainly by Schlichter's talented arm then withstood the fire of Elway for a 24-19 victory, the Buckeyes got it.

"A lot of people said we couldn't beat Stanford," said a happy Bruce. "A lot of people said we couldn't win on the West Coast. Well, we did."

Particularly satisfying was the performance of the Ohio State defense, which yielded Elway's two second-half touchdown passes but stopped Stanford when it had to. Stanford moved the ball from its own 16 with 1:33 left and had the ball at midfield, but runningback Vincent White caught a pass in the flat and was hit hard. He fumbled and Marcus Marek recovered with 44 seconds remaining to seal the win.

"We hung in there for a victory when we needed to," said Bruce "and that could be a turning point for us."

That was when the first real down caught the Buckeyes by surprise. Florida State, the nation's No. 2 team the season before it lost the Orange Bowl game to Oklahoma, visited Ohio Stadium the following week and because of wholesale departures, had not been expected to be that big of a problem. At least that was the scenario until the Seminoles took advantage of some obvious weaknesses in the Ohio State secondary that were to become well known nationally by the end of the year.

Florida State had three weeks of game films and a week off before the game to prepare for the Buckeyes, and it was clear afterwards that the cram course had done the trick.

"It's a young, inexperienced secondary," said Florida State coach Bobby Bowden, when asked to explain his team's passing success in an exciting 36-27 FSU victory, "and they drive you back so you don't get the cheap one behind them. They drop the linebackers so you can't throw under the secondary. We were able to dump the ball in front of the linebackers, and when they were pulled in, we were able to beat the deep men.''

What that added up to was a 25 for 41, 299-yard passing day for quarterback Rick Stockstill. He was outdone by Schlichter, who threw for an Ohio State record 31-52 for 412 yards, but unlike the Seminoles, the Buckeyes were unable to generate anything on the ground. Therein lay the difference. The Buckeyes ran 31 times against the Seminoles and gained just 38 yards, the third lowest total in modern OSU football history.

But if the Buckeyes thought their bad luck was over, they were to find out otherwise the next week. Although Wisconsin had been something of a doormat for Ohio State since 1959, this Badger team was different, as wins over Purdue and Michigan the previous two weeks suggested. The Buckeyes found out for themselves when Wisconsin handed them a 24-21 loss. It was the first time that Ohio State had lost two straight games since 1971.

Bruce, growing tired of criticism from the media and fans, grew testy in the post-game interview session.

''Now just what would you do if you were coach?'' he asked. ''What changes should we make?''

No one made any suggestions, but Bruce made enough changes on his own for his Buckeyes to beat Illinois 34-27 the following week.

''We hid ourselves,'' said Bruce. ''We were trying to conceal our coverages as much as possible so they couldn't see what we were in. But we wanted to stay in three-deep as much as possible.''

It was the beginning of an up period for the Buckeyes. Ohio State beat Indiana 29-10 the following week, which, when coupled with Minnesota's victory over Iowa, tied OSU for the Big Ten lead. Then, the following week, Ohio State beat Purdue 45-33 on regional television, as Schlichter completed 19 of 33 passes for 336 yards that included seven passes and 126 yards to Gary Williams. It was only the second time in 26 games that an opponent had beaten the Boilermakers at Ross-Ade Stadium.

''This is one of the great victories since I've been at Ohio State,'' said Bruce. And considering the circumstances—it put OSU alone atop the Big Ten standings with three games left—he was probably right.

Unfortunately, it was at that point that another of the

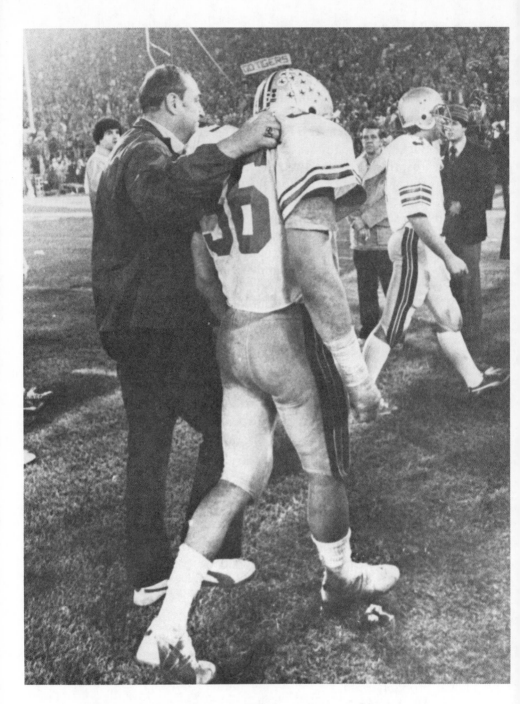

Ohio State defensive coordinator George Hill consoles All-American linebacker Tom Cousineau after the Buckeyes' 17-15 loss in the 1978 Gator Bowl in Jacksonville. Even at that point, it was obvious that Woody Hayes' tenure as Buckeye football coach was nearing a tragic end.

season's biggest downers hit. A pass defense that ranked 136th out of 137 Division I teams in yardage yielded had dodged the bullet more often than not in previous weeks, but Minnesota hit it squarely between the eyes the following week in Memorial Stadium in Minneapolis. Gopher quarterback Mike Hohensee, only a so-so passer to that point, completed 37 of 67 passes for 444 yards and five touchdowns as Minnesota upset the Buckeyes 35-31 and knocked OSU out of the Big Ten lead.

"They're very predictable and easy to read," said Hohensee, who shattered five school records in the onslaught. "Even before they call the play, you can tell what kind of coverage the guys are going into. They haven't changed much all year. Even on the films, you can see what they're going to run, and they did the same things today."

The evidence was damning, but Bruce and his coaches continued to shelter their young secondary and shield it from attacks.

"They got good field position because of our kicking game," said Bruce. "They put a lot of stress on our defense in the second half. You can't continually give the ball to a football team on the short side of the 50."

Dennis Fryzel, the defensive coordinator, agreed.

"I'm not discouraged with the play of our secondary," said Fryzel. "When your opponent gets the ball on the plus side (of the 50), it's tough to have to bend and not break in that situation."

It appeared at that point that Ohio State's Rose Bowl hopes were all that was broken, although the Buckeyes crushed Northwestern 70-6 the next week and waited for the other Big Ten results to trickle in. When they did, it was clear that the Buckeyes could still earn a Big Ten championship the final week of the season with a victory over Michigan, but that would not necessarily earn OSU a berth in the Rose Bowl. Iowa, the only Big Ten team that Ohio State did not face in 1981, could clinch that with a victory over Michigan State.

And as it turned out, that's exactly what happened. Despite the defense's increasingly vocal critics, the Buckeyes put together one of their best games of the season at Ann Arbor, beating Michigan 14-9 for their second share of the Big Ten championship in the past three years. But when Iowa also won,

USC linebacker Dennis Johnson stacks up Art Schlichter near the goal line during the 1980 Rose Bowl game, won by USC.

earning the Rose Bowl honors, the Buckeyes were repaid for their losses at Wisconsin and Minnesota earlier. It was the biggest win of the season and maybe even the biggest win of Bruce's three years' reign as OSU coach, but all the Buckeyes received was a Liberty Bowl bid.

Still, it did not dampen the Buckeyes' enthusiasm. The fact that Ohio State had to come from a 9-7 fourth-quarter deficit on an 80-yard drive capped by a brilliant six-yard run by Schlichter did not hurt.

"He's a big play football player," said Bruce. "Given the opportunity, he'll come through."

The Buckeye coaches were saying the same things about their defense, although it must be said that Michigan quarterback Steve Smith's abominable passing had something to do with that. Smith was only nine of 26 on the afternoon, not because of pass defense, but because the passes often missed receivers by 10-15 yards.

"We didn't execute," said Smith. "We just didn't make the big plays. I'm not going to say it was all my fault. I mean, they made some nice plays too. But this was just one of those games when things don't go so well."

Michigan's Bo Schembechler said basically the same thing.

"The Ohio State defense didn't do anything special," said Schembechler. "I was pleased with the way we moved the ball until we got down there close. We just messed up when we got down there. My feeling is that the offense squandered its opportunities."

What the Buckeyes needed after that round of no-credit comments was a bowl game opponent who provided an opportunity for proof, but the Liberty Bowl and Navy did not provide it. The world accorded Ohio State a role as overwhelming favorite going in and immediately decided that anything short of a Buckeye romp in Memphis would be viewed with the same disdain as losses to Wisconsin and Minnesota.

After a Gargantuan win over Michigan in the season finale, the Buckeyes definitely deserved a better chance.

"I might have been able to write a better ending," said senior quarterback Art Schlichter. And he could have too, although the Liberty Bowl turned out to be the only bowl game in his four years at Ohio State that the sensational quarterback won. It was just that 31-28 win over an unranked team that already had three losses and a tie on its record was not exactly the happy ending that everyone had in mind.

"We fought and scraped all the way and we came out ahead," said Bruce, not wasting a lot of words on the victory that snapped a four-game bowl game loss streak. "We had more points."

"Obviously, Ohio State has a better football team, but they (Navy) played together as a team and that's what helped them stay close," said OSU tight end John Frank.

But Frank, like many others, found a way to appreciate any kind of bowl win.

"It's a win," said Frank. "Everybody talked about how the seniors on this team hadn't won a bowl game. What would it have been like for Art Schlichter never to have won a bowl game? Or Mike D'Andrea? Nick Miller? Ben Lee? They won."

The 9-3 Rut

No one knew it at the time, but by winning the Liberty Bowl, the Ohio State football team had fallen into a rut that would last for six years.

The Liberty Bowl victory gave Ohio State a 9-3 record. The next four years would bring three bowl victories in four appearances, a Big Ten championship, two victories over arch-rival Michigan and a difficult road win over then-No. 2 Oklahoma. But it would bring no improvement, or deterioration, in the record. Starting in 1980, the Buckeyes finished 9-3 six consecutive seasons.

A change seemed likely in 1982, if for no other reason than a change in quarterbacks. When Ohio State opened against Baylor with sophomore Mike Tomczak at quarterback, it marked the first time in 49 games that someone other than Art Schlichter had started a game for OSU at that position.

"Until he gets his feet on the ground," said OSU Coach Earle Bruce, "we are going to run the ball, because we have a big offensive line and a good running combination at the tailback spot."

In a 21-14 win over Baylor, Bruce fulfilled his promise. Senior tailback Tim Spencer, coming off a 1981 season that saw him rush for 1,217 yards, gained 147 yards in 30 carries. Junior fullback Vaughn Broadnax gained 101 in 18, the first 100-yard rushing performance by an OSU fullback since Ricardo Volley gained 132 yards against Michigan State in 1979. It would have been cause for celebration 10 years earlier, but times had changed in the Big Ten.

Teams were finding it difficult to contend for the conference championship without a strong passing attack and Tomczak, his inexperience showing, completed only 6 of 15 passes for 93 yards and was intercepted twice.

"If we're going to be any good," Bruce said afterwards, "we're going to have to throw the ball to Gary Williams, Cedric Anderson and John Frank."

The Buckeyes rolled over a Michigan State destined to win only two games all season the following week, before their offensive problems caught up with them. Stanford quarterback John Elway completed 35 of 63 passes for 407 yards and the game-winning touchdown with 37 seconds left in a 23-20 win over the Buckeyes in Ohio Stadium. But he wasn't responsible for the OSU loss, the Buckeyes' offense was. Aside from the four interceptions Tomczak threw, the Ohio State offense was also flagged for three critical penalties and lost two critical fumbles.

"I was very proud of our defensive football team," Bruce said. "It just didn't get much help from the offense."

When the offense sputtered again against Florida State, Bruce tried to help it out, replacing Tomczak with Brent Offenbecher, a junior who had ridden the bench since transferring from Wake Forest in 1980. Offenbecher threw a 31-yard touchdown pass to Spencer to cut the Seminoles' lead to 21-17 just before halftime, but the magic ended there. He threw interceptions on the Buckeyes' first two possessions of the second half and Florida State blew to a 34-17 win that marked Ohio State's first consecutive losses in Ohio Stadium since 1971.

Things went from bad to worse the following week. A steady rain stopped a home sellout streak at 86 and Wisconsin stopped an Ohio State home winning streak over the Badgers that extended to 1981 with a 6-0 victory that branded the 2-3 Buckeyes with their worst start since 1967. One streak was extended: Ohio State hadn't scored a point in six quarters.

"If you went back and evaluated this year as compared to last year," OSU offensive coordinator Glen Mason said, "the big play is obviously absent from our offense."

It returned, with Tomczak, the following week against Illinois and Ohio State's season turned around. Tomczak completed a 74-yard pass to Cedric Anderson for the game's first touchdown and short passes when his team needed them most. And other contributors were just as timely. Freshman kicker Rich

Spangler missed three field goals, from 35, 36 and 23 yards, then hit one when it counted, drilling a 27-yard field goal that gave Ohio State a 26-21 win in Champaign.

"Relief," a grinning Bruce said afterwards.

And his players must have felt it too. With the pressure relieved, the Buckeyes pounded Indiana (49-25), Purdue (38-6), Minnesota (35-10) and Northwestern (40-28) in preparation for their annual clash with Michigan, which had already clinched the conference title because of a quirk in the league schedule which called for it to play nine Big Ten games to OSU's eight.

Ohio State's 24-14 win, achieved with the aid of six Michigan turnovers and a relentless first half rain, was the Buckeyes' sixth straight. It gave them a 7-1 Big Ten record to Michigan's 8-1. For the second straight year, Ohio State's failure to play Iowa had cost it a chance at a New Year's Day in Pasadena; the Hawkeyes had gone to the Rose Bowl the previous year with a 6-2 record identical to OSU's.

"Today was our Rose Bowl game," said Marcus Marek, an All-American and four-year starter at linebacker. "We proved to ourselves, in our minds, that we are Big Ten champs."

They convinced Brigham Young of that in the Holiday Bowl, scoring 17 points in the first nine minutes of the second half in a 47-17 beating of the Western Athletic Conference champions. Tim Spencer, crowned the Big Ten rushing champion by a narrow margin over Michigan's Lawrence Ricks, was honored as the game's most valuable player after rushing for 167 yards. Tomczak, the early season goat, was an efficient custodian of the offensive assault, which outclassed the high-powered offense engineered by Cougar quarterback Steve Young.

"We knew with the type of team Brigham Young had, we had to keep putting points on the board," Tomczak said. "But 47 points? Yeah, that was a pretty good number."

One good number led to another: the Buckeyes, with a year under Tomczak's belt and an experienced stable of receivers for him to throw to, were ranked No. 6 in the 1983 pre-season poll; after a 31-6 win over Oregon and a nationally-televised 24-14 win over No. 2 Oklahoma in Norman, it seemed for a while that the prognosticators might have even underestimated them.

Against Oklahoma, Ohio State totaled 412 yards offense, rushing for 178 on the legs of sophomores Keith Byars and Kelvin Lindsey, and getting 234 yards passing from Tomczak, who was 15 of 25 with only one interception. Senior tight end John Frank was his primary target, snaring two touchdown passes in the first two periods as the Buckeyes jumped to a 14-0 lead.

The Sooners struck back, launching an 80-yard second quarter drive that culminated with a 37-yard touchdown run by fullback Spencer Tillman. But Oklahoma failed to capitalize on a Tomczak interception on the ensuing series, and when Ohio State drove for a touchdown on its first possession of the second half, the die was cast. In the public's eye, the Buckeyes had reached a height that hadn't been experienced since Bruce's first year.

"We really haven't had a chance to play a team like Oklahoma for a while," senior cornerback Shaun Gayle said. "This was the perfect opportunity to show people, to prove to them that the Bucks aren't dead."

Unfortunately, as so often happened during the 9-3 years, the team's hour of triumph was followed by one of failure. For two years, Iowa's football team had read of Ohio State's frustration over its inability to play the Hawkeyes; now, Iowa had a chance to show the No. 3 Buckeyes what they had missed. The 20-14 Ohio State loss in Iowa City, sealed on a 73-yard fourth quarter touchdown pass from Chuck Long to Dave Moritz, quickly took the steam out of a promising season.

"We heard all the talk about how they didn't go to the Rose Bowl the last two years because they didn't play us," Iowa Coach Hayden Fry said. "Maybe that's true. But you decide it on the field... You don't put out that kind of garbage. You can, against me, but I'm going to use it. Our guys weren't playing for one game out there today, they were playing for the last two years, too."

The Buckeyes rebounded with wins over Minnesota (69-18) and Purdue (33-22) the next two weeks, but more trouble was lurking. Illinois, down 13-10 with 1:43 left, drove 83 yards in 37 seconds on the strength of the passing — and running — of quarterback Jack Trudeau. Trudeau completed passes of 24 and 22 yards to wide receiver Scott Golden on the sideline, then scrambled out of the pocket for 16 yards to the OSU 21. Sensing a blitz, Trudeau changed plays at the line of scrimmage from a draw to a pitchout to running back Thomas Rooks, who turned the right corner and scored standing up for a 17-13 victory. The Illini were on their way to their first Rose Bowl since 1964, the Buckeyes to another 9-3 season. Although Ohio State would win its next four games leading up to Michigan, a 24-21 loss to the Wolverines in

Mike Tomczak started at quarterback for three years and passed for more yards (5,569) than all other Ohio State quarterbacks except for Art Schlichter. Here, he uses a block from Keith Byars to complete a pass against Michigan.

Ann Arbor doomed Ohio State to a fourth place Big Ten finish, the lowest in five years under Earle Bruce.

"Three losses," said senior tight end John Frank, after two interceptions and two fumbles had done them in at Michigan Stadium, "and all three losses were games we could have won. We could have been 11-0 right now."

Their second trip to the Fiesta Bowl in four years was their reward for a season of could-have-beens. The Buckeyes, picked by most to win the Big Ten, needed a win over 8-2-1 Pitt to salvage a 9-3 season.

"Our record says we had a good season," linebacker Rowland Tatum said. "But at Ohio State, it just doesn't go over. Me and the other seniors are out to redeem ourselves."

If the Buckeyes couldn't make up for the heart-breaking losses which had cost them a promising season, they could at least concoct one of their own for Pitt. Bruce, who blamed himself for a conservative offense in the loss to Michigan, opened it up in Tempe and allowed Thad Jemison to haul in eight Tomczak passes and tie a Fiesta Bowl record. The last, a 39-yarder with 39 seconds left, gave Ohio State a 28-23 victory.

"We were just trying to get 10 yards closer so we could kick the field goal," Bruce said. "It was a complete shock. We were supposed to throw the outlet (to Cedric Anderson on the other side.)"

"Cedric was covered," Tomczak said. "I was going to take off and run and I'm glad I didn't. I pumped backside and I thought Thad had a step on the guy, so I put it out there and let Thad run under it."

Jemison's catch dealt the Panthers the kind of hand OSU had grown used to. Pitt quarterback John Congemi had brought his team back from a 14-7 halftime deficit with a Fiesta Bowl record 31 completions in 44 attempts for 341 yards. Included in that was 5 of 8 in a 67-yard drive capped by a 37-yard Snuffy Everett field goal that had given the Panthers a 23-21 lead with 2:39 left.

Understandably, the Buckeyes offered no sympathy.

"We deserved it," said Frank, recipient of a clutch, 13-yard pass on a fourth and 10 three plays prior to Jemison's game-winner. "We've been on the short end of the stick in the big game for four years. The seniors deserved this."

The graduating seniors, which included all-Big Ten players, John Frank, cornerback Garcia Lane and linebacker Rowland

Tight end John Frank won all-Big Ten honors in 1982 and 1983 and is the school's third leading pass receiver with 121 catches for 1,481 yards.

Tatum, were the first Ohio State class since 1967 to pass four years without a Rose Bowl trip. The 1984 class would avoid that distinction, yet couldn't avoid another: their Rose Bowl excursion resulted in a 20-17 loss to USC that ended yet another 9-3 year.

A broken leg Tomczak suffered in spring practice seemed a harbinger of another frustrating season. Tomczak wasn't ready for the opener and heavy underdog Oregon State took a 14-3 lead at the half. Then Ohio State rallied, with Jim Karsatos as

Despite an injury-plagued senior year, Keith Byars still finished third on Ohio State's list in career rushing yards with 3,200, behind only Archie Griffin and Tim Spencer. Byars is the Buckeyes' single season (1,764) and single game rushing leader. He had 274 yards against Illinois in 1984.

quarterback, for a 22-14 victory. Tomczak returned the following week and the Buckeyes again kicked it in gear. They reeled off victories over Washington State (44-0), Iowa (45-26) and Minnesota (35-22), before a trip to Purdue added to the frustrations of the previous four seasons.

Junior tailback Keith Byars ran for a career-high 191 yards and caught eight passes for 102 and Tomczak passed for 280 as the Buckeyes outgained the Boilermakers 570 total yards to 376. But Purdue made big plays when it counted and Ohio State didn't. After coming back from a 17-7 lead to go up 21-17 early in the fourth quarter, Ron Woodson plucked a Tomczak pass from the hands of receiver Doug Smith and raced 55 yards for a touchdown that made it 28-17. A Tomczak TD pass to Cris Carter cut the lead 28-23 with 2:38 left, and a little over a minute later, the Buckeyes got the ball at their own 20 for a final chance to score. They moved the ball to the Purdue 28, but Byars was unable to get a first down or get out of bounds to stop the clock on a third down pass that took them there. With five seconds left, Tomczak took the snap and threw the ball out of bounds to stop the clock, unaware that it was fourth down.

"You get caught up in the game of football," Tomczak said later. "What can I say? I'm human."

Byars, on the other hand, seemed a different species. After his 191-yard performance against Purdue, the 6-foot-2, 236-pound Dayton Roth product gave an even more memorable performance in Ohio Stadium against Illinois. After the Buckeyes fell behind 24-0 in the second quarter, Byars took over, scoring a school-record-tying five touchdowns and gaining an OSU-record 274 yards in a miraculous 45-38 victory. Byars rushing performance, which topped Archie Griffin's 246-yard day against Iowa in 1973, included a 67-yard TD run in the third quarter and a three-yard jaunt on a pitch-sweep with 36 seconds left that broke a 38-38 tie.

"I just had to suck it up and go," Byars said. "I just put my ears back and said 'You've got to go get it. Stop me.'"

Stopping the Buckeyes proved easier. They escaped a tie the following week in East Lansing, Michigan, when Ralf Mojsiejenko missed a 43-yard field goal with six seconds left to preserve a 23-20 OSU win, but lost, 16-14, in the rain at Wisconsin the next Saturday. Although the loss put the Buckeyes' Big Ten title hopes in jeopardy, subsequent losses by Iowa and Purdue gave the Buckeyes an opportunity to earn their first Rose Bowl bid since the 1979 season with a win over Michigan.

In the end, getting to Pasadena seemed almost too easy. The Wolverines, en route to a 6-6 record that was their worst of the Bo Schembechler era, made it interesting for three quarters, before the Buckeyes turned a 7-6 lead into a 21-6 victory.

Byars, the nation's leading rusher entering the game, rushed for 93 yards on 28 carries and all three OSU touchdowns, the second of which was made possible by a diving catch by Mike Lanese for a 17-yard gain on a third-and-12 from the Michigan 43.

"To be truthful with you, this is something I've dreamed about all my life," Byars said. "And we're getting to play USC.....That was half of the dream — playing USC in the Rose Bowl. The other half is going out there and being victorious."

That half of the dream wasn't to be. In Pasadena, the Buckeyes upheld what had become a conference tradition, becoming the 10th Big Ten team in 11 years to lose to the Pac-10 champion.

This time, turnovers in general and interceptions in particular were the name of the game. Senior quarterback Mike Tomczak threw three of them, and two of them led to touchdowns in a 20-17 USC win. Byars, the nation's rushing, all-purpose yardage and scoring champ, gained 109 yards and finished with a school record 1,764 yards for the season, but didn't get into the end zone, the first time that had happened in 21 games. He made it from the four on the Buckeyes' first drive, but the play was called back because offensive tackle Mark Krerowicz jumped offside. The Buckeyes were forced to settle for a field goal instead of a touchdown, a four-point difference, counting the extra point, in a three-point game.

"I think that was probably one of the turning points," Byars said. "We didn't put it into the end zone.....That hurt and it came back and haunted us at the end of the game."

At the end, the Buckeyes still had hopes of a come-from-behind victory. With 56 seconds left, Ohio State had the ball on the USC 38 yard line and on its previous possession it had driven 88 yards, Cris Carter concluding it with an 18-yard TD pass from Tomczak keeping for a two-point conversion. But with third and five at the 38, defensive tackle Brent Moore knocked the ball from Tomczak's hand for a fumble, and though the OSU quarterback recovered, it didn't help. A fourth-and-14 pass fell incomplete.

"You don't make mistakes and win ballgames," Bruce said. "Today, we made mistakes."

296

Statistics showed a strong correlation between mistakes and Ohio State's fifth straight 9-3 season. In its three losses, Tomczak was intercepted a total of eight times.

But Ohio State's fourth consecutive Rose Bowl loss was not without its bright spots. Two players, Carter and place-kicker Rich Spangler, set Rose Bowl records. Carter's 172 yards receiving on nine catches broke Don Hutson's record of 164, set with Alabama in 1935. And Spangler kicked a record 52-yard field goal in the third quarter, one of three which tied a record held by former Ohio State kicker Vlade Janakievski, who booted three in the 1980 game.

Both Carter and Spangler were members of a star-studded group expected to break Ohio State's 9-3 habit in 1985, and they might have done it were it not for a pre-season injury to tailback Keith Byars, the odds-on-favorite to become Ohio State's first Heisman Trophy winner since Archie Griffin.

Byars broke a bone in his right foot before the season opener with Pitt, and although OSU won that game, the school's first night game in Ohio Stadium, 10-7, the effect of the loss was obvious. The Buckeyes, with Junior Jim Karsatos as their new quarterback, were forced to the air. Karsatos passed for 246 yards; the OSU running attack finished with 48, the poorest showing since 1981.

"Obviously, you saw something you haven't seen too many times before," Bruce said. "You saw a lot of yards in the air by Ohio State."

It was the beginning of a season that had a lot in common with Byars' foot— neither was at all predictable. Because of Karsatos, spectacular junior split end Cris Carter, tailback John Wooldridge, fullback George Cooper and an inexperienced, but improving line anchored by Bob Maggs, the Ohio State offense recovered and covered up the loss of Byars, who hobbled in and out of the lineup all season. But the defense, which promised to be Bruce's best, proved disappointing.

After beating Colorado 36-13 and escaping Washington State 48-32, an old nemesis reared its head in Champaign, Illinois. The Fighting Illini, struggling after losses to USC and Nebraska in its first three games, gave quarterback Jack Trudeau some new plays and he used them to lead Illinois to a 31-28 victory. The game was won when Chris White, Illini Coach Mike White's son, kicked a 38-yard field goal as time expired.

"I thought we had the team to go all the way this year," OSU linebacker Eric Kumerow said. "We were looking toward a national championship and losing a game like this will hurt."

It did hurt, but not as much as a loss six weeks later at Wisconsin. After the Illinois loss, the Buckeyes went on a roll, winning five straight games and making it possible for the poll voters to almost overlook the last second loss to the Illini. Included in that streak was a 22-13 win over No. 1 Iowa in Ohio Stadium that pulled the Buckeyes into a first-place tie and gave some respect to the oft-maligned OSU pass defense, which shut down national passing efficiency leader Chuck Long. Sophomore linebacker Chris Spielman intercepted two of Long's passes; cornerbacks William White and Greg Rogan swiped one pass each.

"The motivational factor was that we were underdogs in Ohio Stadium," Spielman said. "If somebody wants to fight me in my own backyard, he had better bring an army with him."

Wisconsin needed no army. When Ohio State lost three fumbles in a game that was supposed to be a mere tuneup for a battle for another Rose Bowl berth the following week against Michigan, the Badgers had all the help they needed to post a 12-7 victory that ended a 20-game OSU home win streak. It was Wisconsin's fourth victory over Ohio State in five seasons.

"We did it in 1982, 6-0," Wisconsin Coach Dave McClain said. "And now we're the first team to beat them here since."

While the Buckeyes retained a slim shot at a trip to Pasadena, Michigan took care of that in Ann Arbor, sending OSU to a 27-17 loss which dropped it into a fourth-place tie with Michigan State. Wolverine quarterback Jim Harbaugh sealed it with a 77-yard touchdown pass to freshman John Kolesar with 9:19 left, one final, fatal jolt for the Buckeye defense.

The defense was given its last opportunity to redeem itself in the Citrus Bowl and did, stopping Brigham Young's high-powered offense in a 10-7 OSU victory. But the effort, led by noseguard Larry Kolic and linebacker Thomas "Pepper" Johnson, only inspired dreams of what might have been.

Keith Byars, expected to be close to 100 percent after a five-week layoff, re-injured his right foot in the Buckeyes' second offensive series and was done for the game and his career. After gaining 2,967 yards rushing during his sophomore and junior years, Byars had played in only four games — and gained 213 yards — in his senior season.

"We wanted him to show what he could do," Kolic said. "But it wasn't to be."

That the OSU defense showed what it could do against quarterback Robbie Bosco and a Cougar offense ranked No. 1 nationally, only made the season all the more painful.

For all the early promise, Ohio State was left to celebrate a sixth consecutive 9-3 season.

New Record, New Duds

After six years of monotony, it took an outside influence to break Ohio State's string of 9-3 seasons.

When officials of the Kickoff Classic in East Rutherford, New Jersey, invited the Buckeyes to meet Alabama in the season-opening game that doesn't count against the 11-game regular season maximum allowed by the NCAA, Ohio State was assured -- if it participated in a bowl game — that it wouldn't finish 9-3.

There was no guarantee for improvement, however, and even with a crop of returnees that included linebacker Chris Spielman and wide receiver Cris Carter, the beginning of the season didn't bode well for the Buckeyes' chances.

Alabama Coach Ray Perkins noted that his team's 16-10 win in Giants Stadium "wasn't a pretty victory," but it was an even uglier loss. Ohio State suffered from two interceptions and a fumble, several key penalties, a pair of missed field goals by freshman place-kicker Pat O'Morrow and a botched snap by center Tom Moore on a field-goal attempt that holder Cris Carter couldn't handle.

"When we had the opportunities, we piddled them away," OSU Coach Earle Bruce said. "We're nowhere near a good football team yet."

As if to emphasize the point, the Buckeyes suffered their worst loss since 1967 the following week at Washington. Ohio State's performance in a 40-7 loss to the 17th-ranked Huskies was as dismal as the weather, a steady first-half rain which provided a perfect backdrop for the play of OSU.

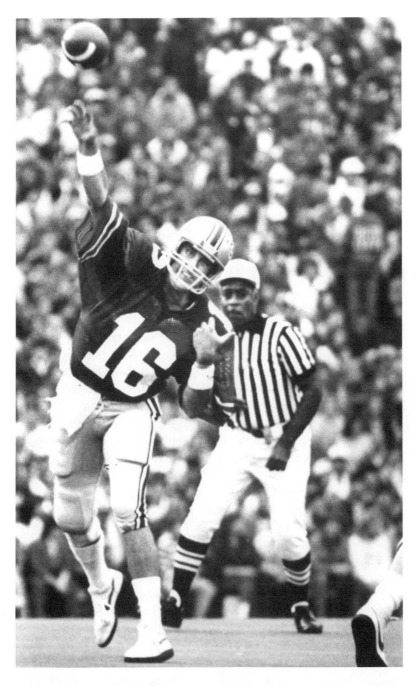

Jim Karsatos passed for 5,089 yards and 36 touchdowns in a career from 1983 to 1986.

"I didn't dream this could happen," Washington Coach Don James said. "Even if they were playing the Chicago Bears, you wouldn't expect it."

Regardless of whom they played, the Buckeyes suddenly looked very human. The Huskies outgained OSU 408-186. Sophomore tailback Vince Workman lost two fumbles and senior quarterback Jim Karsatos was ineffective. The only touchdown Ohio State scored came in the fourth quarter, after Washington led 27-0.

"He (Karsatos) can't put the ball in the end zone," Bruce said. "I can't put my finger on it."

Off to an 0-2 start that was Ohio State's worst since 1894, it suddenly became imperative that Bruce do that soon. Winless Colorado didn't figure to provide much opposition in the home opener; as it was, it provided an excellent barometer to just how critical the Buckeyes' offensive problems had become. A wobbly 19-yard field goal by O'Morrow with 25 seconds left was necessary for a 13-10 Ohio State victory.

"I said 'Thank God,'" O'Morrow said. "I didn't think I hit as well as I should have."

It remained for an outmanned Utah team to straighten Ohio State out. After three weeks of almost no offense at all, the Buckeyes steamrolled the Utes with a Big Ten record 715 yards, breaking a mark of 713 set by Iowa against Northwestern in 1983. Workman rushed for 168 yards and freshman tailback Jim Bryant rushed for 145, the first time since 1982 that two OSU backs had gained more than 100 yards in the same game. With 394 yards rushing and 321 passing, OSU became the first team in conference history to top the 300 mark in both categories in a game.

The score? 64 - 6.

"I didn't think it would be that easy," Bryant said.

Suddenly, things came easier. The Buckeyes blanked Illinois 14-0, then built a 24-14 lead over Indiana and hung on for a 24-22 win. Victories over Purdue (39-11), Minnesota (33-0), Iowa (31-10) and Northwestern (30-9) gave Ohio State a 6-0 Big Ten record entering a game at Wisconsin, which had made a recent habit of spoiling the Buckeyes' season.

But this time, Ohio State's momentum was stronger than the Badger hex. OSU jumped to a 17-0 first quarter lead on two touchdowns by Workman, on his way to a career rushing high of 172 yards, and the Buckeyes held on for a 30-17 win.

"It would be foolish to say I wasn't concerned about this football game, the way they have beaten us four out of the last five years," Bruce said. "And they were talking up here about how they were going to do it again."

When they didn't, the Buckeyes not only had their ninth straight win, but a date with Michigan to decide the league's Rose Bowl berth the following weekend in Columbus. Michigan took some of the lustre from the matchup by losing its first game to Minnesota, 20-17, but the game still had many of the characteristics of the old Michigan-OSU clashes. Ohio State was 9-2 overall and 7-0 in the league; Michigan 9-1 and 6-1.

"That's the way it should be," Bruce said. "We are going to be playing for a Big Ten championship and a Rose Bowl berth. . . That's what makes it a humdinger of a football game, and it will be that. I guarantee it."

Bruce's guarantee was met. Michigan's 26-24 win proved to be one of the more memorable in the recent history of the rivalry.

The week began with Michigan quarterback Jim Harbaugh "guaranteeing" the Wolverines would produce a victory and ended with a game that produced an afternoon of offense, dramatics and big plays.

"I can't recall in all my years (against Ohio State) so many points being scored, so much yardage and so many big plays." Michigan Coach Bo Schembechler would say.

It began as if it would be an OSU day. When Vince Workman took an option pitch, cut back behind a block by tight end Ed Taggart and raced 46 yards for a touchdown with 3:03 left in the first quarter, Ohio State had a 14-3 lead. Inside linebacker Mike Kee's interception of a Harbaugh pass at the goal line just before halftime held the line at 14-6, before Michigan running back Jamie Morris, who rushed for 210 yards, scored a touchdown at the end 93-yard Michigan drive to start the second half.

A 27-yard Matt Frantz field goal gave OSU a 17-13 lead, but an eight-yard Morris touchdown run, set up by a 52-yard run by Morris, gave Michigan a 19-17 lead. Even though a touchdown by Thomas Wilcher early in the fourth quarter gave the Wolverines a 26-17 advantage, the Buckeyes weren't finished. After OSU defensive tackle Darryl Lee blocked a 47-yard field goal attempt by Mike Gillette that could have ended it, Jim Karsatos hit Cris Carter with a 17-yard touchdown pass and Frantz's kick made it 26-24 with 9:42 left in the game.

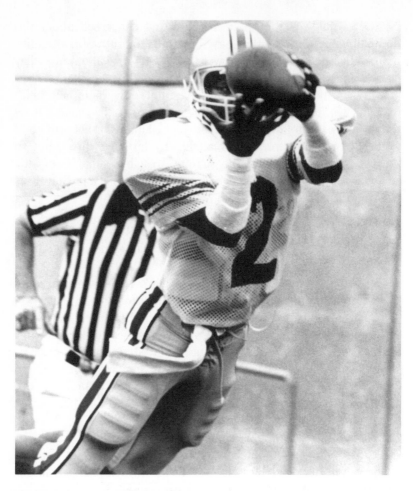

Cris Carter is school's career pass reception leader with 168, despite playing only three seasons.

When Wilcher lost a fumble to Sonny Gordon at the OSU 38 with 3:17 remaining, the dramatics were set. The Buckeyes moved the ball into Michigan territory, where an eight-yard, third down pass from Karsatos to Carter was two yards short at the Michigan 28. With 1:01 on the clock, Matt Frantz' 45-yard field goal attempt was wide to the left by a few feet, and Michigan's victory was preserved.

"I thought it was good," Frantz said. "I got good leg into it, but it hooked a little bit to the left."

A few feet made a big difference in the Buckeyes' holiday travel plans. Instead of going to the Rose Bowl for the second time in three years, Ohio State was invited to the Cotton Bowl to play No. 8 Texas A&M in a first-ever appearance by a Big Ten team.

It was a special occasion that the Buckeyes were more than ready for. Bruce, sometimes criticized for making his excess poundage all too visible in the tight-fitting golf shirts he wore on the sidelines, emerged from the locker room in an expensive charcoal suit, black shoes, black and white diagonally striped tie, and black fedora with a scarlet feather on the side.

Were his players surprised?

"Hell, yes," linebacker Chris Spielman said. "The hat got me."

The players were also decked out for the occasion, wearing bright red shoes that were salient against their gray uniforms.

"I've got to be honest," Bruce said. "It was a Nike promotion. They thought the red shoes were flashy. You win some, you lose some. It might be red shoes from now on. I think 70 or 80 or 90 percent liked them."

But of all the new looks, the one that mattered most was the one Ohio State presented on defense: The Buckeyes played fronts unseen on game films all season. Linebacker Scott Leach was the wild card, the other linebackers the enforcers in an attack designed to confuse A&M quarterback Kevin Murray. It did its job in a 28-12 Ohio State win.

"Everything Ohio State did confused him," Texas A&M offensive coordinator Lynn Amedee said. "He didn't read the zones very well."

Because of that, the Buckeyes intercepted five of Murray's passes, a Cotton Bowl record. Junior linebacker Chris Spielman, named the game's most valuable player after tying a school record by participating in 29 tackles against Michigan, snared two, including one he took for a 24-yard touchdown in the second half. Linebacker Michael Kee also took an interception 49 yards for a touchdown.

"You take away those two touchdowns they got with their defense," Aggie cornerback Terrance Brooks said, "and it's 14-12."

But the Ohio State offense also had its moments. Buckeye

junior All-American wide receiver Cris Carter contributed a couple of spectacular leaping catches en route to a four-catch, 61-yard day. OSU junior flanker Nate Harris had six receptions for 105 yards that included a 51-yard reception from Karsatos on the Buckeyes' first possession.

The significance of the win, which gave the team a rut-ending 10-3 record, wasn't lost on the now-stylish Bruce.

"There won't be any more of this 9-3 crap," he said. "This is a new year, a new start for the Ohio State Buckeyes. We needed this one."

Earle's Last Stand

The new start the Ohio State football program experienced in 1987 wasn't the one Earle Bruce had envisioned.

Spectacular senior wide receiver Cris Carter, expected to be the foundation of the Buckeyes' offense, admitted he had accepted money from an agent, a violation of NCAA rules, and the Middletown, Ohio, product was declared off the team in July, before fall practice began.

At first, his absence wasn't all that noticeable. West Virginia turned over the ball on each of its first three plays in the season opener as the Buckeyes jumped to a 17-0 first quarter lead. The Mountaineers turned it over eight times in all, six on interceptions, as Ohio State coasted to a 24-3 win. Cornerback William White tied a school record with three interceptions and linebacker Chris Spielman had two.

No offense? No problem.

"It's a big blow to a football team," Spielman said. "We seen it in their eyes. They couldn't move the ball on us with consistency. Three turnovers on the first three plays—it's tough to come back, especially here."

The offense, without the passing of departed quarterback Jim Karsatos or the catching of Carter, sputtered. Senior quarterback Tom Tupa had a fair day passing, completing 12 of 25 passes that included one touchdown and one interception, but didn't really get the offense moving. When the afternoon was over, the Buckeyes had only 12 first downs and one sustained touchdown drive.

"I said we'd be bad offensively," Bruce said. "And we were."

The problem became critical, not in a 24-14 win over Oregon the following week, but in a 13-13 tie against fourth-ranked LSU in Baton Rouge two weeks later. Ohio State, up to No. 7 in the polls, was able to score only one touchdown. Two interceptions by cornerback Greg Rogan in the final 2:03 of the game kept the Buckeyes from losing; they could have won if Matt Frantz's 47-yard field goal attempt with five seconds left hadn't been deflected by LSU defensive tackle Karl Dunbar.

"It felt great," Dunbar said. "I felt like we had won."

Bruce didn't feel good about it at all, despite his team's escape from LSU without a loss.

"We don't normally have ties at Ohio State," he said, "and we don't like them."

But a tie, though distasteful, isn't much of a blemish on your record if it comes on the road against a highly-ranked team. The first real blemish — in this case call it an ugly scar — came two weeks later in Ohio Stadium after the Buckeyes survived a 10-6 scare at Illinois.

Indiana, which hadn't beaten Ohio State since 1951, Woody Hayes' first year, slipped into Columbus almost unannounced and embarrassed the Buckeyes 31-10 in their own stadium. It was no fluke. It was a shock.

"This year, it was us against them," Indiana linebacker Van Walters said. "Forget the streak."

Forgetting a once-proud Ohio State offense proved easier. After escaping from 10- and 13-point games the previous two weeks with a win and a tie, the Buckeyes scored 10 points in the first half — it was 10-10 at halftime — and didn't score another. After Tony Buford returned a Tupa punt 40 yards to the OSU 19 to set a six-yard touchdown run by fullback Tom Polce, the Hoosiers didn't look back. Two Tupa interceptions in the fourth quarter led to Indiana's last two touchdowns.

"The last two games had been just a little close for comfort," OSU sophomore tailback Jim Bryant said. "I could see, in the back of my head, something like this was going to happen."

No one could foresee the troubles which lay ahead. The Buckeyes seemed to get back on the right track when Matt Frantz, who had missed two field goal attempts earlier, kicked a 50-yarder with 3:10 left to give Ohio State a 20-17 win at Purdue. Minnesota offered little opposition in losing 42-9. Then, on the first play from scrimmage against Michigan State, Tupa threw a

79-yard touchdown pass to split end Everett Ross. The patient seemed to be well at last.

"That first play worked just like we'd planned, just like we'd practiced it," Ross said. "At that moment, we thought all of our plays were going to work the same way."

As it turned out, very little worked for the Buckeyes for the rest of the season. After that first touchdown, the Buckeye offense did another one of its celebrated shutdowns, only this time the Spartans pulled the switch. A strong defense which would eventually carry Michigan State to the Rose Bowl held OSU to two yards rushing, the lowest team total since 1965. The Buckeyes made only six first downs and ran just 49 plays. The Buckeyes threw for 145 yards, 79 of which came on the first play.

When you take all that into account, Michigan State's 13-7 victory wasn't at all surprising.

"When we ran, we gained two yards," Bruce said. "When we passed, we either got sacked or dumped."

The obvious question was why?

"It wasn't a matter of strength, it was a matter of intensity," Ohio State right guard Greg Zackeroff said. "I don't think all of us were at the intensity we should have been."

The Buckeyes had no trouble getting up for Wisconsin, their old nemesis, but a new problem emerged. After Ohio State took a 24-13 lead over the 2-6 Badgers at the half, it turned the ball over six times in the second half and fell behind 26-24. Despite all that, Frantz could have salvaged the game with a 22-yard field goal with 6:57 left. He missed.

"The missed field goal," Bruce said, "should have been the game-winning field goal."

But six second half turnovers and seven in all indicated that the Ohio State offensive problems were more serious than an erratic place-kicker. Bruce, sensing that, had replaced Tupa with redshirt freshman Greg Frey late in the third quarter, and Frey found freshman tight end Jeff Ellis on a pass, only to have Ellis fumble and lose it at the OSU 29. Later, Bruce replaced freshman tailback Carlos Snow, one of the few successful offensive cogs, with Bryant, and Bryant bombed. It wasn't a good afternoon to be an Ohio State player or coach.

"We're just in a state of shock," linebacker Chris Spielman said. "It's hard to face. It's kind of embarrassing. It's the lowest point of my career."

309

Another low lay just ahead. Ohio State, 5-3-1 and playing for pride, took a 14-3 lead against Iowa the following Saturday on Tupa touchdown passes of 24 and 60 yards to Ross. The Hawkeyes rallied to take a 15-14 lead at the half, but the Buckeyes seemed determined to right their course. A 20-yard Tupa to Ellis touchdown pass, Ellis' first TD as a collegian, again gave OSU the lead. When the Hawkeyes regained the lead 22-31 with 9:11 remaining, Ohio State bounced back again. Tupa directed a time-consuming, 75-yard drive, Snow finally going in from the 14 with 2:45 left. A two-point conversion failed, but a 27-22 lead still gave Ohio State a clear upper hand.

"We were feeling confident," linebacker Eric Kumerow said.

The Hawkeyes made it sticky, eventually moving the ball to a first down at the Ohio State 15 with less than a minute to play, but the OSU defense seemed equal to the challenge. Kumerow sacked Iowa quarterback Chuck Hartlieb for an eight-yard loss on second down. On third and 23, Kumerow and blitzing rover Ray Jackson pressured Hartlieb into a bad pass. With 16 seconds left, at fourth and 23 from the OSU 28, the Hawkeyes were down to their last play.

For the Buckeyes, the play unfolded like a microcosm of a frustrating season. Tight end Marv Cook ran a sideline route, slowed up to let defensive back Sean Bell run by, caught the ball at the 10 and crashed into the end zone with six seconds left. Iowa 29, Ohio State 27. The Buckeyes had lost four Big Ten games for the first time since 1966.

"I just don't quite understand myself how we can lose like we lose," Bruce said, "but we keep doing it."

The Ohio State players were equally befuddled, but tried to steer the blame away from Bruce, increasingly under fire from the fans as a once-promising season turned into the school's worst in 22 years.

"It's not his fault," said Spielman, whose long-shot Heisman Trophy candidacy had been misplaced among the team's four losses. "He didn't suit up. He didn't play. We had the defense to stop them. We didn't stop them. If you're going to blame anybody, blame the players."

The blame was assigned two days later. A few hours after a determined Bruce told the press, "I am staying," at his weekly news conference, OSU Athletic Director Rick Bay read a 17-line statement from OSU President Edward Jennings announcing that

Bruce had been fired, effective after the final game of the season. Bay, who had loyally supported his coach in the face of mounting criticism, then resigned in protest over the move, which came with a year still remaining on Bruce's contract.

"It's a shame," Bay said. "It's a dark day for Ohio State."

It was, in fact, considerably darker than Jennings thought it was. When he dropped the curtain on a coach who had the best overall record (80-26-1) among Big Ten coaches since 1979, criticism of his action was immediate and widespread. Bruce, who had seemed so unpopular with the fans before his abrupt dismissal, suddenly seemed to have supporters in every corner. Many who had criticized him before switched sides, angered that a successful coach with a program untainted by scandal had been fired with a game left in the season and a year left on his contract. The fact that Bruce had honored his commitment to OSU by turning down a lucrative offer from Arizona the previous January only upset the critics more.

"I don't understand why I am being fired," Bruce said on the night of his firing. Thousands of other people asked the same thing.

"This is a sad day for college football," Michigan Coach Bo Schembechler said.

"I hate that," said Purdue Coach Fred Akers, fired himself from Texas in 1986. "He hasn't even had a losing season."

Ohio State students staged rallies for Bruce's support, and the university was severely criticized in newspapers and magazines and on network newscasts.

Bruce said he was as confused by the firing as anybody. "I'm at a loss," he said. "If I was a crud, or a cheater, or a lousy coach...I consider myself a damn good football coach."

Jennings, who did not appear at the news conference, only added to the growing mystery later. He said Bruce knew why he was fired, and indicated that it was for reasons other than the poor season. Whatever the reasons, he refused to divulge them publicly.

"Those are personnel issues," he said. "In our judgment, it was time to make a change. That's all there is to it. It was a personnel matter."

The furor continued for days. In the meantime, Bruce and his staff tried to work through the tempest and prepare for a season-ending game at Michigan, which was to be Bruce's last at Ohio State.

311

A game between Big Ten also-rans suddenly was awash in emotion. The Ohio State players wore headbands which read "Earle," and backed up their sentiments with their play. Two third quarter touchdowns, one on a short pass from Tupa that Carlos Snow turned into a 70-yarder, gave the Buckeyes a 20-13 lead, before Michigan tied the game on a 10-yard run by Leroy Hoard with 1:14 to go in the third quarter.

It was left to Matt Frantz, who had missed an extra-point attempt after a school-record 52 straight, to give Bruce his final win. His 26-yard field goal with 5:18 left did it.

"If he's not coming back," Frantz said, "this is one hell of a way to go out."

Bruce agreed.

"I had a knot in my stomach I guess all week," he said. "But I'm a professional. We teach our players that when they get knocked down, they have to get up and go again. I guess this is the ultimate test for me."

Even while Bruce was passing that test, his lawyer, John Zonak, was announcing a legal test he and Bruce had planned for Jennings and the university. Zonak filed a $7.4 million dollar lawsuit in Franklin County Common Pleas Court on Bruce's behalf against Jennings and Ohio State, charging them with breach of contract. In announcing the lawsuit, Zonak accused Jennings of firing Bruce because the coach disapproved of Jennings' lifestyle, although that accusation wasn't mentioned in the nine-page suit. The suit accused Jennings "as a part of a scheme... and in bad faith made false and untrue statements about... Earle D. Bruce."

The case was never heard in court. A week later, Ohio State agreed to settle suit by paying Bruce $471,000 dollars within three business days. The amount represented 18 months salary and benefits, a retirement buyout of $195,000 dollars and $119,184 dollars Bruce would have received from OSU and outside sources if he had remained a coach through June, 1989, the end of his contract.

Jennings and Bruce are "both interested in Ohio State University," attorney John C. Elam, representing OSU, said in announcing the settlement, "and they both regret the fact that it was necessary for there to be litigation. But they're both pleased with what has been accomplished."

Cooper Comfort

The search for a new coach, conducted by new Ohio State Athletic Director Jim Jones, dragged on for over a month.

Finding a man who could guarantee improvement on Earle Bruce's nine-year 81-26-1 record, 5-4 against Michigan and four Big Ten championships wouldn't be easy. But as Jones, promoted from senior associate athletic director when Rick Bay resigned, scoured the nation for suitable candidates, it became obvious that, in itself, wasn't necessarily the only goal. Other factors were also going to weigh heavily in the decision.

At times, Bruce had come under criticism, not so much for his coaching, but for his lack of marketing and communication skills. If it could get one, Ohio State wanted a good football coach who was also a good communicator. Then, on the evening of December 30th, in Anaheim, California, it became obvious that it had found him. Immediately following Arizona State's 33-28 win over Air Force in the Freedom Bowl, ASU Coach John Cooper confirmed he was leaving the Pac-10 school for "one of the premier jobs in college football." At the same time, Ohio State confirmed through its sports information department that Cooper had accepted the job and would be introduced at a news conference in Columbus the next day.

"He didn't tell until after the games but we knew," Arizona State free safety Jeff Mahlstede said in a somber Sun Devil locker room. "We had been hearing these things for quite a while. It was a sad thing."

The new Ohio State coach, who had taken the Sun Devils to a

New Ohio State football coach John Cooper enjoys a laugh with reporters during the press conference announcing his hiring.

22-15 Rose Bowl victory over Michigan the season before, had emerged from a field which included West Virginia's Don Nehlen, Kent State's Glen Mason, Howard's Willie Jeffries, Boston College's Jack Bicknell, Marshall's George Chaump and former Cleveland Browns' Coach Sam Rutigliano. Most of the others also possessed the blend of communication and coaching skills Ohio State sought, but the outgoing Cooper was a standout. He was 82-

314

40-2 in 11 seasons, including eight at Tulsa, and 25-9-2 in three seasons at Arizona State.

"We're going to give it our best shot," said Cooper, the next day. "I think we can win the national championship. I felt like we could win the national championship at Arizona State; that's a goal we had every year. That's the goal we'll have at Ohio State."

The university's goal in hiring him was just as clear. Cooper, 50, is talkative and personable, a Tennessee native who knows how to charm a crowd. If the crowd includes the press, that's all the better.

The perception of Bruce was that he couldn't do that, he could win football games but not win enough friends to give the program the image OSU President Edward Jennings wanted. The perception of Cooper is that he can do both.

"Whenever you do a national search and whenever you see outstanding people the result is there is one person who stands out head and shoulders," Jennings said. "John Cooper did. Obviously, I think a coach has an awful lot of responsibilities, as do I. I think John Cooper will represent us very well."

First impressions seemed to confirm that. The new coach said all the right things in his introductory press conference.

"I'm a greater believer in aiming for the sky and hitting an eagle, than in aiming for an eagle and hitting the ground," Cooper said. "So our goal will be to win the national championship, to win the Big Ten championship, to win the Rose Bowl. There's a big difference between going to the Rose Bowl and winning the Rose Bowl."

By talking about winning the Rose Bowl, Cooper struck a responsive chord. Michigan State's 20-17 victory over Southern California the next day in the 1988 Rose Bowl was the Big Ten's first win there in seven years and only the second in the last 14 games. Ohio State had lost in its last four Rose Bowl appearances.

But there were more immediate matters at hand. Following the question and answer session, Cooper hit the recruiting trail, intent on making up for lost time.

"The big thing now is to get in here, get our staff together and get on with recruiting," he said. "I recognize that we probably are behind in recruiting, but we are going to catch up in a hurry."

Shortly after the press conference, Cooper called his first recruit, highly-touted quarterback Kirk Herbstreit of Centerville, Ohio. Herbstreit, who had been asked to delay making his announcement until a new coach was named, told him he was coming to Ohio State.

I've always wanted to go to Ohio State, to be a Buckeye, to go to the Rose Bowl," said Herbstreit, whose father, James, played for OSU from 1958-60. "There was no doubt ever, no matter who the coach was going to be, that I was always going to Ohio State."

The machinery was in place. Now, it was Cooper's turn to man the controls.

APPENDIX

Appendix Material Updated 1988
Courtesy Sports Information Office
Ohio State University

Ohio State's All-Opponent Record
1890-1986

Team	OSU Won	OSU Lost	Tied	First Game	Last Game
Akron	4	1	0	1891	1895
Alabama	0	2	0	1978	1986
Antioch	1	0	0	1894	1894
Arizona	0	1	0	1967	1967
Arizona State	1	0	0	1980	1980
Auburn	0	0	1	1917	1917
Baylor	2	0	0	1978	1982
Brigham Young	2	0	0	1982	1985
California	5	1	0	1920	1972
Camp Sherman	1	0	0	1917	1917
Carlisle Indiana	0	1	0	1904	1904
Case	11	10	2	1894	1918
Central Kentucky	0	1	0	1895	1895
Chicago	10	2	2	1920	1939
Cincinnati	9	2	0	1893	1930
Clemson	0	1	0	1978	1978
Colgate	1	0	1	1923	1934
Colorado	3	1	0	1971	1986
Columbia	2	0	0	1925	1926
Columbus Barracks	2	1	0	1894	1897
Cornell	0	2	0	1939	1940
Dayton YMCA	1	0	0	1892	1892
Denison	14	1	2	1890	1927
De Pauw	1	0	0	1905	1905
Drake	1	0	0	1935	1935
Duke	3	1	0	1955	1981
Florida State	0	2	0	1981	1982
Fort Knox	1	0	0	1942	1942
Great Lakes	1	1	0	1943	1944
Heidelberg	3	0	0	1898	1907

Team	OSU Won	OSU Lost	Tied	First Game	Last Game
Illinois	50	21	4	1902	1986
Indiana	50	10	4	1901	1986
Iowa	32	11	2	1922	1986
Iowa Seahawks	1	1	0	1942	1943
Kentucky	3	0	0	1895	1935
Kenyon	17	6	0	1890	1929
Marietta	6	2	0	1892	1902
Miami (O.)	2	0	0	1904	1911
Miami (Fla.)	1	0	0	1977	1977
Michigan	32	46	5	1897	1986
Michigan State	15	8	0	1912	1984
Minnesota	24	6	0	1921	1986
Missouri	8	1	1	1939	1976
Mount Union	1	0	0	1930	1930
Muskingum	7	0	0	1899	1928
Navy	3	0	0	1930	1981
Nebraska	2	0	0	1955	1956
New York University	2	0	0	1936	1938
North Carolina	3	1	0	1962	1975
Northwestern	44	13	1	1913	1986
Notre Dame	0	2	0	1935	1936
Oberlin	13	9	3	1892	1922
Ohio Medical	5	2	1	1896	1906
Ohio University	4	0	0	1899	1902
Ohio Wesleyan	26	2	1	1890	1932
Oklahoma	1	1	0	1977	1983
Oregon	6	0	0	1957	1983
Oregon State	2	0	0	1974	1984
Otterbein	13	2	3	1893	1912
Pennsylvania	3	0	0	1932	1953
Pennsylvania State	2	6	0	1912	1980
Pittsburgh	15	4	1	1929	1985
Princeton	0	1	1	1927	1928
Purdue	24	9	2	1919	1986
Seventeenth Regiment	1	0	0	1894	1894
Southern California	9	9	1	1937	1985
Southern Methodist	7	1	1	1950	1978
Stanford	2	3	0	1955	1982
Syracuse	2	1	0	1911	1980
Texas A. & M.	3	0	0	1963	1987
Texas Christian	4	1	1	1937	1973
U.C.L.A.	3	3	1	1961	1980
Utah	1	0	0	1986	1986
Vanderbilt	3	1	0	1908	1933
Virginia	1	0	0	1933	1933
Washington	4	2	0	1957	1986
Washington State	6	0	0	1952	1985
Western Reserve	5	6	1	1891	1934
West Virginia	3	1	0	1897	1903
Wilmington	1	0	0	1926	1926
Wisconsin	41	11	4	1913	1986
Wittenberg	12	3	0	1893	1929
Wooster	4	2	2	1890	1925
Total	608	239	48	1890	1986

Winning Percentage .706

All-Time Big Ten Standings (1896-1986)

(Conference Games Only)

Team	Won	Lost	Tied	Pct.
OHIO STATE (1913)	321	118	20	.721
Michigan (1896)	330	132	15	.707
Michigan State (1953)	133	107	6	.553
Chicago (1896-1939)	120	99	14	.545
Minnesota (1896)	263	228	26	.534
Illinois (1896)	254	267	27	.488
Purdue (1896)	232	244	28	.488
Wisconsin (1896)	233	264	38	.471
Iowa (1900)	185	266	21	.414
Northwestern (1896)	177	339	20	.349
Indiana (1900)	134	318	23	.306

All-Time Football Letter Winners

"A"

Abbott, Albert G, 1898
Ackerman, Cornelius, 1925-26-27
Adamle, Anthony, 1946
Adams, Douglas O., 1968-69-70
Adams, J. J., 1900
Adderly, Nelson W., 1965
Addison, Evert, 1918-22
Adkins, David, 1974-75-76-77
Adulewicz, Casimir T., 1959
Alber, George H., 1926-27-28
Alders, Gary, 1981-82-84
Aleskus, Joseph P., 1937-38
Allegro, Joe, 1975-76-77
Allen, Paul, 1983
Allen, Robert M., 1932
Amlin, George P., 1966
Amling, Warren E., 1944-45-46
Anders, Billy J., 1965-66-67
Anderson, Charles C., 1939-40
Anderson, Cedric, 1980-81-82-83
Anderson, Kim, 1964-65-66
Anderson, Richard L., 1964-65
Anderson, Richard, 1952
Anderson, Thomas L., 1964
Anderson, William T., 1968-69-70
Andrako, Steven F., 1938-39
Andrews, Lawrence F., 1951
Andria, Ernest, 1975-77-78-79
Andrick, Theodore K., 1964-65
Antenucci, Frank L., 1934-35-36
Anthony, Thomas, 1981-82
Appleby, Gordon E., 1942-43-44
Applegate, Richard, 1974-75
Arledge, Richard, 1951
Armstrong, Billy J., 1960-61-62
Armstrong, Ralph A., 1949-50-51
Arnold, Birtho, 1957-58-59
Arnold, George A., 1907
Aston, Daniel B., 1969
Atha, Robert, 1978-79-80-81
Auer, John J., 1953
Augenstein, Jack G., 1953
Ayers, Ronald, 1974-75-76

"B"

Baas, James W., 1965-66
Bach, Terry, 1977-78
Bachman, Stanley, 1908-09-10
Backhus, Tom A., 1967-68-69
Backus, Clark, 1982-83
Bahin, Michael, 1895
Bailey, Ralph, 1958
Baird, Charles H., 1893
Baker, Ray G., 1945
Baldacci, Thomas G., 1955-56-57
Balen, Alan, 1981
Ballmer, Paul E., 1958
Bargerstock, Douglas, 1974
Barnes, Robert L., 1890
Barnett, Orlando T., 1963-64-65
Barratt, Fred W., 1928-29
Barricklow, Donald B., 1910-11-12
Barrington, Thomas G., 1963-64-65
Barrington, Walter D., 1905-06-07-08

Bartley, Thomas A., 1967-68
Bartoszek, Mike, 1972-73-74
Bartschy, Ross D., 1937-38-39
Barwig, Ronald, 1977-78-79-80
Baschnagel, Brian, 1972-73-74-75
Bates, Roman, 1983-84
Battista, Thomas, 1971
Baumgarten, Eugene H., 1930-31
Baxa, Thomas L., 1972
Beatty, Hobart, 1890
Beatty, Hugh G., 1909-10
Beam, William D., 1959
Beamon, Eddie, 1974-75-76-77
Bear, C. L., 1911
Bechtel, Earl R., 1952
Beecroft, Charles, 1971-72
Beekley, Marts E., 1951-52
Beerman, Raymond O., 1957
Beetham, Rupert R., 1899
Belgrave, Earl, 1972
Bell, Farley, 1975-76
Bell, Frederick J., 1917-18
Bell, Kelvin, 1981-82-83
Bell, Robert R., 1925-26-27
Bell, Robin A., 1925-26-27
Bell, Sean, 1985
Bell, Todd, 1977-78-79-80
Bell, William M., 1929-30-31
Belmer, Cliff, 1978-79
Beltz, Richard H., 1934-35
Bender, Edward A., 1968
Benedict, Charles Y., 1897
Benis, Joe V., 1930-31
Benis, Michael K., 1960
Berner, Joseph, 1981
Bettridge, John W., 1934-35-36
Betz, Wayne O., 1961-62
Biel, William J., 1945
Bilkie, Edward R., 1950
Biltz, John W., 1949-50
Birdseye, Claude H., 1901
Blaine, Ernest D., 1910-11
Blair, Howard H., 1920-21-22
Blair, Kenneth, 1984
Blanchard, Bruce J., 1925
Bledsoe, John, 1971-72
Bliss, Harry W., 1919-20
Bliss, Keith H., 1937-38
Blinco, Thomas, 1976-77-79
Blose, M. L., 1896-97
Bobo, Hubert L., 1954
Bodenbender, David G., 1964
Boesel, Richard, 1915-16-17
Boesel, Stephen W., 1909-10
Bolen, Charles W., 1915-16-17
Bolin, Stuart R., 1895
Bolser, Harvey J., 1938
Bombach, Jaren D., 1967
Bompiedi, Carl J., 1933
Bond, Robert J., 1952-53-54-55
Bonica, Charles, 1970-71-72
Bonnie, Dale B., 1947
Bonnie, David M., 1946-47
Boone, Chelsea A., 1909
Booth, William J., 1953-54-55
Booth, William R., 1936
Boothman, Dale M., 1900-01
Borton, John R., 1951-52-53-54
Boucher, Arthur F., 1934-35
Boughner, Richard J., 1937-38
Boughton, Ivan B., 1913-14-15

Bowermaster, Russell L., 1956-57-58
Bowers, Brian, 1973-74
Bowman, Howard, 1890
Bowsher, Gerald J., 1959
Boxwell, Kenneth E., 1944
Boynton, A. J., 1893-94
Bradley, Robert T., 1925
Bradshaw, Morris, 1971-72-73
Braun, Don, 1982
Breehl, Edward L., 1957
Breese, Clarence, 1899-00
Bridge, Brooklyn B., 1912
Briggs, Maurice, 1912-13
Brindle, Arthur B., 1905
Broadnax, Vaughn, 1980-81-82-83
Brockington, John S., 1968-69-70
Bronson, A. P., 1890
Brophy, James F., 1897-98
Brown, Aaron, 1974-75-76-77
Brown, Bernard, 1979
Brown, David, 1986
Brown, G. W., 1902
Brown, Henry, 1983-85-86
Brown, Jeff, 1972
Brown, Leo M., 1955-56-57
Brown, Matthew, 1943-44-45
Brown, Stanley, 1902
Brown, Timothy, 1978-79
Brubaker, Carl R., 1953-54
Bruckner, Edwin, 1940-41
Brudzinski, Robert, 1973-74-75-76
Brugge, Robert S., 1944-46-47
Bruney, Fred K., 1950-51-52
Bruney, Robert O., 1962-63
Brungard, David A., 1967-68
Brungard, George, 1935
Bryant, Charles S., 1959-60-61
Bryant, Jaymes, 1986
Bryce, Chalmers K., 1906-07-08
Bugel, Thomas E., 1963-64-65
Bulen, Elwood J., 1900-01
Bullock, William M., 1938
Buonamici, Nicholas, 1973-74-75-76
Burgett, Richard K., 1941
Burgin, Asbury L., 1965-66
Burke, Timothy, 1978-79
Burris, Scott, 1978-79-80
Burrows, Norman, 1978-79-80
Burrows, Roger W., 1970
Burton, Arthur F., 1967-68-69
Busich, Sam, 1934-35
Buss, Charles, 1891
Butts, Robert W., 1960-62
Butcher, Fred E., 1895-96-97-00
Byars, Keith, 1982-83-84-85
Byrne, Edward G., 1903-04

"C"

Cairns, Gary L., 1966-67
Calkins, George H., 1894-95
Cameron, George D., 1924
Campana, Thomas, 1969-70-71
Campanella, Joseph A., 1950
Campbell, Paul, 1976-77-78-79
Cannavino, Joseph P., 1955-56-57
Cannavino, Michael L., 1946-47-48

Cappell, Richard A., 1969-70-71
Cargile, Jeff, 1983-84
Carlin, Earl V., 1939-40
Carlin, Oscar E., 1927-29
Carroll, Paul B., 1911-12
Carroll, William M., 1930-31-32
Carson, James, 1981-82-83
Carson, Samuel K., 1893-94
Carter, Cris, 1984-85-86
Carter, David W., 1928-29
Carver, Rolly J., 1904
Case, Claude H., 1902-03
Cassady, Craig, 1973-74-75
Cassady, Howard (Hop), 1952-53-54-55
Castignola, Gregory, 1977-78-79
Cato, Byron, 1975-76-77-78
Cheney, David A., 1968-69-70
Cheroke, George, 1941
Cherry, Boyd V., 1912-13-14
Chonko, Arnie, 1962-63-64
Chrissinger, Warren O., 1936-37
Cicero, Chris, 1983
Cisco, Galen, 1955-56-57
Cisco, Jeff, 1981-82
Claflin, Walter N., 1906-07-08
Claggett, Edward F., 1904-06-07
Clair, Frank J., 1938-39-40
Clare, Robert L., 1909-10
Clark, James, 1947-48-49
Clark, David B., 1902-03-04
Clark, Donald, 1956-57-58
Clark, Eugene L., 1943
Clark, Myers A., 1924-25-26
Cleary, Thomas J., 1942
Cline, Oliver M., 1944-45-47
Cline, W. D., 1895
Clotz, Dennis R., 1961
Cobb, Glen, 1979-80-81-82
Coburn, James A., 1970
Cochran, Kenneth L., 1931
Cochran, Terrence A., 1965
Coffee, Charles B., 1927-28-29
Cole, George N., 1891
Cole, Robert, 1956
Coles, Karl, 1986
Collmar, William J., 1954-55
Colzie, Cornelius, 1972-73-74
Conley, William N., 1970-71
Conlin, Ray, 1984
Connor, Daniel D., 1961
Conrad, Frederick B., 1931-32-33
Conroy, James, 1969
Conway, Blair, 1972-73
Cooke, Clement C., 1910
Cook, Ronald L., 1955-57
Cooper, George, 1984-85-86
Coover, Winifred F., 1900-01-02
Cope, Harry, 1898
Cope, James, 1972-73-74
Cornell, Fred A., 1902
Cory, Lincoln T., 1927-28
Cott, Richard S., 1919-20-21
Cottrell, Ernest A., 1944
Courtney, Harold J., 1915-16-17
Courtney, Howard G., 1915-16-17
Cousineau, Tom, 1975-76-77-78

All-Time Football Letter Winners—Con't

Cox, Garth, 1976-77
Cox, Joseph E., 1926-27-28
Cox, Joseph F., 1909-10-11
Cox, Melvin B., 1934
Cowman, Randy, 1972
Craig, Orlando, 1986
Cramer, Carl F., 1931-32-33
Cramer, William E., 1917
Crane, Jameson, 1945-46-47
Crapser, Steven R., 1969
Crawford, Albert K., 1956-57-58
Crawford, Thomas E., 1957
Crecelius, David, 1981-82-83-84
Crecilius, Arthur W., 1894-95
Crow, Fred., 1936-37
Csuri, Charles A., 1941-42-46
Culbertson, Claude L., 1897
Cumiskey, Frank S., 1934-35-36
Cummings, John, 1972
Cummings, William G., 1956
Cunningham, Charles, 1971
Cunningham, Harold B., 1923-24-25
Cunningham, John F., 1896
Cunningham, Leo, 1943
Curcillo, Anthony, 1950-51-52
Curren, Michael F., 1904
Curtis, Clarence, 1981-82-83
Current, Michael, 1965-66
Curto, Patrick, 1973-74-75
Cusick, Martin, 1977
Cusick, Peter, 1972-73-74
Cutillo, Dan, 1971-72-73
Czyzynski, Richard, 1981-82-83

"D"

Dale, Michael D., 1970
D'Andrea, Michael, 1979-80-81
Daniell, James L., 1939-40-41
Dannelley, Scott, 1972-73-74-75
Dansler, Kelton, 1975-76-77-78
Darst, Lester D., 1907-11
Datish, Michael, 1975
Daugherty, Harold R., 1945
Daughters, Charles G., 1916
Davidson, James, 1963-64
Davidson, James, 1985
Davidson, Jeff, 1986
Davies, Thomas C., 1918-19
Davis, Jeff, 1971-72-73
Davis, Jerome, 1973-74
Davis, Paul J., 1943
Davis, Vernon H., 1898
Dawdy, Donald A., 1953
Dawson, Jack S., 1948
Dean, C. A., 1902
Dean, Hal S., 1941-42-46
Debevc, Mark C., 1968-69-70
DeCree, Van, 1972-73-74
Delaney, Kevin, 1985
DeLeone, James, 1979-80-81
DeLeone, Thomas D., 1969-70-71
Delich, Peter D., 1931-32-33
DeLong, A. Z., 1895-96
Demmel, Robert C., 1947-50
Dendiu, Traian T., 1944-46
Denker, Irv., 1952
Denman, Edgar, 1894
Detrick, Roger, 1959-60
DeVoe, Keith E., 1923-24-25
Diehl, William, 1932
Dike, Ed, 1904

Dill, M. R., 1928-29
Dill, Raymond, 1901
Dillman, Thomas M., 1954-55-56
Dillon, Daniel D., 1966
Diltz, Charles R., 1901-02-03-04
DiPierro, Ramon F., 1944-46-47-48
Disher, Larry L., 1957
Dixon, Joe, 1975-76-77
Dixon, Ken, 1970-71
Dixon, Thornton D., 1939-40-41-45
Doig, Hal F., 1920-21
Doll, John, 1972
Donley, Douglas, 1977-78-79-80
Donley, Fred, 1908
Donovan, Brian P., 1968-69-70
Dooley, Joseph, 1981-82-83
Doolittle, Francis W., 1946-47
Dorris, Victor, 1937
Dorsey, Robert S., 1947-48
Dove, Robert E., 1944-45
Doyle, Richard A., 1950-52
Drake, Phillip B., 1942
Drakulich, Samuel, 1933
Dreffer, Stephan D., 1962-63-64
Drenik, Douglas J., 1962-63-64
Dreyer, Carl A., 1924
Dreyer, Virgil O., 1915-16
DuBois, Wilbur L., 1900
Dugger, Dean, 1952-53-54
Dugger, John R., 1942-43-44
Dulin, Gary, 1976-77-78-79
Dumas, Zack, 1986
Dunlap, John H., 1895-96
Dunlap, Nelson H., 1921-22-23
Dunlap, Renick W., 1891-93-94-95
Dunn, Craig, 1981-82
Dunsford, Jan H., 1904-05
Duncan, Howard D., 1946-47
Durtschi, William R., 1942
Dwelle, Brad, 1979-80-81-82
Dwyer, Donald W., 1965-66-67
Dwyer, R. E., 1898
Dye, William H., 1934-35-36

"E"

Eachus, William N., 1965-66
Eagleson, John H., 1898
Early, Ellis T., 1921
Eberle, John J., 1908-09
Eberts, Mark, 1981
Ebinger, Elbert C., 1955
Eby, Byron, 1926-27-28
Echols, Reginald, 1979-80
Edwards, Karl, 1981-82-83
Edwards, William R., 1949
Egbert, Archie D., 1910
Ehrensberger, Carl H., 1930
Ehrsam, Gerald R., 1966-67-68
Ehrsam, John H., 1944-45
Elder, Walter W., 1901-02
Elgin, Edward G., 1922
Elia, Bruce, 1972-73-74
Elliott, Samuel, 1965-66-67
Ellis, Ray, 1977-78-79-80
Ellis, Richard T., 1890-91-92
Ellison, Leon, 1980
Ellwood, Franklin D., 1955-56
Ellwood, Richard P., 1949-50
Endres, George J., 1950
Endres, Robert L., 1951
Engensperger, Albert, 1896-97

Englebeck, Amos, 1904-06
Epitropoulos, John, 1978-79-80
Ernst, L. C., 1891-92
Ervin, Terry L., 1966-67
Espy, Bennie E., 1962-63
Ewalt, Dwight S., 1913
Ewart, Kenneth L., 1917-19
Ewing, Harry E., 1905
Ezzo, Billy, 1972-73-74

"F"

Facchine, Richard, 1955
Faehl, Paul J., 1950
Fair, Robert F., 1963
Farcasin, Constantine J., 1918-19-22
Ferrall, Junius B., 1930-31-32
Farrell, John R., 1960
Fay, Sherman, 1899-00-01-02
Fazio, Charles A., 1945-46-47-48
Fedderson, Jerold V., 1943
Federle, Tom, 1963-64
Fekete, Eugene, 1942
Feldwisch, Henry W., 1911
Fender, Paul E., 1967
Ferguson, Keith, 1978-79-80
Ferguson, Robert E., 1959-60-61
Ferko, Richard, 1970-71
Ferrelli, Jeffrey, 1975-76
Fertig, Dwight L., 1967
Fesler, Wesley E., 1928-29-30
Fields, Jerry E., 1958-59
Fiers, Alan, 1959-60
Fill, John M., 1964-65-66
Fioretti, Anthony R., 1922-23
Fisch, Frank, 1933-34-35
Fischer, Louis C., 1950-51
Fisher, Richard, 1939-40-41-45
Fitz, Thomas, 1964
Flanagan, Richard E., 1944
Fletcher, Kevin, 1970-71-72
Flowers, James T., 1919
Foley, David, 1966-67-68
Foley, W. J., 1893
Fontaine, Lawton L., 1929
Fontes, Arnold P., 1965-66
Fontes, Leonard J., 1958-59
Fordham, Forrest P., 1937-38
Fortney, Harrison, 1963
Foster, Jerome, 1979-80-81-82
Foster, Rodney, 1961-62
Foster, Thomas B., 1905
Foss, Clarence M., 1902-03-04-05
Foss, Earl D., 1910-11
Fouch, George E., 1927-28-29
Foulk, Charles W., 1890-91-92
Fout, James E., 1945
Fox, Samuel S., 1940-41
Fox, Tim, 1972-73-74-75
France, Doug, 1972-73-74
Francis, David L., 1960-62
Frank, John, 1980-81-82-83
Frantz, Matthew, 1986
Frayer, Leo A., 1894
Frechtling, Arthur G., 1899-00
French, Edward H., 1893-94-95
Fried, Lawrence L., 1930
Friedman, Max, 1918
Fritz, Kenneth, 1976-77-78-79
Fronk, Daniel A., 1957-58
Frye, Robert H., 1941-42
Fulton, William S., 1899
Funk, Robert, 1964-65

Funkhauser, Samuel K., 1908-12

"G"

Gaffney, Mike, 1972
Gage, Ralph G., 1958
Gailus, Joseph T., 1931-32-33
Galbos, Richard, 1971-72
Gales, Charles P., 1935-36-38
Gales, Richard, 1971-72
Gandee, Charles F., 1945-49-50
Gandee, Sherwin K., 1948-50-51
Garber, Joseph, 1986
Gaudio, Angelo R., 1946
Gayle, James, 1979-80-81-82
Gayle, Shaun, 1980-81-82-83
Geib, J.R., 1911-12
Geissman, W. I., 1911-12-13
Gentile, Jim M., 1968-69-70
George, August, 1935
Gerald, Rod, 1975-76-77-78
German, William, 1959-60
Gibbs, George C., 1893
Gibbs Jack G., 1954
Gibson, Millard F., 1906-07-08
Giessen, Carl, 1894-95
Gilbert, Charles R., 1948-49
Gill, Arthur G., 1904
Gillam, Neal, 1918
Gillard, James H., 1905-06
Gillian Lonnie R., 1967-68-69
Gilliam, Neil, 1918-21
Gillie, George W., 1905-06-07
Gillis, Clarence, 1901
Gillman, Sidney, 1931-32-33
Gilmore, James, 1981-83-84-85
Ginn, Dwight G., 1914-15
Giuliani, Anthony, 1983-84
Givens, Dan O., 1971
Glasser, Chester F., 1928-29
Godfrey, Ernest R., 1914
Gordon, Denman "Sonny", 1983-84-85-86
Goodsell, Douglas R., 1951-52
Gordon, George D., 1944
Gordon, Les, 1975
Gorby, Herbert L., 1945
Gorley, Rodney, 1979-80-83
Gorrill, Charles V., 1923-24-25
Gottron, Jeff, 1982
Gradishar, Randy, 1971-72-73
Grady, Robert J., 1929-30-31
Graf, Campbell J., 1912-13-14
Graf, Campbell R., 1939
Graf, Jack R., 1939-40-41
Graf, Lawrence, 1973
Graves, Reggie, 1986
Graves, Rory, 1983-84-85
Greenberg, Jack Z., 1931-32
Greene, Cornelius, 1973-74-75
Greene, Horatius A., 1969
Griffin, Archie, 1972-73-74-75
Griffin, Duncan, 1975-76-77-78
Griffin, Ray, 1974-75-76-77
Griffith, A. G., 1892
Griffith, William A., 1928-29-30
Griffith, William N., 1924
Griggs, Anthony, 1981
Grim, Fred, 1925-26-27
Grimes, Robert L., 1950-51-52
Griswold, Francis H., 1927
Groza, Judd, 1982-83-84
Grundies, Arthur J., 1938-40
Guess, Michael, 1976-77-78-79
Guthrie, George P., 1951-52
Guy, Richard S., 1954-55-56
Guzik, Frank A., 1953

All-Time Football Letter Winners—Con't

Stuart, John D., 1921
Stungis, John J., 1943-46
Sturtz, Karl L., 1949-50
Sullivan, John, 1984
Sullivan, John K., 1916
Sullivan, John L., 1985-86
Sullivan, Mark, 1975-76-77-78
Sullivan, Mark P., 1979-80
Sullivan, Michael F., 1985-86
Summers, Merl G., 1908-09-10
Surface, Frank M., 1902-03-04-05
Surington, Cyril T., 1927-28
Sutherin, Donald P., 1955-56-57
Swan, Earl G., 1902-03-04
Swartz, Donald C., 1952-53-54
Swartzbaugh, Charles B., 1913
Swartzbaugh, John D., 1943
Swinehart, Rodney E., 1946-47-48-49
Sykes, W. E., 1897

"T"

Taggart, Ed, 1983-84-85-86
Takacs, Michael J., 1951-52-53
Tangeman, Theodore H., 1899-1900-01-05
Tanski, Victor T., 1932
Tarbill, John W., 1899
Tatum, Jack D., 1968-69-70
Tatum, Rowland, 1981-82-83
Taylor, Alvin, 1978
Taylor, Charles A., 1919-20-21
Taylor, John L., 1920
Taylor, Russell E., 1928-29
Teague, Willie M., 1970-71-72
Teifke, Howard A., 1943-46-47-48
Templeton, David I., 1946-47-48
Ternent, William A., 1952
Theis, Franklyn B., 1955
Thies, Wilfred L., 1933
Thom, Leonard, 1939-40
Thomas, Aurelius, 1955-56-57
Thomas, George B., 1905
Thomas, James, 1949
Thomas, John R., 1943-44-45
Thomas, Joseph R., 1933
Thomas, Richard J., 1951-52
Thomas, Will C., 1965-66
Thompson, Ed, 1974-75-76
Thompson, Kenneth, 1955
Thompson, R. E., 1905-07
Thompson, Rollin H., 1892
Thornton, Robert F., 1952-53-54
Thrower, John D., 1900-02-03-04
Thurman, A. G., 1893-95
Tidmore, Samuel E., 1960-61
Tillman, J. H., 1901-02
Tilton, Josephus H., 1898-99-1900-01
Tingley, David R., 1959-61
Titus, Clarence H., 1896
Tobik, Andy Bill, 1940
Tolford, George K., 1959-60-61
Tomczak, Michael 1981-82-83-84
Toneff, George, 1944-48-49
Tracy, William P., 1906
Trapuzzano, Robert, 1969
Trautman, George M., 1911-12-13

Trautwein, Henry Bill, 1948-49-50
Treat, W. G., 1910
Trivisonno, Joseph J., 1955-57
Troha, Richard J., 1969
Trott, Dean W., 1919-20-21
Turner, E. C., 1902
Turner, Irwin, 1916
Tucci, Amel, 1939
Tupa, Thomas, 1984-85-86
Tyler, Julius B., 1896
Tyrer, James E., 1958-59-60

"U"

Uhlenhake, Jeff, 1985-86
Ujhelyi, Joseph A., 1928-29
Ullery, Jack C., 1925-27
Ulmer, Edward, 1960-61
Unverferth, Donald V., 1963-64-65
Updegraff, Winston R., 1922
Urban, Harry N., 1897
Urbanik, William J., 1967-68-69
Uridil, Leo R., 1925-26-27

"V"

Van Blaricom, Robert P., 1932
Van Buskirk, Lear H., 1907-08
Van Dyne, Kelley, 1916-17
Van Horn, Douglas C., 1963-64-65
Van Raaphorst, Richard W., 1961-62-63
Vanscoy, Norman J., 1960
Vargo, Kenneth W., 1953-54-55
Vargo, Thomas W., 1965
Varner, Martin D., 1930-31-32
Varner, Thomas A., 1960
Vavroch, William B., 1952
Vecanski, Milan, 1970-71
Verdova, Alex S., 1945-46-47-48
Vickroy, William E., 1941-42
Vicic, Donald J., 1954-55-56
Vogel, Robert L., 1960-61-62
Vogelgesang, Donald A., 1960
Vogler, Terry 1977-78
Vogler, Tim, 1975-76-77-78
Volley, Ricardo 1977-78-79
Volzer, Donald H., 1920
Von Schmidt, Walter G., 1927
Von Swearingen, Fiske, 1909
Vuchinich, Michael N., 1931-32-33

"W"

Wagner, Jack, W., 1950-51
Wakefield, Richard, 1969-70-71
Walden, Robert L., 1964-65-66
Walker, Barry, 1983-84-85-86
Walker, Dow H., 1902-03-04
Walker, Gordon H., 1928
Walker, Jack E., 1960
Walker, Stephen E., 1971
Wallace, Robert H., 1944
Walther, Bernard E., 1950-51
Wandke, Richard A., 1944
Ward, Chris, 1974-75-76-77
Ward, Grant P., 1912
Warden, Leonard G., 1894
Warfield, Paul D., 1961-62-63
Warner, Duane A., 1960
Warren, Lee G., 1905
Warwick, Herbert S., 1904
Washington, Alvin, 1977-78-79-80
Wassmund, James A., 1956
Wasson, Harold, 1922

Wasson, Richard, 1963
Wasson, Robert E., 1895-96-97
Wasylik, Nicholas, 1935-36-37
Waters, E. C., 1904
Watkins, Jene, 1959
Watkins, Robert A., 1952-53-54
Watson, Otha, 1978
Watson, Thomas G., 1945-48-49-50
Watts, Robert S., 1922-23-24
Waugh, Charles A., 1970
Waugh, Thomas 1976-77-78-79
Way, Rex D., 1907
Wears, Leland H., 1934
Weaver, C. Robert, 1920-21
Weaver, David A., 1953-54-55
Weaver, J. Edward, 1970
Weber, Fred C., 1898-99-1900
Wedebrook, Howard N., 1936-37-39
Weed, Thurlow, 1952-53-54
Welbaum, Thomas A., 1938-39
Welch, John W., 1947
Welever, Arthur W., 1931
Wells, Leslie H., 1908-09-10
Wendler, Harold, 1923-24-25
Wendt, Merle E., 1934-35-36
Wentz, Burke B., 1925
Wentz, William A., 1959-60
Wersel, Timothy, 1972
Wertz, George P., 1948-49
West, Edward F., 1936
Westwater, James G., 1896-99-1900-01
Wetzel, Charles J., 1908
Wetzel, Damon H., 1932-33-34
Wharton, Homer F., 1898-99-1900
Wheeler, T. L., 1902
Whetstone, Robert E., 1953-55
Whipple, Charles A., 1905-06-07
Whisler, Joseph G., 1946-47-49
Whitacre, H.J., 1890
White, C. C., 1892
White, Claude, 1938-40
White, Jan, 1968-69-70
White, John T., 1942
White, Loren R., 1957-58-59
White, Stanley R., 1969-70-71
White, Terry, 1984-85
White, William, 1984-85-86
Whitehead, Stuart F., 1938-39
Whitfield, David A., 1967-68-69
Whitmer, Doug, 1982-83-84
Wible, Calvin D., 1945
Widdoes, Richard D., 1948-49-50
Wieche, Robert, 1917-19-20
Wiggins, Larry, 1972
Wilder, Thurlow C., 1920
Wiles, A. O., 1902
Wilkins, Dwight, 1972
Wilks, William C., 1951
Willaman, Frank R., 1917-19-20
Willaman, Samuel S., 1911-13
Willard, Robert, 1973
Williams, Albert C., 1943
Williams, David M., 1953-54
Williams, Donald W., 1939
Williams, Gary, 1979-80-81-82
Williams, Lee E., 1955-58
Williams, Joe J., 1935-36
Williams, Robert D., 1968

Williams, Shad, 1970-71-72
Willott, Louis, 1974-75
Willis, Leonard, 1974-75
Willis, William K., 1942-43-44
Wilson, Andrew J., 1946-47-48-49
Wilson, C. R., 1899
Wilson, Donald A., 1932-33
Wilson, John B., 1922-23-24
Wingert, Albert C., 1930
Winters, Harold A., 1915
Winters, Sam C., 1945
Wiper, Donald W., 1920-21
Wiper, Harold A., 1917-18-20
Withoft, Clarence, 1891-92
Wittman, Julius W., 1949-50-51
Wittmer, Charles G., 1959-60-61
Wolf, Ralph C., 1936-37
Wolfe, Russell H., 1946
Wood, Charles L., 1892
Wood, Michael, 1984-85
Woodbury, Chester, 1905
Wooldridge, John, 1983-84-85-86
Worden, Dirk J., 1966-67-68
Workman, Harry H., 1920-22-23
Workman, Noel, 1920-21
Workman, Vince, 1985-86
Wortman, Robert C., 1964
Wright, David W., 1970
Wright, Ernest H., 1958
Wright, Ward, 1945
Wright, William E., 1909-10-11
Wuellner, Richard W., 1938-39

"Y"

Yards, Ludwig, 1932-33-34
Yassenoff, Leo, 1914-15
Yassenoff, Sol, 1913-14
Yerges, Howard E., Sr., 1915-16-17
Yerges, Howard S., Jr., 1943
Yingling, Walter E., 1928
Yonclas, Nicholas, 1963-64
Yost, Benjamin P., 1898
Young, Donald G., 1958-59-60
Young, Francis D., 1921-23-24
Young, Louis C., 1938
Young, Richard A., 1953-54
Young, William G., 1925-27-28

"Z"

Zackeroff, Greg, 1985-86
Zadworney, Frank S., 1937-38-39
Zalenski, Scott, 1981-82-83-84
Zangara, Donald, 1945
Zarnas, Gust C., 1935-36-37
Zavis, George J., 1941
Zavistoske, George, 1941
Zawacki, Charles E., 1955
Zelina, Larwrence P., 1968-69-70
Ziegler, Randall K., 1963
Zima, Albert J., 1962
Zimmer, Frank E., 1931
Zincke, Clarence F., 1929
Zinsmaster, John L., 1930
Zizakovic, Srecko, 1986

Ohio State Scores through the Years

1890
Coaches Alexander S. Lilley
Jack Ryder

20	Ohio Wesleyan	14
0	*Wooster	64
0	Denison	14
10	*Kenyon	18
30		110

Won 1, Lost 3

1891
Coach: Alexander S. Lilley

6	*Western Reserve	50
0	Kenyon	26
8	*Denison	4
6	Akron	0
20		80

Won 2, Lost 2

1892
Coach: Jack Ryder

0	Oberlin	4
62	*Akron	0
80	*Marietta	0
32	Denison	0
42	*Dayton YMCA	4
18	Western Reserve	40
26	*Kenyon	10
260		94

Won 5, Lost 2

1893

16	Otterbein	22
36	*Wittenberg	10
10	*Oberlin	38
6	Kenyon	42
16	*Western Reserve	30
32	*Akron	18
38	*Cincinnati	0
40	*Marietta	8
8	*Kenyon	10
202		178

Won 4, Lost 5

1894

6	Akron	12
0	Wittenberg	6
32	*Antioch	0
6	Wittenberg	18
30	Columbus Barracks	0
4	*Western Reserve	24
10	*Marietta	4
0	Case	38
6	Cincinnati	4
46	*17th Regiment	4
20	*Kenyon	4
160		114

Won 6, Lost 5

1895

14	*Akron	6
6	Otterbein	14
6	*Oberlin	12
4	Denison	4
8	*Ohio Wesleyan	8
4	Cincinnati	0
8	Kentucky	6
0	Central Kentucky	18
0	Marietta	24
12	*Kenyon	10
62		102

Won 4, Lost 4, Tied 2

1896
Coach: Charles A. Hickey

24	*Ohio Medical	0
6	Cincinnati	8
12	Otterbein	0
0	Oberlin	16
30	*Case	10
4	*Ohio Wesleyan	10
10	*Columbus Barracks	0
0	*Ohio Medical	0
6	*Wittenberg	24
12	*Ohio Medical	0
18	*Kenyon	34
122		104

Won 5, Lost 5, Tied 1

1897
Coach: David F. Edwards

6	*Ohio Medical	0
0	*Case	14
0	Michigan	34
12	*Otterbein	12
0	*Columbus Barracks	6
0	*Oberlin	44
0	West Virginia	28
0	Cincinnati	24
0	*Ohio Wesleyan	6
18		168

Won 1, Lost 7, Tied 1

1898
Coach: Jack Ryder

17	*Heidelberg	0
0	*Ohio Medical	10
34	*Denison	0
0	*Marietta	10
0	Western Reserve	49
5	*Case	23
0	*Kenyon	29
24	*Ohio Wesleyan	0
80		121

Won 3, Lost 5

1899
Coach: John B. C. Eckstorm

30	*Otterbein	0
28	*Wittenberg	0
5	Case	5
41	*Ohio University	0
6	Kentucky	0
6	*Western Reserve	0
17	*Marietta	0
12	*Ohio Medical	0
34	Muskingum	0
5	*Kenyon	0
184		5

Won 9, Lost 0, Tied 1

1900

20	*Otterbein	0
20	*Ohio University	0
29	Cincinnati	0
47	*Ohio Wesleyan	0
17	*Oberlin	0
27	*West Virginia	0
24	*Case	10
6	*Ohio Medical	11
0	Michigan	0
23	*Kenyon	5
213		26

Won 8, Lost 1, Tied 1

1901

0	*Otterbein	0
30	*Wittenberg	0
17	*Ohio University	0
24	*Marietta	0
6	*Western Reserve	5
0	*Michigan	21
0	Oberlin	6
6	*Indiana	18
11	*Kenyon	6
94		56

Won 5, Lost 3, Tied 1

1902
Coach: Perry Hale

5	*Otterbein	0
17	*Ohio University	0
30	*West Virginia	0
34	*Marietta	0
0	Michigan	86
51	*Kenyon	5
12	*Case	23
0	*Illinois	0
17	Ohio Wesleyan	16
6	*Indiana	6
172		136

Won 6, Lost 2, Tied 2

Marcus Marek (36) is Ohio State's career leader in tackles with 572.

Ohio State Scores Through the Years—Cont'd

1903

18	*Otterbein	0
28	*Wittenberg	0
24	*Denison	5
30	*Muskingum	0
59	*Kenyon	0
0	Case	12
34	*West Virginia	6
0	Michigan	36
27	*Oberlin	5
29	*Ohio Wesleyan	6
16	*Indiana	17
265		87

Won 8, Lost 3

1904
Coach: E. R. Sweetland

34	*Otterbein	0
80	*Miami	0
24	*Denison	0
46	*Muskingum	0
6	*Michigan	31
16	*Case	6
0	Indiana	8
0	*Illinois	46
2	Oberlin	4
11	*Kenyon	5
0	*Carlisle Indians	23
219		123

Won 6, Lost 5

1905

6	*Otterbein	6
28	*Heidelberg	0
40	*Muskingum	0
17	*Wittenberg	0
2	*Denison	0
32	*DePauw	6
0	*Case	0
23	*Kenyon	0
0	Michigan	40
36	*Oberlin	0
15	*Wooster	0
0	*Indiana	11
199		63

Won 8, Lost 2, Tied 2

1906
Coach: A. E. Herrnstein

41	*Otterbein	0
52	*Wittenberg	0
16	*Muskingum	0
0	*Michigan	6
6	Oberlin	0
6	*Kenyon	0
9	Case	0
12	*Wooster	0
11	*Ohio Medical	8
153		14

Won 8, Lost 1

1907

28	*Otterbein	0
16	*Muskingum	0
28	*Denison	0
6	*Wooster	6
0	Michigan	22
12	*Kenyon	0
22	*Oberlin	10
9	*Case	11
23	*Heidelberg	0
16	*Ohio Wesleyan	0
160		49

Won 7, Lost 2, Tied 1

1908

18	*Otterbein	0
0	*Wooster	8
16	*Denison	2
0	*Western Reserve	18
6	*Michigan	10
20	*Ohio Wesleyan	9
8	Case	18
17	Vanderbilt	6
14	*Oberlin	12
19	*Kenyon	9
118		92

Won 6, Lost 4

1909

14	*Otterbein	0
39	*Wittenberg	0
74	*Wooster	0
6	Michigan	33
29	*Denison	0
21	*Ohio Wesleyan	6
3	*Case	11
5	*Vanderbilt	0
6	Oberlin	26
22	*Kenyon	0
219		76

Won 7, Lost 3

1910
Coach: Howard Jones

14	*Otterbein	5
62	*Wittenberg	0
23	*Cincinnati	0
6	*Western Reserve	0
3	*Michigan	3
5	*Denison	5
10	Case	14
6	*Ohio Wesleyan	0
0	*Oberlin	0
53	*Kenyon	0
182		27

Won 6, Lost 1, Tied 3

1911
Coach: Harry Vaughn

6	*Otterbein	0
3	*Miami	0
0	*Western Reserve	0
0	Michigan	19
3	*Ohio Wesleyan	0
0	*Case	9
24	*Kenyon	0
0	Oberlin	0
0	*Syracuse	6
11	*Cincinnati	6
47		40

Won 5, Lost 3, Tied 2

1912
Coach: John R. Richards

55	Otterbein	0
34	*Denison	0
0	*Michigan	14
45	*Cincinnati	7
31	Case	6
23	*Oberlin	17
0	*Penn State	37
36	Ohio Wesleyan	6
20	*Michigan State	35
244		122

Won 6, Lost 3

1913
Coach: John W. Wilce

58	*Ohio Wesleyan	0
14	*Western Reserve	8
0	*Oberlin	0
6	*Indiana	7
0	Wisconsin	12
18	*Case	0
58	*Northwestern	0
154		27

Won 4, Lost 2, Tied 1

1914

16	*Ohio Wesleyan	2
7	Case	6
0	Illinois	37
6	*Wisconsin	7
13	Indiana	3
39	*Oberlin	0
27	*Northwestern	0
108		55

Won 5, Lost 2

1915

19	*Ohio Wesleyan	6
14	*Case	0
3	*Illinois	3
0	Wisconsin	21
10	*Indiana	9
25	*Oberlin	0
34	Northwestern	0
105		39

Won 5, Lost 1, Tied 1

Howard "Hop" Cassady twice won All-America honors and was a Heisman Trophy winner in 1955. He ran for 2,466 career yards and is Ohio State's all-time kickoff return leader.

1916

12	*Ohio Wesleyan	0
128	*Oberlin	0
7	Illinois	6
14	*Wisconsin	13
46	*Indiana	7
28	Case	0
23	*Northwestern	3
258		29

Won 7, Lost 0
Big Ten Champions

1917

49	*Case	0
53	*Ohio Wesleyan	0
40	*Northwestern	0
67	*Denison	0
26	Indiana	3
16	Wisconsin	3
13	*Illinois	0
0	Auburn	0
28	*Camp Sherman	0
292		6

Won 8, Lost 0, Tied 1
Big Ten Champions

1918

41	*Ohio Wesleyan	0
34	*Denison	0
0	*Michigan	14
56	*Case	0
0	Illinois	13
3	*Wisconsin	14
134		41

Won 3, Lost 3

1919

38	*Ohio Wesleyan	0
46	*Cincinnati	0
49	*Kentucky	0
13	Michigan	3
20	*Purdue	0
3	Wisconsin	0
7	*Illinois	9
176		12

Won 6, Lost 1

1920

55	*Ohio Wesleyan	0
37	*Oberlin	0
17	*Purdue	0
13	*Wisconsin	7
7	Chicago	6
14	*Michigan	7
7	Illinois	0
0	†California	28
150		48

Won 7, Lost 1
Big Ten Champions
† Rose Bowl

1921

28	*Ohio Wesleyan	0
6	*Oberlin	7
27	*Minnesota	0
14	Michigan	0
7	Chicago	0
28	*Purdue	0
0	*Illinois	7
110		14

Won 5, Lost 2

1922

5	*Ohio Wesleyan	0
14	*Oberlin	0
0	*Michigan	19
0	Minnesota	9
9	*Chicago	14
9	*Iowa	12
6	Illinois	3
43		57

Won 3, Lost 4

1923

24	*Ohio Wesleyan	7
23	*Colgate	23
0	Michigan	23
0	*Iowa	20
42	*Denison	0
32	Purdue	0
3	Chicago	17
0	*Illinois	9
124		99

Won 3, Lost 4, Tied 1

1924

7	*Purdue	0
0	Iowa	0
10	*Ohio Wesleyan	0
3	*Chicago	3
7	*Wooster	7
7	*Indiana	12
6	*Michigan	16
0	Illinois	7
40		45

Won 2, Lost 3, Tied 3

1925

10	*Ohio Wesleyan	3
9	*Columbia	0
3	*Chicago	3
0	*Iowa	15
17	*Wooster	0
7	*Indiana	0
0	Michigan	10
9	*Illinois	14
55		45

Won 4, Lost 3, Tied 1

1926

40	*Wittenberg	0
47	*Ohio Wesleyan	0
32	Columbia	7
23	*Iowa	6
18	Chicago	0
13	*Wilmington	7
16	*Michigan	17
7	Illinois	6
196		43

Won 7, Lost 1

1927

31	*Wittenberg	0
13	Iowa	6
13	*Northwestern	19
0	Michigan	21
13	*Chicago	7
0	Princeton	20
61	*Denison	6
0	*Illinois	13
131		92

Won 4, Lost 4

1928

41	*Wittenberg	0
10	Northwestern	0
19	*Michigan	7
13	Indiana	0
6	*Princeton	6
7	*Iowa	14
39	*Muskingum	0
0	*Illinois	8
135		35

Won 5, Lost 2, Tied 1

1929

Coach: Sam S. Willaman

19	*Wittenberg	0
7	*Iowa	6
7	Michigan	0
0	*Indiana	0
2	Pittsburgh	18
6	*Northwestern	18
54	*Kenyon	0
0	*Illinois	27
95		69

Won 4, Lost 3, Tied 1

1930

59	*Mt. Union	0
23	*Indiana	0
2	Northwestern	19
0	*Michigan	13
0	*Wisconsin	0
27	Navy	0
16	*Pittsburgh	7
12	Illinois	9
139		48

Won 5, Lost 2, Tied 1

1931

67	*Cincinnati	6
21	*Vanderbilt	26
20	Michigan	7
0	*Northwestern	10
13	Indiana	0
20	*Navy	0
6	Wisconsin	0
40	*Illinois	0
7	Minnesota	19
194		68

Won 6, Lost 3

1932

34	*Ohio Wesleyan	7
7	*Indiana	7
0	*Michigan	14
0	Pittsburgh	0
7	*Wisconsin	7
20	Northwestern	6
19	*Pennsylvania	0
3	Illinois	0
90		41

Won 4, Lost 1, Tied 3

1933

75	*Virginia	0
20	*Vanderbilt	0
0	Michigan	13
12	*Northwestern	0
21	*Indiana	0
20	Pennsylvania	7
6	Wisconsin	0
7	*Illinois	6
161		26

Won 7, Lost 1

1934

Coach: Francis A. Schmidt

33	*Indiana	0
13	Illinois	14
10	*Colgate	7
28	Northwestern	6
76	Western Reserve	0
33	*Chicago	0
34	*Michigan	0
40	*Iowa	7
267		34

Won 7, Lost 1

1935

19	*Kentucky	6
85	*Drake	7
28	*Northwestern	7
28	Indiana	6
13	*Notre Dame	18
20	Chicago	13
6	*Illinois	0
38	Michigan	0
237		57

Won 7, Lost 1
Big Ten Co-Champions

1936

60	*New York University	0
0	*Pittsburgh	6
13	Northwestern	14
7	*Indiana	0
2	Notre Dame	7
44	*Chicago	0
13	Illinois	0
21	*Michigan	0
160		27

Won 5, Lost 3

Ohio State Scores Through the Years—Cont'd

1937

14	*Texas Christian	0
13	*Purdue	0
12	Southern California	13
7	*Northwestern	0
39	Chicago	0
0	*Indiana	10
19	*Illinois	0
21	Michigan	0
125		23

Won 6, Lost 2

1938

6	*Indiana	0
7	*Southern California	14
0	Northwestern	0
42	*Chicago	7
32	New York University	0
0	*Purdue	12
32	Illinois	14
0	*Michigan	18
119		65

Won 4, Lost 3, Tied 1

1939

19	*Missouri	0
13	*Northwestern	0
23	Minnesota	20
14	*Cornell	23
24	*Indiana	0
61	Chicago	0
21	*Illinois	0
14	Michigan	21
189		64

Won 6, Lost 2
Big Ten Champions

1940

30	*Pittsburgh	7
17	*Purdue	14
3	Northwestern	6
7	*Minnesota	13
7	Cornell	21
21	*Indiana	6
14	Illinois	6
0	*Michigan	40
99		113

Won 4, Lost 4

1941
Coach: Paul E. Brown

12	*Missouri	7
33	Southern California	0
16	*Purdue	14
7	*Northwestern	14
21	Pittsburgh	14
46	*Wisconsin	34
12	*Illinois	7
20	Michigan	20
167		110

Won 6, Lost 1, Tied 1

1942

59	*Fort Knox	0
32	*Indiana	21
28	*Southern California	12
26	*Purdue	0
20	Northwestern	6
7	Wisconsin	17
59	*Pittsburgh	19
44	Illinois (Cleveland)	20
21	*Michigan	7
41	*Iowa Seahawks	12
337		114

Won 9, Lost 1
Big Ten Champions
National Champions

1943

13	*Iowa Seahawks	28
27	*Missouri	6
6	Great Lakes	13
7	Purdue (Cleveland)	30
0	*Northwestern	13
14	*Indiana	20
46	Pittsburgh	6
29	*Illinois	26
7	Michigan	45
149		187

Won 3, Lost 6

1944
Coach: Carroll C. Widdoes

54	*Missouri	0
34	*Iowa	0
20	Wisconsin	7
26	*Great Lakes	6
34	*Minnesota	14
21	*Indiana	7
54	*Pittsburgh	19
26	Illinois (Cleveland)	12
18	*Michigan	14
287		79

Won 9, Lost 0
Big Ten Champions

1945

47	*Missouri	6
42	*Iowa	0
12	*Wisconsin	0
13	*Purdue	35
20	Minnesota	7
16	*Northwestern	14
14	Pittsburgh	0
27	*Illinois	2
3	Michigan	7
194		71

Won 7, Lost 2

1946
Coach: Paul O. Bixler

13	*Missouri	13
21	Southern California	0
7	Wisconsin	20
14	*Purdue	14
39	*Minnesota	9
39	Northwestern	27
7	*Pittsburgh	13
7	Illinois	16
6	*Michigan	58
166		170

Won 4, Lost 3, Tied 2

1947
Coach: Wesley E. Fesler

13	*Missouri	7
20	Purdue	24
0	*Southern California	32
13	*Iowa	13
0	Pittsburgh	12
0	*Indiana	7
7	*Northwestern	6
7	*Illinois	28
0	Michigan	21
60		150

Won 2, Lost 6, Tied 1

1948

21	*Missouri	7
20	*Southern California	0
7	*Iowa	14
17	Indiana	0
34	*Wisconsin	32
7	Northwestern	21
41	*Pittsburgh	0
34	Illinois	7
3	*Michigan	13
184		94

Won 6, Lost 3

1949

35	*Missouri	34
46	*Indiana	7
13	Southern California	13
0	*Minnesota	27
21	Wisconsin	0
24	*Northwestern	7
14	Pittsburgh	10
30	*Illinois	17
7	Michigan	7
17	†California	14
207		136

Won 7, Lost 1, Tied 2
Big Ten Co-Champions
† Rose Bowl

1950

27	*Southern Methodist	32
41	*Pittsburgh	7
26	Indiana	14
48	*Minnesota	0
83	*Iowa	21
32	Northwestern	0
19	*Wisconsin	14
7	Illinois	14
3	*Michigan	9
287		111

Won 6, Lost 3

1951
Coach: W. W. "Woody" Hayes

7	*Southern Methodist	0
20	*Michigan State	24
6	Wisconsin	6
10	*Indiana	32
47	*Iowa	21
3	*Northwestern	0
16	Pittsburgh	14
0	*Illinois	0
0	Michigan	7
109		104

Won 4, Lost 3, Tied 2

1952

33	*Indiana	13
14	*Purdue	21
23	*Wisconsin	14
35	*Washington State	7
0	Iowa	8
24	Northwestern	21
14	*Pittsburgh	21
27	Illinois	7
27	*Michigan	7
197		119

Won 6, Lost 3

1953

36	*Indiana	12
33	California	19
20	*Illinois	41
12	Pennsylvania	6
20	Wisconsin	19
27	*Northwestern	13
13	*Michigan State	28
21	*Purdue	6
0	Michigan	20
182		164

Won 6, Lost 3

1954

28	*Indiana	0
21	*California	13
40	Illinois	7
20	*Iowa	14
31	*Wisconsin	14
14	Northwestern	7
26	*Pittsburgh	0
28	Purdue	6
21	*Michigan	7
20	†Southern California	7
249		75

Won 10, Lost 0
Big Ten Champions
National Champions
† Rose Bowl

1955

28	*Nebraska	20
0	Stanford	6
27	*Illinois	12
14	*Duke	20
26	Wisconsin	16
49	*Northwestern	0
20	*Indiana	13
20	*Iowa	10
17	Michigan	0
201		97

Won 7, Lost 2
Big Ten Champions

1956

34	*Nebraska	7
32	*Stanford	20
26	Illinois	6
6	*Penn State	7
21	*Wisconsin	0
6	Northwestern	2
35	*Indiana	14
0	Iowa	6
0	*Michigan	19
160		81

Won 6, Lost 3

1957

14	*Texas Christian	18
35	Washington	7
21	*Illinois	7
56	*Indiana	0
16	Wisconsin	13
47	*Northwestern	6
20	*Purdue	7
17	*Iowa	13
31	Michigan	14
10	†Oregon	7
267		92

Won 9, Lost 1
Big Ten Champions
National Champions
† Rose Bowl

1958

23	*Southern Methodist	20
12	*Washington	7
19	Illinois	13
49	*Indiana	8
7	*Wisconsin	7
0	Northwestern	21
14	*Purdue	14
38	Iowa	28
20	*Michigan	14
182		132

Won 6, Lost 1, Tied 2

1959

14	*Duke	13
0	Southern California	17
0	*Illinois	9
15	*Purdue	0
3	Wisconsin	12
30	*Michigan State	24
0	*Indiana	0
7	*Iowa	16
14	Michigan	23
83		114

Won 3, Lost 5, Tied 1

1960

24	*Southern Methodist	0
20	*Southern California	0
34	Illinois	7
21	Purdue	24
34	*Wisconsin	7
21	Michigan State	10
36	*Indiana	7
12	Iowa	35
7	*Michigan	0
209		90

Won 7, Lost 2

1961

7	*Texas Christian	7
13	*U.C.L.A.	3
44	*Illinois	0
10	Northwestern	0
30	Wisconsin	21
29	*Iowa	13
16	Indiana	7
22	*Oregon	12
50	Michigan	20
221		83

Won 8, Lost 0, Tied 1
Big Ten Champions
National Champions

1962

41	*North Carolina	7
7	U.C.L.A.	9
51	Illinois	15
14	*Northwestern	18
14	*Wisconsin	7
14	Iowa	28
10	*Indiana	7
26	*Oregon	7
28	*Michigan	0
205		98

Won 6, Lost 3

1963

17	*Texas A.&M.	0
21	Indiana	0
20	*Illinois	20
3	Southern California	32
13	Wisconsin	10
7	*Iowa	3
7	*Penn State	10
8	*Northwestern	17
14	Michigan	10
110		102

Won 5, Lost 3, Tied 1

1964

27	*Southern Methodist	8
17	*Indiana	9
26	Illinois	0
17	*Southern California	0
28	*Wisconsin	3
21	Iowa	19
0	*Penn State	27
10	*Northwestern	0
0	*Michigan	10
146		76

Won 7, Lost 2

1965

3	*North Carolina	14
23	Washington	21
28	*Illinois	14
7	Michigan State	32
20	Wisconsin	10
11	*Minnesota	10
17	*Indiana	10
38	*Iowa	0
9	Michigan	7
156		118

Won 7, Lost 2

1966

14	*Texas Christian	7
22	*Washington	38
9	Illinois	10
8	*Michigan State	11
24	*Wisconsin	13
7	Minnesota	17
7	*Indiana	0
14	Iowa	10
3	*Michigan	17
108		123

Won 4, Lost 5

During a four-year career, Tom Skladany averaged 42.7 yards per punt to become Ohio State's all-time leading punter. Skladany was an All-American three years.

1967

7	*Arizona	14
30	Oregon	0
6	*Purdue	41
6	Northwestern	2
13	*Illinois	17
21	Michigan State	7
17	*Wisconsin	15
21	*Iowa	10
24	Michigan	14
145		120

Won 6, Lost 3

1968

35	*Southern Methodist	14
21	*Oregon	6
13	*Purdue	0
45	*Northwestern	21
31	Illinois	24
25	*Michigan State	20
43	Wisconsin	8
33	Iowa	27
50	*Michigan	14
27	‡Southern California	16
323		150

Won 10, Lost 0
Big Ten Champions
National Champions
‡ Rose Bowl

1969

62	*Texas Christian	0
41	Washington	14
54	*Michigan State	21
34	Minnesota	7
41	*Illinois	0
35	Northwestern	6
62	*Wisconsin	7
42	*Purdue	14
12	Michigan	24
383		93

Won 8, Lost 1
Big Ten Co-Champions

1970

56	*Texas A.&M.	13
34	*Duke	10
29	Michigan State	0
28	*Minnesota	8
48	Illinois	29
24	*Northwestern	10
24	Wisconsin	7
10	Purdue	7
20	*Michigan	9
17	†Stanford	27
290		120

Won 9, Lost 1
Big Ten Champions
National Champions
† Rose Bowl

1971

52	*Iowa	21
14	*Colorado	20
35	*California	3
24	Illinois	10
27	Indiana	7
31	*Wisconsin	6
14	Minnesota	12
10	*Michigan State	17
10	*Northwestern	14
7	Michigan	10
224		120

Won 6, Lost 4

1972

21	*Iowa	0
29	*North Carolina	14
35	California	18
26	*Illinois	7
44	*Indiana	7
28	Wisconsin	20
27	*Minnesota	19
12	Michigan State	19
27	Northwestern	14
14	*Michigan	11
17	†Southern California	42
280		171

Won 9, Lost 2
Big Ten Co-Champions
† Rose Bowl

Ohio State Scores Through the Years—Cont'd

1973

56	*Minnesota	7
37	*Texas Christian	3
27	*Washington State	3
24	Wisconsin	0
37	Indiana	7
60	*Northwestern	0
30	Illinois	0
35	*Michigan State	0
55	*Iowa	13
10	Michigan	10
42	†Southern California	21
413		64

Won 10, Lost 0, Tied 1
Big Ten Co-Champions
† Rose Bowl

1974

34	Minnesota	19
51	*Oregon State	10
28	*Southern Methodist	9
42	Washington State	7
52	*Wisconsin	7
49	*Indiana	9
55	Northwestern	7
49	*Illinois	7
13	Michigan State	16
35	Iowa	10
12	*Michigan	10
17	†Southern California	18
437		129

Won 10, Lost 2
Big Ten Co-Champions
† Rose Bowl

1975

21	Michigan State	0
17	*Penn State	9
32	*North Carolina	7
41	U.C.L.A.	20
49	*Iowa	0
56	*Wisconsin	0
35	Purdue	6
24	*Indiana	14
40	Illinois	3
38	*Minnesota	6
21	Michigan	14
10	†U.C.L.A.	23
384		102

Won 11, Lost 1
Big Ten Champions
† Rose Bowl

1976

49	*Michigan State	21
12	Penn State	7
21	*Missouri	22
10	*U.C.L.A.	10
34	Iowa	14
30	Wisconsin	20
24	*Purdue	3
47	Indiana	7
42	*Illinois	10
9	Minnesota	3
0	*Michigan	22
27	†Colorado	10
305		149

Won 9, Lost 2, Tied 1
Big Ten Co-Champions
† Orange Bowl

1977

10	*Miami (Fla.)	0
38	*Minnesota	7
28	*Oklahoma	29
35	Southern Methodist	7
46	*Purdue	0
27	Iowa	6
35	Northwestern	15
42	*Wisconsin	0
35	Illinois	0
35	*Indiana	7
6	Michigan	14
6	†Alabama	35
343		120

Won 9, Lost 3
Big Ten Co-Champions
† Sugar Bowl

1978

0	*Penn State	19
27	Minnesota	10
34	*Baylor	28
35	*Southern Methodist	35
16	Purdue	27
31	*Iowa	7
63	*Northwestern	20
49	Wisconsin	14
45	*Illinois	7
21	Indiana	18
3	*Michigan	14
15	†Clemson	17
339		216

Won 7, Lost 4, Tied 1
†Gator Bowl

1979

Coach: Earle Bruce

31	*Syracuse	8
21	Minnesota	17
45	*Washington State	29
17	U.C.L.A.	13
16	*Northwestern	7
47	*Indiana	6
59	*Wisconsin	0
42	*Michigan State	0
44	Illinois	7
34	*Iowa	7
18	Michigan	15
16	†Southern California	17
390		126

Won 11, Lost 1
Big Ten Champions
† Rose Bowl

1980

31	*Syracuse	21
47	*Minnesota	0
38	*Arizona State	21
0	*U.C.L.A.	17
63	Northwestern	0
27	*Indiana	17
21	*Wisconsin	0
48	Michigan State	16
49	*Illinois	42
41	Iowa	7
3	*Michigan	9
19	†Penn State	31
387		181

Won 9, Lost 3
†Fiesta Bowl

1981

34	*Duke	13
27	*Michigan State	13
24	Stanford	19
27	*Florida State	36
21	Wisconsin	24
34	*Illinois	27
29	*Indiana	10
45	Purdue	33
31	Minnesota	35
70	*Northwestern	6
14	Michigan	9
31	†Navy	28
387		253

Won 9, Lost 3
Big Ten Co-Champions
† Liberty Bowl

1982

21	*Baylor	14
31	Michigan State	10
20	*Stanford	23
17	*Florida State	34
0	*Wisconsin	6
26	Illinois	21
49	Indiana	25
38	*Purdue	6
35	*Minnesota	10
40	Northwestern	28
24	*Michigan	14
47	†Brigham Young	17
348		208

Won 9, Lost 3
† Holiday Bowl

1983

31	*Oregon	6
24	Oklahoma	14
14	Iowa	20
69	*Minnesota	18
33	*Purdue	22
13	Illinois	17
21	*Michigan State	11
45	*Wisconsin	27
56	Indiana	17
55	*Northwestern	7
21	Michigan	24
28	†Pittsburgh	23
410		206

Won 9, Lost 3
† Fiesta Bowl

1987

24	West Virginia	3
24	Oregon	14
13	*LSU	13
10	*Illinois	6
10	Indiana	31
20	*Purdue	17
42	Minnesota	9
7	Michigan State	13
24	*Wisconsin	26
27	Iowa	29
23	*Michigan	20

Won 6, Lost 4, Tied 1

1984

22	*Oregon State	14
44	*Washington State	0
45	*Iowa	26
35	Minnesota	22
23	Purdue	28
45	*Illinois	38
23	Michigan State	20
14	Wisconsin	16
50	*Indiana	7
52	Northwestern	3
21	*Michigan	6
17	†Southern California	20
391		200

Won 9, Lost 3
Big Ten Champions
† Rose Bowl

1985

10	*Pittsburgh	7
36	Colorado	13
48	*Washington State	32
28	Illinois	31
48	*Indiana	7
41	*Purdue	27
23	Minnesota	19
22	*Iowa	13
35	Northwestern	17
7	*Wisconsin	12
17	Michigan	27
10	†Brigham Young	7
325		212

Won 9, Lost 3
† Citrus Bowl

1986

10	†Alabama	16
7	Washington	40
13	*Colorado	10
64	*Utah	6
14	*Illinois	0
24	Indiana	22
39	Purdue	11
33	*Minnesota	0
31	Iowa	10
30	*Northwestern	9
30	Wisconsin	17
24	*Michigan	26
28	#Texas A&M	12
347		179

Won 10, Lost 3
Big Ten Co-Champions
† Kickoff Classic
(Meadowlands, N.J.)
Cotton Bowl